The Men We Long to Be

The Men We Long to Be

BEYOND LONELY WARRIORS
and DESPERATE LOVERS

Stephen B. Boyd

THE PILGRIM PRESS
CLEVELAND, OHIO

The Pilgrim Press, Cleveland, Ohio 44115

*The Men We Long to Be: Beyond Domination to a New Christian
Understanding of Manhood.* Copyright © 1995 by Stephen B. Boyd.
Preface and introduction copyright © 1997 by Stephen B. Boyd.

Permissions acknowledgments begin on page 259.

First edition published 1995 by HarperSanFrancisco. Paperback
edition published 1997 by The Pilgrim Press by arrangement with
HarperSanFrancisco, a division of HarperCollins Publishers, Inc. All
rights reserved.

Printed in the United States of America on acid-free paper

02 01 00 99 98 97   5 4 3 2 1

Library of Congress Cataloging-in-Publication Data

Boyd, Stephen Blake.
    The men we long to be : beyond lonely warriors and desperate
lovers / Stephen B. Boyd.
        p.   cm.
    Originally published: 1st ed. [San Francisco] :
HarperSanFrancisco, c1995. With new introd.
    Includes bibliographical references and index.
    ISBN 0-8298-1201-6 (pbk. : alk paper)
    1. Men (Christian theology)   2. Men's movement.   I. Title.
    [BT701.2.B68   1997]
    248.8'42—dc21
                                                        97-29641
                                                          CIP

To THE MEN of the Monday Night Men's Group:

John Collins, Richard Fireman, Jay Foster, Chris Ingalls, Russ McGhee, and Mark Retherford

Contents

Preface to the Paperback Edition   *ix*

Acknowledgments   *x*

Introduction   *1*

PART ONE

The Men We Have Become

ONE   Lonely Warriors: The Public, Responsible Self   *18*

TWO   Desperate Lovers: The Private, Separative Self   *44*

THREE   A House Divided: The Punishment of Adam   *69*

PART TWO

The Love of God and the Men We Long to Be

FOUR   "A New Creation": The Call to a Center and Over the Barricades   *100*

FIVE   Losing Ourselves to Find Ourselves: Faith   *123*

PART THREE

Our Longing for Connection and a Ministry of Reconciliation

SIX   Love Casts Out Fear   *146*

SEVEN   On Being Body-selves: Body Wisdom and Body Care   *155*

EIGHT   On Loving Our Brothers   *177*

NINE   On Loving Our Sisters   *202*

Epilogue   *224*

Endnotes   *234*

Index   *252*

Permissions Acknowledgments   *259*

Preface to the Paperback Edition

SINCE THE FIRST publication of this book, I have become even more convinced that finding a third way beyond the dual identities of lonely warrior and desperate lover requires sharing the visions, support, and challenges of other men committed to a similar path. But many of us, particularly liberal, "kenotic" masculine men do not do well in groups and often choose to navigate the waters of change alone. Many traditionally oriented groups of men have tended to reinforce or even inculcate some of the very masculine patterns that we know have hurt us and others. Consequently, we shy away from men in groups (e.g., Promise Keepers) because we perceive, often rightly, that, while addressing certain of our needs, they also contribute to our own and others' difficulties. However, leaving old habits—the thoughts, feelings, and behaviors required by these identities—and learning new ones produces a kind of disorientation, or vertigo, as we let go of the plausibility structures provided by our various communities that have held those habits in place. There is tremendous pressure from almost every quarter for us to change back to the behaviors and attitudes that others have come to expect from us. I see now in a more profound way why James Cone has said that conversion means changing communities.[1] Personal transformation toward a "new creation" is mediated and sustained by transformed and transforming communities.

In response to the first edition, I have been contacted by men seeking further resources for their journeys and looking for traveling companions. Therefore, I have compiled on my home page some bibliographies, links to helpful Internet sites, and information about networking with others (http://www.wfu.edu/~boyd; for those without a personal computer, access to the Internet is available at many local libraries).

Acknowledgments

WITH A BOOK like this one, it is difficult to thank everyone who has had a hand in it and in my development. In the text and footnotes I mention a number of people from whom I have learned much—both personally and from their publications. Here I want to mention people without whose support, challenge, love, and friendship I could not have written what I have.

Mark Muesse, a beloved friend and colleague, has read the entire manuscript several times and given sage and encouraging advice about the book's form and content. In addition, he has been a midwife for some of the spiritual labor from which this book has emerged. Russ McGhee has given generously the gift of listening and has been a constant source of brotherly love, inspiration, and provocative insights. In rape prevention workshops we have led together, Lisa Allred has helped develop the chart on gender roles in chapter 2. In relating to her, I have discovered, with gratitude, a lot about the hard work and rewards that come when women and men try to treat each other with respect. I am deeply grateful to my sister, Beth Boyd, for her sustaining sisterly love, her advice, and her hard-won thoughts about the effects of sexism in the business world. I thank Joe Foster for his courage to be out, his fierce insistence that he and his gay and lesbian brothers and sisters be treated with respect, the largeness of his heart, and the depth of his spiritual maturity. I am grateful to those who have read and commented on parts or all of the manuscript in one stage or another: Lisa Allred, Merle Longwood, Russ McGhee, Mark Retherford, David Schoeni, and Mahan Siler.

I am also grateful to: Margaret Miles, for an early conversation about the situation for men and her encouragement to write about it; Meg Davis, for her contributions in clarifying the alternative theological paradigms that appear in chapters 3 and 4; Steve Hanselman, for his early encouragement and subsequent support for this book; Lynn Rhoades, for her friendship, pastoral support, and help with what it means for women in Christian communities to appropriate critically traditions that are both hurtful and life-giving; Linda McFarland, for her regular and compassionate attention; Ben Paden, for his enthusiasm and support; Cecil Murphey, for his encouragement to put this in the form of a book and for his invaluable advice about the publishing world; Mike Absher, for his meticulous work on the notes; Delta Lightner, for sharing her life's journey with me for a time; John Loudon, executive editor at HarperSanFrancisco, for his enthusiasm for and editorial advice on the hardcover edition; and Tim Staveteig at Pilgrim, for his vision and support.

I want, also, to acknowledge my debt and gratitude to the various groups of men and women with whom I have worked on this material: the students in the Gender and Religion courses at Wake Forest University; the Christian Education classes at St. Paul's Episcopal Church, Winston-Salem, North Carolina; Shalom Place Retreat Center, Topsail Island, North Carolina; the Presbyterian Counseling Center, Greensboro, North Carolina, especially Bob Herron; In the Oaks Conference Center, Black Mountain, North Carolina; Hartford Theological Seminary, especially Betty Secord and Miriam Therese Winter; the Center for Life Enrichment, Winston-Salem; the Presbyterian, USA, conference titled "Ministry to, for, and with Men," especially David Lewis; and the North Carolina Baptist Chaplains' Association, especially Jay Foster and Gerald Richards.

I have also been inspired and informed by the commitment and clarity of my colleagues in the American Men's Studies Association; the National Organization for Men Against Sexism and its task group, the Men's Studies Association; the Men's Studies in Religion group of the American Academy of Religion; the Gay Men's Issues group of the AAR; the Women's Studies Program at Wake Forest University, especially Mary DeShazer; the conference titled "Male Sexuality and Masculine Spirituality" at Stony Point, New York; the Piedmont Religious Network for Gay and Lesbian Equality, Winston-Salem; and Citizens United for Justice, Winston-Salem.

It is impossible to see and do the kinds of things I write about in this book without the empowerment of communities of faith, both large and small. The book is dedicated to one such group—my weekly men's group. In addition, I have been meeting monthly with a leadership group, the members of which—Russ McGhee, Frederick Whitmeyer, and John Rowe—have been a constant source of brotherly support, challenge, and peace. I am grateful, too, to the members of the Wake Forest Baptist Church, especially the Spiritual Journeys Sunday School Class, who struggle with what it means to be faithful to Christ's call in a confusing and exciting world. I realize, also, my profound debt to the folks of the First Baptist Church, Bristol, Virginia, especially William P. Tuck, Emily C. Tuck, and Joann Feazell, who embodied for me a deeply compassionate and intellectually fearless faith. And from people like Billy and Lynn Wallace, Jon and Nancy Burnett, and George K. Schweitzer of First Baptist Church, Knoxville, Tennessee, I have learned with admiration the transforming power of loyalty to Christ's cause as expressed in less than perfect Christian communities—the only kind we have.

I am indebted to Wake Forest University for both financial assistance and release time to complete this manuscript.

Finally, I will forever treasure the consistent esteem, love, and care I have received from my father, Donald E. Boyd, and my mother, Maxine D. Boyd. And, though our vocations have taken us in somewhat different directions, I am grateful for the mutual respect there has always been in my relationship with my brother, Sam.

Introduction

IT IS NOT easy these days to be a man and escape feelings of isolation and guilt. Pat Conroy, in his book *The Prince of Tides,* captures very well how disconcerting it sometimes can feel in the 1990s to be simply what I am—a white, heterosexual, middle-class, middle-aged, Protestant, southern, able-bodied, Euro-American male. Tom Wingo, the former high-school quarterback, laments:

> This has not been an easy century to endure. . . . I grew up in South Carolina, a white southern male, well trained and gifted in my hatred of blacks when the civil rights movement caught me outside and undefended along the barricades and proved me to be both wicked and wrong. But I was a thinking boy, a feeling one, sensitive to injustice, and I worked hard to change myself and to play a small, insignificant part in that movement—and soon I was feeling superabundantly proud of myself. Then I found myself marching in an all-white, all-male ROTC program in college and was spit on by peace demonstrators who were offended by my uniform. Eventually I would become one of those demonstrators, but I never spit on anyone who disagreed with me. I thought I would enter my thirties quietly, a contemplative man, a man whose philosophy was humane and unassailable, when the women's liberation movement bushwhacked me on the avenues and I found myself on the other side of the barricades once again. I seem to embody everything that is wrong with the twentieth century.

Everywhere we look we seem to be on the top of the oppression pyramid—the objects of implicit and explicit critiques by liberationists of almost every perspective and social location.

The voices of women of our social class; men and women of color; gay, lesbian, and bisexual persons; two-thirds-world persons; Native Americans; and persons with physical disabilities, among others, demand our attention and insist on inclusion in public institutions, and in public and private discourse. Since we lead many of these institutions, we might feel that we are being accused of being "wicked and wrong"; we seem to be the universal bad guys. Often we respond in one of two polarized ways—defensive denial or guilty silence—or we might oscillate between them. That is, we deny we have personally hurt others or participate in institutions that do so; we might say things like, "It is not so bad; I've got it worse; God intended it to be this way, there's nothing I can do; and I'm tired of all this 'politically correct' business!" Or we internalize the criticism in such a way that it leads to a pervasive sense of shame, guilt, and even self-hatred. Some of us might respond by saying or thinking, "You're right; this is terrible; something must be done; men are jerks; I'm not like the other guys, so please don't hold their [sexism, racism, homophobia] against me." But it is difficult for us to figure out what to do because we are paralyzed with guilt. Some of us fluctuate between these two responses—sometimes feeling hurt and angry and other times feeling paralyzed with guilt. Neither response leaves us feeling very good about ourselves, because, on some level of our being, we sense that neither response is entirely truthful, nor do they seem to do justice to others' demands or contribute to our own well-being. I'll say more about how these two responses are exhibited in the church in chapter 3.

There is, I am coming to believe, a way out of this dilemma—a third response. The first step is simple, but it has profound implications: we must learn to make a distinction between who we are as male human beings and the expectations our culture imposes on us as men. In other words, we must start by distinguishing our maleness from our masculinity. This is important because, as men in this culture, we have been socialized, even violently conditioned, to masculine roles in which we come to believe we must be dominant in so many areas of our lives; we believe that our survival depends on our being in control of "unruly" aspects of ourselves, of others, and of the earth and its creatures. This conditioning and these roles produce in many of us feelings, thoughts, and behaviors that are deadly to others, to our earth, and to us. We find ourselves facing numbing isolation, substance addiction, divorce court, the criminal justice system, and/or suicidal depression not because we are not man enough, but because, often, we are too much of a man. That is, we are playing out masculine roles that have unhealthy, unjust, and dysfunctional aspects to them.

THESES

In this book, there are several points I want to make; I will list them here as seven theses. They are closely related and, in many ways, interlocking:

1. We men are not inherently or irreversibly violent, relationally incompetent, emotionally constipated, and sexually compulsive. To the extent that we manifest these characteristics, we do so not because we are male, but because we have experienced violent socialization and conditioning processes that have required or produced this kind of behavior and we have chosen to accept, or adopt, these ways of being, thinking, and acting.

2. This dominative form of masculinity can be theologically construed to be a punishment or, better put, a manifestation of human sin.[1] That is, it exhibits an alienation from our truest selves, from God, and from others. It is a captivity from which we need release.

3. We men, as men, are victims of a systemic oppression. Recognizing this and organizing with all other men to resist it are necessary for our full participation in the ending of all other forms of oppression.

4. It is possible for us to experience transformation and make different choices. For that to occur, we will need new kinds of communities and visions of ourselves and of the world free from the profound alienations we have mistaken for reality.

5. Our well-being is inextricably linked to the well-being and flourishing of all others—human and nonhuman. One of the ways in which we are mystified by what I call "dominative masculinity" is the mistaken belief that our well-being is somehow in competition with that of others. We are convinced that the progress of another somehow diminishes us. Not only is this not true, but it is one aspect of this form of masculinity that itself contributes to the very attitudes and behaviors that diminish us and others.

6. Certain aspects of Christian theology and practice, particularly aspects of the dominant theology and practice that have served the ruling classes since the marriage of church and state with the emperor Constantine, have not had salutary effects on men. There are, however,

alternative traditions and less visible expressions of the dominant traditions that call us to personal and interpersonal reconciliation and communion with God.

7. The pursuit of our bliss is our duty. Or, put the other way around,
our duty is our bliss. It is the means by which God calls us to wholeness
and participation in God's realm of justice and love.

Using the rhetorical style of the "obedient rebel," Martin Luther, seems
appropriate for a couple of reasons.[2] First, I think we may be at a point
similar to where the Western church was in the sixteenth century. One of
the problems in that period was the sacramental system of the church; it
wasn't, in the opinion of some, offering the healing and reconciliation
that it was originally intended to offer. In the sacrament of penance, the
sale of indulgences short-circuited the healing process. It may be that a
similar "works righteousness" (i.e., we need to *achieve* masculine expectations, not simply *be* men) in our churches is short-circuiting the healing
process for men. Second, these theses, like those of Luther, are offered
by someone who loves the church and, therefore, feels compelled to try
to figure some of this out. I have come to realize that I can't live without
the church, though some days I have wished I could. I am not alone.

These theses and this book have emerged from an ongoing process of
self-examination prompted by several painful experiences in my own life.
Those experiences—the collapse of what I thought was my vocation and
a divorce—led me to begin a journey to understand what had shaped
them and me. When these things happened, I felt sick, helpless, disori-
ented, and hopeless. I was also angry; I had done everything I felt had
been expected of me—done them very well—and still these things happened. I see now that they precipitated for me what St. John of the Cross,
the sixteenth-century mystic, called "the dark night of the soul."

I am a recovering officer. Martin Luther, the Protestant reformer, believed that God had ordained three estates—the church, the family, and
the state—to keep order in the world after the fall into sin. Because of
the self-centeredness resulting from human sin, Luther believed that,
without these ordering institutions, we would constantly be at each other's
throats—anarchy would reign. In his view, God gave men the responsibility to fill the offices of husband/father, pastor, and civil magistrate; we
are the keepers of the gates against the forces of barbarism. When I say I
am a recovering officer, I do not mean to say that these institutions are

not important or that responsible participation in them is not needed. They are and it is. What I am realizing is that some of the ways we men participate in them can themselves be harmful (theologically: sinful) and contribute to greater, rather than less, alienation and enmity in the world and in ourselves. Part 1 of this book will explore why that is, but first I want to say a little bit about the way I came to be an officer and how I came to step back from those offices and take a look at them and me.

I grew up in a Southern Baptist church, where I was president of the youth group and where I spent most of my social time. In college, I was an officer in the Baptist Student Union and in my senior year served on the staff of a downtown church as an outreach coordinator to the campus. I married the first woman president of the BSU (we were both virgins) and went off to Harvard Divinity School to prepare to be a pastor. While there, I was ordained and served as a campus minister and then as assistant pastor (my wife was the first woman to chair the board of deacons), and I worked really hard in school. This describes part of my ascent (as Robert Bly would say)—I worked a lot and found favor with a select group of men, many women, and, I assumed, God. Things seemed to be going well; I was doing what I was supposed to be doing and doing it very well.

And then the wheels started to come off; I began a descent. Near the end of my doctoral program, in the middle of my dissertation, I accepted a job as the education minister of a church near where I grew up. I had other opportunities—to teach at a Baptist seminary or to get into the (really terrible) university job market. I did a complex decision chart, weighing these options very rationally, prayed a lot, and decided that the education minister job was right for me, vocationally, and for us, financially. I committed in January and was to begin in June, after completing my dissertation.

In April, however, I grew increasingly restless—I couldn't sleep, had heart palpitations, couldn't concentrate on my dissertation, and was generally miserable. One night, I bolted up in bed and said to my wife, "I want to teach! If I go to the church, I'll never be able to teach in a university or seminary other than Baptist ones." I had already decided not to go to one of the Southern Baptist seminaries to teach, because at the time a fundamentalist takeover was under way that was purging the seminaries of professors who were not biblical inerrantists.

After several days of excruciatingly intense conversations and reflections, I called the pastor and told him that I would keep my commitment for a year but that I would send out applications for teaching jobs. Because the church needed more of a commitment than that, he said I should not come. End of conversation. I was in shock. We had no money; I now had no job. Because I had trained completely in a nondenominational seminary and Baptists are not exactly ecumenical, I not only did not have a job, but I felt there would not be another opportunity for ministry among Southern Baptists. In one fell swoop, I had no job, no career, no place to pursue my vocation, and no identity. I felt I had no people among whom my life made sense.

After having previously served as a teaching fellow and as supervisor of the field education program for master's students at the divinity school, I now took a job on a painting crew and tried to finish my dissertation at night. These were some of the darkest days of my life. It felt as if someone had reached in and turned me inside out—with all my nerve endings exposed and no way to get relief. I had one primary person to talk to about all of this, and she was tired of talking about it.

So, I wanted to teach. I remember talking, during that time, to a friend of mine who had been a Presbyterian minister and had come back to graduate school. He said, "Steve, you have to tell the church how you are feeling; they have a right to know." And I said, "What if they don't want me to come? What will I do? The job market for professors is terrible for guys like me." He said, "Steve, I know guys who go through their whole lives and never know what they want to do; at least you know." It seemed to me a high price for what people like Joseph Campbell call "following your bliss," but I knew I couldn't go back.

I had other friends in church who took a different attitude.

One friend said to me, "So, how does God 'uncall' you to a church?"

He articulated the indictment that I was internally leveling at myself—I was being selfish and refusing to be a dutiful, responsible officer.

As I view this period from where I am now, I am struck by some of my incapacities: how out of touch I was with what I wanted—my body knew, but my mind didn't; how limited my reference group was—if I didn't serve among Southern Baptists my life meant nothing; and how small and fragile my network of support was—I had very few people beyond my wife with whom I felt comfortable talking about the things that meant the most to me.

But I am also impressed with the fact that I did know, on some level, what I wanted and that I listened to my body—a relatively new and scary thing for me; that I went on and put one foot in front of the other in the face of a sense of loneliness and meaninglessness; and that I reached out to other people, such as my Presbyterian minister friend, to get some help with what I was dealing with.

About eighteen months later, my wife, confidante, and partner of ten years told me that she wanted to live alone and that she did not want to be married. It was like I had the emotional breath knocked out of me—for months. The world turned dark, cold, and rainy—sometimes I wondered if it would ever be sunny again. What was I going to do? Who would see it? Whom would I tell about it? After about a year, I realized that I did not want to be married to someone who did not want to be married to me and we got a divorce and then I got mono. I entered therapy during this time and slowly discovered how enmeshed I was with her. One day I started crying, and my therapist (who was a pastor's son and is not now affiliated with a church) patiently attended to me. When I paused to catch my breath and looked at him, he said, "Steve, I can't figure out whose pain you are feeling—yours or hers." This bowled me over. I had always prided myself on my empathy—it seemed so caring, so good, so Christian. I can't remember anyone ever giving me that kind of permission to feel my own pain, or challenging me to. My reflex was to assume that all the problems were hers. Only slowly did I begin to understand the difficulties I had caused. It took a while to begin to identify my own feelings as distinguished from other people's feelings and to take responsibility for my own patterns of behavior, but I did and am. My world began to brighten; I began to find a way out.

Again, I am struck now with my lack of clarity about my boundaries in those days. That is, it was very difficult for me to see clearly those things for which I was responsible and about which I could do something and those things for which other people were responsible. I think much stress comes from feeling responsible for things over which one has no control. I felt a lot of that then. I'm also struck by my lack of compassion for myself. At the same time, I appreciate my willingness, in the midst of a great deal of confusion and guilt, to act on my own behalf and to begin to care for myself.

At the time, I wished desperately that these things had not happened to me, but I now see that they initiated a journey in which I began to understand why I had come to that point in my life; why I was sick and felt powerless, confused and hopeless; and what I could begin to do about it. With the help of books, students, friends, and a group of men that has been meeting weekly for nine years, I began to sort out the influences that shaped my life—some in positive, healthy ways and others in negative, unhealthy ways.

This book is a "coming out" of sorts; in it, I am bringing to light things about myself that I have kept carefully hidden.[3] For example, it has not been easy for me to admit to myself, much less to other people, that fear too often motivates much of what I do and what I do not do; that I am tired and want to rest; that I am tired of being tired; that I want more pleasure, including sensual and sexual pleasure, in my life; that I feel isolated and alone and am sick to death of it; that I want things to be right in the world and I want everyone to be treated fairly; that I want to be close to women and men who are both like me and different from me; that I want to be close to other men, enjoy their company, and feel as if I can trust them; that I want to be powerful and act powerfully without hurting others; that I want to recapture the feelings of mystery, wonder, and belongingness I had as a boy when I look at trees; and that I want to figure out why I haven't said many of these things before and acted on them.

In the midst of my own "midlife crisis," I found a growing body of literature that came out of what the media commonly call the "men's movement." As I read, went to retreats, and joined organizations, I discovered two important things: (1) there is a pervasive restlessness, or stirring, among men these days; and (2) underneath this stirring is a profound spiritual longing, though many men are seeking its fulfillment outside the institutional church.

Something is happening today among men. Bill Moyers's interview with Robert Bly on PBS elicited a great deal of excitement and conversation among many men and between men and women. Bly's *Iron John* and Sam Keen's *Fire in the Belly* were on bestseller lists for most of 1991. In addition, there is a growing resentment, mostly among men, about perceived demands to be "politically correct" in the academy and in the wider culture. This restlessness and stirring have spawned various and diverse efforts at organizing men to act, think, and be together. For example, the *National Review* recently published a series of articles aimed at restoring respect for traditionally masculine roles; tens of thousands of men are attending Promise Keepers rallies in stadiums, followed by small group experiences in churches across the nation; men's rights organizations are lobbying against what they see as reverse sexism in divorce cases, custody decisions, and military requirements; profeminist organizations like NOMAS (National Organization for Men Against Sexism) sponsor working groups for the purpose of dismantling personal and institutional sexism, homophobia, domestic violence, and sexual assault; mythopoetic leaders, like Bly, are leading workshops, retreats, and gatherings aimed at helping men recover neglected aspects of themselves through storytelling and ritual; scholars of the "new" men's studies are critically examining culturally specific social constructions of masculinity in order to determine their influence on men's lives, on women, on institutions, and on ideas; leaders, such as Cornel West, Louis Farrakhan, Ben Chavis Muhammad, Jesse Jackson, and Jacob Gordon, among many others, have focused attention (most prominently with the Million Man March) on the situation of African American men and are organizing nationally and locally for leadership development for social change; and gay men and their allies are organizing around civil rights legislation, the AIDS crisis, and the reshaping of academic scholarship from gay perspectives.

The media often refer to a "men's movement" as though there were just one. There isn't. What is usually referred to is the so-called mythopoetic wing of what is happening among men today.[4] As I have indicated, however, a lot of different things are going on among men these days. Therefore, I prefer to speak of the movement, or movements, among men. There are some commonalities, but there are also many barriers and divisions that separate us—notably, race and ethnicity, homophobia, and class.

Because of these divisions among us, I want to say a word here about the perspective from which this book is written and the audience that might find it most helpful. I am a white, heterosexual, Anglo-Saxon, Protestant (evangelical), middle-class, middle-aged, southern, able-bodied male; I think and speak from that location, and this book is written from that perspective. I have become aware that I cannot speak for "men" generally. Women have taught us in recent years that when a man says "man" he doesn't often include, or speak for, women. Just so, my gay, African American, and Jewish male friends have helped me see that when I say "men," I don't always speak for them. I have realized that believing that you speak for everyone, or even for all men, betrays a naive assumption that your perspective is not conditioned significantly by your social location (i.e., where you grew up, what your economic opportunities and constraints have been, what the contents of the sermons you heard as a boy were, whom you knew personally and whom you did not, to whom you were attracted sexually and what you felt you were allowed to do with that attraction, and many other things). Mostly, then, this book is about white, heterosexual, Anglo-Saxon, Protestant (evangelical), middle-class, middle-aged, southern, able-bodied men. So, when I say men, understand that this is the group to which I am referring. In an earlier version of the manuscript, I had used *-men to designate this particular group of men. My editor thought that would be too cumbersome and distracting. It was, however, a good exercise for me constantly to remind myself that what I am experiencing, thinking, and writing emerges from this particular set of circumstances and may not be true for other men.

This being the case, I could write a strictly autobiographical book; I could speak only of my own experiences. I have done and will do some of that. However, that approach would assume that my experience is completely idiosyncratic, that all the things that have shaped my life are unique to me. This, I believe, exhibits another kind of naivete concerning the pervasive institutional realities and structures of consciousness that shape in similar ways me and other men who are and are not like me. The problem is that without recognizing these larger realities, we are isolated and powerless to change them. We can go to all the consciousness-raising events, individual therapy, drumming retreats, and recovery programs we want, but we will have to go frequently because we will continue to be hurt and our characters will continue to be distorted until some of the greater social realities are changed. And they will not change until those of us similarly distorted by them join hands in solidarity and demand their change. Personal "soul work" is indispensable, but so is unified work to alter the institutions and structures that are harming all of us. I am convinced that we can't make much progress in one without the other.

One of the pitfalls of an author's personal sharing is that some readers may focus on the author's life to diagnose it or to displace their attention from their own lives. That is precisely what I hope you will not do. My theses and the illustrations from my own life story are intended to be, not an end product, but a beginning. They are an invitation to dialogue, conversation, correction, and revision.[5] My hope is that some of the things I say about myself and others here will serve as a seed for your thinking about your own life and others you know. I believe it is important for us men to begin to look at our lives, to tell our stories, and to give each other permission to do that. This moves us to a different level of consciousness and is critical in our movement toward wholeness.

In the face of the divisions among different groups of men, it seems the best thing we each can do is to examine critically and in dialogue with other men and women like and unlike us how we have been shaped, the difficulties we face, the difficulties we cause for others, the opportunities we have, and the common ground we share that will enable us to work together for a more just, compassionate, and pleasurable world.[6]

MEN'S RESTLESSNESS

The causes of the restlessness among men are many. I think the most prevalent are: (1) guilt about our role in the mistreatment of others, (2) resentment about being overburdened and enervated, (3) anger at being unfairly blamed for things that are not our responsibility, and (4) deep feelings of isolation.

As I have said, in the face of justifiable objections to our oppressive attitudes and behaviors, we rage defensively or sink into a guilty silence. We know we are not responsible for everything that is wrong in the world, but we also sense that, personally and collectively, we act in ways that are unfair and hurtful to others and to ourselves.

However, even in the face of persuasive evidence of our collective public (i.e., political and economic) power, we often feel personally isolated and powerless. It is this isolation and felt sense of powerlessness that constitutes one of our identities—what I am calling the "desperate lover." Some of the questions that need to be asked and that occupy part 1 of this book are: How did Tom Wingo, and many of the rest of us, get on the wrong side of so many barricades? How did we become isolated from so many people? Further, how do we begin to step over the barricades or remove them from our side? That is the focus of parts 2 and 3.

But these voices for liberation are not the only cause for the stirring taking place among men today. Observers like Barbara Ehrenreich and Bly have argued that an increasing unrest or dis-ease was evident among men even before the effects of the most recent wave of the women's and other liberation movements were felt. For some time, increasing numbers of us have experienced a feeling of powerlessness and a vague, often unexamined and inarticulate sense that we are somehow being victimized.

Ehrenreich sees this sense of victimization at the root of the various forms of protest in the 1950s, 1960s, and 1970s. The "gray flannel rebels" resisted conformity to the breadwinner role in alienating jobs, and the playboys resisted or complained about the responsibilities and constraints of traditional marriages. Both were most often middle-class, white-collar men who felt the strains imposed on them by the responsibilities inherent in the male sex role and rejected some, but not all, of those responsibilities. The "beatniks" criticized American consumer culture by rejecting both the white-collar work world and the suburbanized family. They emerged from an underclass, walked away from responsibility in any form without money, ambition, or guilt and took inspiration from blacks— permanent outsiders who "countered their rejection by the white world by creating their own language and art."[7] So, among some men there has been a growing awareness of the constrictions to our lives imposed by the harness of the masculine role.[8] Reactions have ranged from selectively rejecting certain aspects of that role to completely dropping out and contributing to the creation of an alternative, a counterculture. As Ehrenreich points out, those choices have been influenced by opportunities and constraints that are often class-specific. I would add that those choices have been shaped also by one's race, ethnic identity, and sexual orientation.

In addition, Robert Bly, among others, suggests that men, in response to our sense of isolation, particularly from our fathers, experience a profound grief, which he identifies as the door to many men's feeling lives.[9] Many of us need a door to our feeling lives because, in part, of the kind of responsibilities and expectations placed on us as men in this culture. To survive, we have had to deaden much of our psychic and physical feeling. This deadening, or numbing, of our souls and bodies results in a number of compulsive, even addictive, behaviors. These, along with the stress that comes with the burdens of our overresponsibility in certain areas of life, lead many of us to an early grave.[10] In addition, our emotional and physical frozenness desensitizes us to the hurt and injustice done to others.

Some of the roles we are expected to play as men produce in us a "lonely warrior." There is a part of many of us that is highly disciplined, focused, task-oriented, and able to accomplish much; but because of our physical, psychic, and emotional numbness, what we accomplish can sometimes be less than productive, even counterproductive to what we and others really need and want.

There exists in many men a tension between these two identities. One of the consequences is that many of us know how to work or how to play, but not many of us have learned to do both. Because we haven't, our work often goes sour and our play becomes compulsive and not very re-creative.[11] Another consequence is our growing sense that something is terribly wrong in the world for which we bear some responsibility, and that something is terribly wrong in us. Our emotional responses to these realizations tend to be a sense of mostly unexpressed anger, resentment, and confusion, as well as a sense of guilt, shame, depression, paralysis, dullness, and lifelessness.

Whether from listening to the pain of others or listening to our own, many men have a growing awareness that we are caught in a system of behaviors and attitudes that not only don't feel good (when we begin to thaw out from the emotional and physical deep freeze), but are also lethal to us, to others, and to the earth. This is causing us to look at ourselves, our institutions, and our roles in them in new ways.

MEN'S LONGING

The second thing I have realized in my explorations of this stirring among men is that a spiritual, or soulful, longing is fueling much of it. There is a deep desire for more meaningful and compassionate relationships, work, and play. Recently over lunch, a clergy friend said, "I have a job that I like, a good marriage and family, more money than I thought I would have at this point in my life, two cars, and a house at the beach. But none of it means anything to me. I wish I were passionate about something." This man, and many other men like him, yearns for passion, for meaning, for life. Like me, many men are searching for a just order for all; the ability to act powerfully and decisively for that order; a capacity to dream dreams of how things might be; and a renewal of our sense of connection to ourselves, to others, and to our earth. Put another way, we are searching for a vocation, a calling.

This longing is a profoundly religious, or spiritual, issue. Saint Augustine believed that human beings are primarily loving creatures (*homo amans*), so if we want to know who people are, we should not ask them what they think or believe, but look at what they love. For Augustine, God is that absolute Good which draws us through our passion, delight, or bliss to communion, integrates all relative goods, and satisfies our deep spiritual longing for a just world and significant connections to others.[12]

Much of the stirring that is happening among men, however, is happening outside the institutional church. Why is that? I think there are several reasons. First, many men have been hurt by particular uses of Christian scriptures, symbols, and doctrines, which have sometimes been used to instill or, at least, reinforce some of the masculine patterns of feeling, thinking, and acting that have been harmful to us and to others. Second, many hold us collectively and personally responsible for much past and present discrimination. Tom Wingo mentions three of our sins—and sins they are—racism, xenophobic militarism, and sexism. I would add homophobia/heterosexism, classism, and anti-Semitism. The problem is that we haven't gotten much help from the church or anywhere else in understanding how, for example, we came by our sexism, the specific ways it is destructive to women, how it is destructive also to men, and what, concretely, we can do about it. I would say the same thing about our homophobia/heterosexism, racism, classism, and anti-Semitism.[13] Third, many of us have been trained to discipline our psyches and bodies to take whatever comes at us, repress or control our emotional response, and go on with whatever task is before us. However, we haven't had much help from the church in understanding what has happened to us; how we have been hurt and mistreated; and how we can heal so that we do not recycle that violence and mistreatment to others and to aspects of ourselves. In other words, the church has not always been a safe enough place for men to step out of their culturally defined masculine roles in order to redefine themselves and those roles. For this reason, many men are turning to other cultural and religious traditions (African and Native American, among others) for stories, rituals, and perspectives from which to experience needed transformation. Some are doing this with great effect, and I have learned and continue to learn much from them and from those traditions.[14]

I also believe, however, that there is much in the Christian faith and the church that mediates to us a calling and offers profound possibilities and opportunities for healing and transformation. Those of us shaped by Christian traditions cannot turn our backs on that heritage. To do so would be to turn our backs on a significant part of who we are, for we have been shaped—even constituted—by the stories, lives, aspirations, failures, and successes of people who felt, thought, and acted in the name of Christ. For me, in fact, there has been much in my experience and study of Christian traditions that has challenged the alienating masculine behaviors I have described and provided resources for personal and communal healing and wholeness.

The purpose of this book is to begin to explore some of these issues and to address the role that the Christian church and theology have played both in producing some of the destructive behaviors and in resisting them.

OUTLINE OF BOOK

Like me, many men begin to ask themselves questions during a crisis, often at midlife, when the cultural models of masculinity break down or are no longer satisfying. When we begin to look at what these models have done to us, to others we care about, to still others we don't know personally, and to our earth, it can be intensely painful. This awareness can shatter our sense of who we are and our whole system of values. Such a "dark night of the soul" can also be a "severe mercy" (Saint Augustine) that precipitates an "eternal birth" (Meister Eckhart), which "fattens the soul" (Catherine of Siena). I will have more to say about this and these mentors later, but here I acknowledge that their thinking has helped me frame my own experiences in a fruitful way. In fact, I now realize the structure of the book reflects the threefold path described by medieval Christian mystics—purgation, illumination, and union.

Part 1 is an elaboration of the development of the dual identities— the lonely warrior (chapter 1) and the desperate lover (chapter 2). In chapter 3, I argue that these identities are false selves that can be construed to be a consequence of, or punishment for, sin. Part 2 offers an interpretation of Christianity that calls us deeply into ourselves and out over the barricades that isolate us from others (chapter 4). In chapter 5, I look at the ways in which faith challenges our attachments to false selves. In part 3, I describe potentially tranformative processes and spaces (chapter 6) and suggest ways that love leads us to reconciliation with our bodies and the earth (chapter 7), other men (chapter 8), and women (chapter 9).

As for the intended audience for this book, I imagine that other men much like me will find it the most helpful. Others who live with us, work with us, love us, or resent us might also find things here that increase their understanding of us. I pray that it will make us better able to speak and listen to the truth with each other in love (Ephesians 4:15).

The Men We Have Become

Chapter One

Lonely Warriors:
The Public, Responsible Self

I cannot believe that a good judge would approve of the beatings I received as a boy on the ground that my games delayed my progress in studying subjects which would enable me to play a less creditable game later in life.

SAINT AUGUSTINE, *Confessions*

I feel like I spent forty years of my life working as hard as I can to become somebody I don't even like.

RALPH

MUCH OF THE MASCULINE socialization boys receive in our society prepares us to take on the responsibilities of manhood. Among the primary responsibilities we have as men are to protect and to provide for others. We are trained to become officers in the institutions that are intended to give order to our collective lives and help them flourish. The problem is that the ways we are often trained to fill these offices produce in us a "lonely warrior" that alienates us from significant aspects of ourselves and from others. In this chapter, I want to relate the story of one such officer and then explore some of the implications of his story for many of the rest of us.

THE STORY OF RALPH

In his book *Why Men Are the Way They Are,* Warren Farrell tells a story about a man who participated in one of his men's groups. This man, like me, ran into a brick wall in mid-life and describes his confusion, pain, and anger. They are feelings that I and many men I know have felt at one time or another—for many of the same reasons. In fact, reading his story helped me puncture my own denial and added momentum to my growth.

Ralph was a forty-one-year-old man in our men's group. He was married, the father of two children. He had been in the group for three months, and had hardly said a word. One evening he looked up and said, "I think I'd like to speak up tonight. I'm afraid I joined this group only because my wife forced me to. She got involved in one of these women's movement operations and started changing. She called it 'growing.' About three months ago she said, 'Ralph, I'm tired of having to choose between a relationship with you and a relationship with my-self.' Pretty fancy rhetoric, I thought. Then she added, 'There's a men's group forming that's meeting next Tuesday. Why don't you get involved?'

"Well, I kind of laughed her off. But a week later she started again. 'The group's meeting next Tuesday. As far as I'm concerned, if you're not doing some changing in *three* months, that's the end.'

" 'The end! For the sake of a *men's group?*' I asked.

" 'It's symbolic, Ralph,' she said.

"So I figured I'd join this symbol and see what you fags were talking about! But the problem was, you didn't fit my image, and I began identifying with some of the things you were saying. Well, anyway, last night Ginny reminded me the three months were up tomorrow. So I think I'd like to speak up tonight."

We laughed at Ralph's motivation, but encouraged him to continue.

"Well, what struck me was how each of you chose different careers, but you all worried about succeeding. Even you, Jim—even though you're unemployed and have a laid-back facade. That started me thinking about my career.

"All my life I wanted to play baseball. As a pro. When I was a sophomore in high school I was pretty hot stuff, and my uncle came and scouted me. Later he said, 'Ralph, you're good. Damn good. And you might make it to the pros if you really work at it. But only the best make good money for a long time. If you really want to be good to yourself, make use of your intelligence, get yourself a good job—one you can depend on for life.'

"I was surprised when my folks agreed with him. Especially Dad. Dad always called me 'Ralph, who pitched the no-hitter.' Dad stopped calling me that after that conversation. Maybe that turned the tide for me.

". . . Anyway, I was proud of myself for making the transition like a man. I'd always liked reading and learning, but just hadn't focused much on it. But I figured just for a couple of years I'd 'play the system': borrow friends' old term papers, take a look at old exams, focus my reading on the questions different teachers tended to ask, and so on. I never cheated. I just figured I'd 'play the system' for a couple of years, raise my grades, then when I got into college, I could really learn—I could do what I wanted after that.

"Well, 'playing the system' worked. I got into a top-notch university. But it soon became apparent that a lot of people graduated from good universities—if I wanted to really stand out it would help to 'play the system' for just a few more years, get into a good grad school or law school, and then, once I did that, I could do with my life what I wanted after that.

"I decided on law school—but to become a social-work lawyer, so I could make a real contribution to people who most needed it. But about my second or third year of law school—when my colleagues saw I was taking what they called 'missionary law' seriously, they explained that if I really wanted to be effective as a social-work lawyer, I'd better get some experience first in the hard-knocks, reality-based field of corporate law rather than ease into the namby-pamby area of social-work law right away—if I didn't I wouldn't get the respect to be effective. Frankly, that made sense. So I joined a top corporate law firm in New York. I knew I could work there for a couple of years, and then really do what I wanted with my life after that.

"After a couple of years in the firm, I was doing well. But the whole atmosphere of the corporate legal community made it clear that if I dropped out after two years it would be seen as a sign that I just couldn't hack the pressure. If I continued for just a couple more years, and became a junior partner—junior partners were the ones marked with potential—then I could really do what I wanted with my life after that.

"Well, it took me seven years to get the junior partnership offered to me—with politics and everything. But I got it. By that time I had lost some of the desire to be a social-work lawyer—it was considered a clear step backward. In other ways I maintained that ideal—it seemed more meaningful than kowtowing to rich money. But I also knew the switch would mean forfeiting a lot of income. My wife Ginny and I had just bought a new home—which we pretty much had to do with two kids—and I knew they'd be going to college. . . . Ginny's income was only part-time now, and she was aching to travel a bit.

"By that time, I also realized that while junior partners had potential, the people with the real ins in the legal community were not the junior partners, but the senior partners. I figured I had a pretty big investment in the corporate law area now—if I just stuck it out for a couple more years, I could get a senior partnership, get a little money saved for the kids' education and travel, and *then* I could really do with my life what I wanted. . . .

"It took me eight more years to get the senior partnership. I can remember my boss calling me into the office and saying, 'Ralph, we're offering you a senior partnership.' I acted real calm, but my heart was jumping toward the phone in anticipation of telling Ginny. Which I did. I told Ginny I had a surprise. I'd tell her when I got home. I asked her to get dressed real special. I refused to leak what it was about. I made reservations in her favorite restaurant, bought some roses and her favorite champagne.

"I came home real early so we'd have time to sip it together; I opened the door and said, 'Guess what?' Ginny was looking beautiful. She said, 'What is it, Ralph?' I said, 'I got the senior partnership!' She said, 'Oh, fine, that's great,' but there was a look of distance in her eyes. A real superficial enthusiasm, you know what I mean?"

We nodded.

"So I said, 'What do you mean "Oh, fine"—I've been working since the day we met to get this promotion for us, and you say "Oh, fine" '?

" 'Every time you get a promotion, Ralph,' Ginny announced, 'you spend less time with me. I guess I just wish you'd have more time for me. More time to love me.'

" 'Why do you think I've been working my ass off all these years if it isn't to show you how much I love you?' I said.

" 'Ralph, that's not what I mean by love. Just look at the kids, Ralph.'

"Well, I did look at the kids. Randy is seventeen. And Ralph, Jr., is fifteen. Randy just got admitted to college—a thousand miles from here. Each year I keep promising myself that 'next year' I'll really get to know who they are. 'Next year. . . ' 'Next year.' But next year he'll be in college. And I don't even know who he is. And I don't know whether I'm his dad or his piggy bank.

"I don't know where to begin with Randy, but a few weeks ago I tried to change things a bit with Ralph, Jr. He was watching TV. I asked him if he wouldn't mind turning it off so we could talk. He was a little reluctant, but he eventually started telling me some of what was happening at school. We talked baseball, and I told him about some of my days pitching. He said I'd already told him. He told me about some of his activities, and I spotted a couple of areas where I thought his values were going to hurt him. So I told him. We got into a big argument. He said I wasn't talking with him, I was lecturing him . . . 'spying' on him.

"We've hardly talked since. I can see what I did wrong—boasting and lecturing—but I'm afraid if I try again, he'll be afraid to say much now, and we'll just sit there awkwardly. And if he mentions those values, what do I say? I want to be honest, but I don't want to lecture. I don't even know where to begin."

Ralph withdrew from the group. He had struck so many chords it took us more than ten minutes to notice that he was fighting back tears. Finally one of the men picked up on it and asked, "Ralph, is there anything else you're holding back?" Ralph said there wasn't, but his assurance rang false. We prodded.

"I guess maybe I am holding something back," he said hesitantly. "I feel like I spent forty years of my life working as hard as I can to become somebody I don't even like."

Ralph continued: "I was mentioning some of my doubts to a few of my associates at work. They listened attentively for a couple of minutes, then one made a joke, and another excused himself. Finally I mentioned this men's group—which I never should have done—and they just laughed me out of the office. I've been the butt of jokes ever since: 'How are the U.S. Navel Gazers doing, Ralph boy?'

"Suddenly I realized. Ginny has a whole network of lady friends she can talk with about all this. Yet the men I've worked with for seventeen years, sixty hours a week, hardly know me. Nor do they want to."

Ralph withdrew again. But this time he seemed to be taking in what he had just said as if he were putting together his life as he was speaking. Then his face grew sad. . . .

"I guess I could handle all this," Ralph volunteered, fighting back the tears again, "but I think, for all practical purposes, I've lost Ginny in the process. And maybe I could handle that, too. But the only other people I love in this world are Randy and Ralph, Jr. And when I'm really honest with myself—I mean *really* honest—I think for all practical purposes I've lost them too—."

We started to interrupt, but Ralph stopped us, tears silently escaping his eyes, "What really gets me . . . what really gets me angry is that I did everything I was supposed to do for forty years, did it better than almost any other man I know, and I lost everyone I love in the process, including myself. . . .

"In some ways, I feel I could handle all that, too. But look at me—paid more than any two of you guys put together, supposedly one of the top decision-makers in the country, and when it comes to my own home, my own life, I don't even know how to begin."

Ralph cried. For the first time in twenty-two years.[1]

"I feel like I spent forty years of my life working as hard as I can to become somebody I don't even like." How many of us, at one time or another, have felt this way? Farrell says in the book that this story stopped him dead in his tracks, as he thought about the ways in which some of what Ralph said either had been or might be true for him. I have thought about Ralph a lot over the last five years and have shared his story with other men. Ralph is not everyman; he had many, many opportunities other men do not have. Even when compared with those who have had similar opportunities, Ralph achieved unusually high levels of success. Or did he? Well, it depends on what is meant by success.

For Ralph, success was defined for him by his uncle, with the agreement of his father, as making "good money for a long time." If the primary responsibilities of men are to provide for and protect our families, this definition seems reasonable; money helps on both scores. It provides what our families need and want and promises to protect them and us from threats to our physical, emotional, and psychological survival. Ralph suggests that all the guys in the group worried about succeeding; for that matter, most men I know do, too. We do so, not just for the sake of our families, but in order to develop and maintain our own self-respect and the respect of others. For many of us, our sense of worth and belonging is bound up with the degree of this kind of success.

How do we learn to pursue this kind of success in the ways Ralph did? How did he learn it? There are two major influences that shape our sense of what it means to be a good or successful man—our fathers or other older male role models, and the often violent conditioning that comes from our society.

FATHERS AND OTHER MENTORS

Ralph said that the tide turned for him when his father stopped calling him "Ralph, who pitched the no-hitter." For Ralph and for many of us, we learn about being a man from our fathers—either by their presence or by their absence. One of the ways our personalities are developed is through a series of identifications.[2] That is, we identify with someone and take an aspect, characteristic, or property of another into ourselves. Boys look at their fathers and other older men for cues about how they are supposed to be. This was driven home to me by a couple of experiences I had recently.

The first was something I observed during our church's summer vacation Bible school. Besides the program leader, I was the only adult male helper present for most of the week. One day I looked over at a row of five boys in the first or second grade. Each time I looked, I caught at least two of them staring at me; they would look away when I made eye contact. That same afternoon, I saw my neighbor leave his garage with a handsaw to cut up a branch that had fallen in his yard. Right behind him was his four-year-old son carrying a plastic saw. It suddenly struck me—we learn how to be men by watching other men be men. Then I thought, If a little guy was watching me all the time, what would he see; what would he learn that men do? Well, for most of my adult life he would see me go to work, then come home and either work some more or indulge myself in some sort of compensatory activity by which I rewarded myself for working so long and hard. That is a scary thought—this is what he would learn about what men do and who they are— that we are "human doings" and not "human beings"?[3] I'm afraid that is what many of us learned.

For many men in industrial and postindustrial society, we have learned from our fathers by their absence.[4] A recent study shows fathers spending an average of thirty-seven seconds a day interacting with infants in the first three months of life; another found an average of about an hour a day of direct play between fathers and nine-month-old infants, including time spent together on weekends.[5] In an informal survey of seventy-one of his clients, Jack Sternbach found that 23 percent of the men had fathers who were physically absent, 29 percent had fathers who were psychologically absent, 18 percent had psychologically distant fathers who were also austere and moralistic, 15 percent had fathers who were threatening and seemingly out of control, and only 15 percent had fathers who were appropriately involved with their sons.[6] Many fathers work hard; it is not that they don't love their children, but "the curse of fatherhood is distance, and good fathers spend their lives trying to overcome it."[7] For many of us, our father is not around long enough, or if he is, he is not self-disclosing enough, for us to get to know much about the way he thinks and feels.

So, if our fathers are significantly absent to many of us, where else do we learn about becoming men? For many, it is through imitating the cultural images of men presented to us in movies, fairy tales, and stories, on TV, and in athletic arenas. Even for men, like me, whose fathers were physically and emotionally present, there is tremendous peer pressure to adopt cultural images. We are often pushed toward particular images because of the violent conditioning we experience in our early lives.

Violence and Masculine Conditioning

In addition to his identification with his father's goals and values, Ralph was shaped by the emotionally violent responses of his male peers—"How are the U.S. Navel Gazers doing, Ralph boy?" Not only was Ralph expected to continue the never-ending pursuit of respect and credibility by working sixty hours a week without complaint, he was ridiculed for even thinking about stepping back and considering whether this was the way he wanted to spend his life. Such violent conditioning begins very early in our lives and continues throughout.

Many of the ways we come to think, feel, and behave are produced and negatively reinforced by violence we experience at the hands of other boys and men. I have come to believe that we men are surrounded and significantly shaped by forms of violence that, though all around us, are often invisible to us. Perhaps they are invisible because they are so pervasive that we take them for granted as simply the way things are—as the natural order of things. As Hannah Arendt observed, "No one questions or examines what is obvious to all."[8]

Recently Myriam Miedzian has pointed to a strong correlation between physical violence and men—both as perpetrators and as victims: 89 percent of all violent crimes are committed by men; each year 1.8 million women are physically assaulted by their husbands or boyfriends; wars are initiated, conducted, and consummated primarily by men; and three times as many men as women are murdered.[9] However, she steps back and "problematizes" male violence; that is, she rejects the notion that violence is natural to, or inevitable for, males and looks at the ways that masculine norms "such as toughness, dominance, repression of empathy, and extreme competitiveness play a major role in criminal and domestic violence and underlie the thinking and policy decisions of many of our political leaders."[10]

In her discussion of violence Miedzian makes several helpful distinctions. First, she distinguishes three kinds of "aggression": (1) constructive aggression, which is assertiveness and determination; (2) antisocial aggression, exhibited in extreme competitiveness and a concern for dominance; and

(3) destructive aggression, or violence. She further distinguishes offensive violence from defensive violence, which is justified by an unjust attack on oneself.[11]

While some of our masculine socialization involves constructive assertiveness, too much of it is produced by and produces in us antisocial aggression and violence. So much so that we might say that the way we are molded into men is not just through a process of socialization, but also by violent conditioning. This is a distinction made by Judith Kay, who has done a great deal of work with groups who have experienced discrimination and oppression. For her, socialization refers to "the process of living in a social context that accustoms people to certain views of self, others, and world." This process includes the language, symbols, tools, technology, art, narratives, and myths of a society. Two aspects of socialization that bear upon the dynamics of oppression are a lack of information about oneself and others and misinformation about oneself and others. Conditioning, however, is "the process by which people acquire rigid behavioral patterns, emotions, and thoughts from experiences of mistreatment."[12] The point of making this distinction here is to say that many of those masculine ways of thinking, feeling, and behaving, so destructive to others and to us, are not only socialized, but also conditioned in us. Consequently, we need to pay attention to both the socialization processes and the conditioning that have shaped Ralph and men like him to act, think, and feel as we do.

In this section, I want to look at what our culture says men are supposed to be like in four areas of our lives—physical and emotional, intellectual, relational, and sexual—and at the ways we are violently conditioned to exhibit these characteristics. In chapter 2, I have developed a table that schematizes this. See page 52.

PHYSICAL AND EMOTIONAL LIFE

When I am in mixed-gender groups or groups of men, I sometimes ask men what they are supposed to be like physically and emotionally. For the physical aspect, the responses often include strong, hard, tall, powerful, and erect (column 6 in the table). For the emotional aspects, the answers are silent, disciplined, and controlled. Then I ask, "If you do not exhibit these traits, what are you called?" The responses include wimp, sissy, pussy, and girl (column 7).

Charlie Kreiner, a consultant and workshop leader, aptly describes the conditioning that takes place around our physical, emotional, and sexual lives.[13] For most of us there is a time—usually around the beginning of our formal education—when the polarization of gender roles escalates and takes on institutional expression. Do you remember the time in your life when anything associated with girls was offensive? The most horrifying thing you could think of was doing anything like a girl did it—to walk like a girl, to run like a girl, to throw like a girl, to talk like a girl, to look like a girl. Do you remember what happened if you did? Many of us were ridiculed, humiliated, or beaten up—three forms of escalating violence. If you acted in any way like a girl, you would first be ridiculed. If you didn't stop, the ridicule might become more organized, leading to public humiliation. If this emotional violence did not persuade you to change your behavior, you might have to suffer physical violence at the hands of the male enforcers of masculine norms.

This, however, is just the first level of masculine socialization and conditioning, for even if you avoid so-called feminine behavior, you must participate in the violence against other boys who don't. If you don't ridicule other boys who act like girls, you again risk being the target of ridicule, humiliation, and violence. Further, if you don't ridicule those boys who don't ridicule others, you can also be the target of violence yourself. There often is nowhere to go—no place to hide. For many young boys, the choice is either to adopt these kinds of masculine norms and behaviors or to suffer violence at the hands of other boys, and sometimes girls and adults.

I remember my first and only fight with another boy in grade school. I was in the fourth grade and was walking home with a girl I liked. My stomach tightened as I noticed Bobby and a buddy of his walking some distance behind us. After a while, Bobby began to call me a sissy, among other things, and they proceeded to laugh at me. I felt humiliated and believed that I had no choice but to turn and confront them. If I didn't, I felt that the girl would think less of me and that the boys might tell others and the humiliation would spread. Better to do something now and face just these two boys. Well, the girl went on home (she didn't seem very interested in this important confrontation), and Bobby and I, after a number of exchanges consisting of things like, "You going to do something about it?" and "Oh, yeah," went into a yard to fight. I don't think either of us had ever fought before, so we spent a lot of time circling each other. He was, however, able to land a punch to my mouth, which made it swell. As suppertime came, we decided to suspend the fight until the next afternoon and went home.

At home, I got a piece of ice to try to control the swelling so that my family wouldn't notice it. The reason was not so much because they would know that I had been in a fight, but because Bobby had "busted my lip." Well, I was unsuccessful, and my father and brother made fun of me for letting

Bobby do that to me. In fact, that "busted lip" became a part of family lore and a source of continued embarrassment for some time to come. I was glad to have the chance to finish the fight the following day, so that I could do something to redeem myself. As I recall, we probably scheduled the continuation because I wanted to get even for the "busted lip."

The next day, the news that Bobby and I were going to finish our fight spread through school. After a very uneasy day, I left school to meet Bobby at the prearranged place. When I got to the school door I was met, much to my surprise, by my brother (who was two years older) and a bunch of his sixth-grade friends. As they escorted me to the designated yard, they whistled the theme to the sixties television show "Combat." I knew that there wouldn't be the possibility of a truce and resolved to do whatever I had to do to get out of the spotlight. There wasn't much circling this time and I was much more aggressive, probably because I had more face to save (Bobby was accompanied by only one friend). I hit Bobby several times in the stomach and he gave up and went home. I was a big hero.

I felt pretty good about myself until one of my friends told me that I had put Bobby in the hospital and the principal called me to the office over the loudspeaker. She said that Bobby was in the hospital with internal bleeding because of our fight. I was frightened, sick, and worried. I learned later that Bobby went to the hospital for an intestinal virus, not as a result of our fight. I was relieved to find that out, and while it might have tainted my "victory" to know that he was probably already sick when we fought, I didn't really care. In retrospect, I think I was not so concerned about the victory as I was about getting out of the spotlight or, said another way, removing myself from "target" status. Not to say that I didn't want to win; I did. But part of that desire was, I think, related to the desire to stop being the target of my peers' attention and to save face. I have since thought about what many of us men do to avoid such targeting. Establishing oneself as one of the powerful, or at least developing alliances with the powerful, is a crucial strategy in the attempt to avoid targeting.

This violently induced sex-role polarization is often institutionalized by the segregation of boys and girls. In my generation and before, the segregation was more pronounced than it is today. At church the boys went to one Sunday school class and the girls went to another. The boys played organized sports like Little League baseball, midget-league football, and grade-school basketball; the girls went to dance class, took music lessons, and had slumber parties. In many ways we became different creatures in different cultures, barely recognizing each other as belonging to the same species.

Here we see some of the psychosocial roots of our deeply internalized misogyny (hatred of women), femiphobia (fear of the feminine), and restrictive emotionality. It is difficult to like girls if relating to them brings ridicule, humiliation, and physical violence down on you. It is difficult to affirm parts of yourself such as sensitivity and artistic creativity if their expression makes you a target for the enforcers of "boy stuff" (or dominative masculinity). It is difficult to express your feelings if doing so makes you a "baby" or a "loser" in the eyes of your peers and, in too many cases, adults.

Organized sports too often reinforce these norms. A boy who is not competing hard enough, or who cries when he loses, or is uneasy about beating someone else, is ridiculed by being called a "girl," a "sissy," or a "pussy." Physical pain is something that must be numbed or ignored for the sake of performance. The expression of emotion leaves one vulnerable to one's competitor, so the strict control of any emotion that might adversely affect a boy's performance or competitive edge is rewarded and any lack of control is punished. Important skills are learned in the arena of sports, including the ability to focus and accomplish goals in spite of obstacles. The point here is that it is often very difficult for us to recover access to our emotions. And this difficulty has dire effects on us and others around us.

Cultural images of men and masculinity often reinforce this conditioning. In junior high, I read as much as I could about major-league baseball; I particularly liked the pictures of heroes past and present and spent a great deal of time imagining what it would be like to play with them and watch them play. My favorite player was Willie Mays, so on my Little League, Pony League, and high-school teams, I played center field. I loved his speed, power, and grace in the outfield. In football, I wore the number 19 and played quarterback—the number and position of Johnny Unitas, the great quarterback of the Baltimore Colts. I admired his coolness under pressure and his uncanny ability to pull victory from the jaws of defeat. I recall the admiration in the voice of one of Johnny Unitas's linemen when speaking of the way the Hall of Fame quarterback played. He said that when Unitas came off the field, you could not tell from looking at his face whether he had just thrown a touchdown or an interception. He had, as sports reporters like to say, "ice water in his veins."

In high school and college, I had a six-foot poster of Muhammad Ali on the back of my bedroom door. I admired him for his strong religious convictions, his grace and style inside and outside the ring, his determination to regain the heavyweight championship, and his desire to inflict no more physical damage than was necessary to win the fight.

As I look now at my identifications with these men, I can appreciate the positive values I gained from them—the grace, strength, gentleness, discipline, determination, intelligence, resourcefulness, fair play, and pleasure in their profession. I can also see more clearly some of the self-destructive aspects of their lives, and though I don't know much about those around them, I have a sense that some of these things must not have been good for them either.

First, they all lived very public lives; their lives were constantly covered by the media, that is, until they retired. I think that that is one of the reasons it was so difficult for Mays and Ali to retire—the loss of the public gaze and what it provided in terms of a sense of self-worth. For Ali, that meant taking a lot of physical punishment in later fights, which probably should never have taken place. I have come to know what it means to need that kind of external approbation. It brings with it certain expectations of the particular public from which one seeks approval and encourages the meticulous, even compulsive, development and maintenance of a public persona, which may conceal or misrepresent aspects of oneself that do not conform to the popular public image.

Second, their popularity and, I imagine, sense of self-worth depended on their winning or, at least, maintaining a high level of performance vis-à-vis an opponent.

INTELLECTUAL LIFE

When I ask men what they are supposed to be like intellectually, they say things like smart, expert, right, and decisive. If we are not, we are "losers."

I have recently become convinced that we experience about as much violent conditioning in our formal education as we do on the playgrounds and ball fields. The violence often takes a different, less noticeable form, which therefore may be more difficult to see and deal with.

Much to his embarrassment, Saint Augustine could not read Greek as well as he would have liked. The reason, he believed, had to do with the way it was taught in school. This is what he says about the painful memories of his boyhood school days:

O God, my God, I now went through a period of suffering and humiliation. I was told that it was right and proper for me as a boy to pay attention to my teachers, so that I should do well at my study of grammar and get on in the world. This was the way to gain the respect of others and win for myself what passes for wealth in this world. . . . If I was idle at my studies, I was beaten for it, because beating was favored by tradition . . . and then my elders and even my parents, who certainly wished me no harm, would laugh at the beating I got and in those days beatings were my one great bugbear.

. . . if a man clings to you with great devotion, how can his piety inspire him to find it in his heart to make light of these tortures, when he loves those who dread them so fearfully? And yet this was how our parents scoffed at the torments which we boys suffered at the hands of our masters. For we feared the whip just as much as others fear the rack, and we, no less than they, begged you to preserve us from it. But we sinned by reading and writing and studying less than was expected of us. . . . But we enjoyed playing games and were punished for them by men who played games themselves. However, grown-up games are known as "business," and even though boys' games are much the same, they are punished for them by their elders. No one pities either the boys or the men, though surely we deserved pity, for I cannot believe that a good judge would approve of the beatings I received as a boy on the ground that my games delayed my progress in studying subjects which would enable me to play a less creditable game later in life. Was the master who beat me himself very different from me? If he were worsted by a colleague in some petty argument, he would be convulsed with anger and envy, much more so than I was when a playmate beat me at a game of ball.

. . . I sinned, O Lord, by disobeying my parents and the masters of whom I have spoken. . . . I was disobedient, not because I chose something better than they proposed to me, but simply from the love of games. . . . As time went on, . . . I wanted to see the shows and sports which grown-ups enjoyed. The patrons who pay for the production of these shows are held in esteem such as most parents would wish for their children. Yet the same parents willingly allow their children to be flogged if they are distracted by these displays from the studies which are supposed to fit them to grow rich and give the same sort of shows themselves.[14]

"No one pities either the boys or the men, though surely we deserved pity." Indeed they did and so, too, do many of us. Although many public schools have done away with corporal punishment, other things haven't changed very much since the fourth century.

Augustine describes what Paulo Freire, the Brazilian educator and liberation theoretician, calls antidialogical education.[15] This educational method, which prevails in many of our schools today, operates on the assumptions that the teacher knows everything and the students know nothing; the teacher thinks and the students are thought about; the teacher disciplines and the students are disciplined; and the teacher talks and the students listen. So, the teacher talks about, or narrates, reality (as he or she sees it, or as it was narrated to him or her) and the student listens, records, memorizes, and repeats the narration.

The very abstraction of the contents of what is taught, rather than engendering curiosity about reality as the student experiences it and encouraging the development of the student's flexible intelligence, serves to cut the student off from reality. The student relates to the abstracted content of what is presented by the teacher, not the everyday reality that both student and teacher experience and that the class content is supposed to clarify. Often, students who attempt to stay connected with reality as they experience it will be punished with low grades for not sufficiently mastering the teacher's content.

This kind of education has several debilitating effects on those of us who are subjected to it. First, it is most often carried out in a competitive environment. We have to compete with other students for the limited supply of good grades—there must be a curve because we can't all do well; otherwise, the grades would mean nothing—or other forms of the teacher's or the institution's approbation. This pits us against one another and encourages individual achievement and not cooperative learning. This, in turn, inhibits or even damages our ability to empathize, to understand how another person perceives a situation and is reacting cognitively and affectively to it.[16] Again, the competition produces a certain conformity in students; if you must beat someone else, you must do the same thing he or she is doing—often in the same way. There is, in this form of education, less physical violence but no less aggression and hostility. One observer notes:

> One must marvel at the intellectual quality of a teacher who can't understand why children assault one another in the hallway, playground, and city street, when in the classroom the highest accolades are reserved for those who have beaten their peers. In many subtle and some not so subtle ways, teachers demonstrate that what children learn means less than that they triumph over their classmates. Is this not assault? . . . Classroom defeat is only the pebble that creates widening ripples of hostility. It is self-perpetuating. It is reinforced by

peer censure, parental disapproval, and loss of self-concept. If the classroom is a model, and if that classroom models competition, assault in the hallways should surprise no one.[17]

This kind of education goes a long way toward producing what Sam Keen calls a "warrior psyche." He describes that psyche as characterized by the identification of action with force; a paranoid worldview (i.e., one's intellectual powers are mobilized against the enemy); black-and-white thinking that oversimplifies issues and deals with stereotypes that reduce the enemy to an object that can be defeated without remorse; the repression of fear, compassion, and guilt; and an obsession with rank and hierarchy.[18] In other words, this kind of education conditions and shapes in us a belief in the force of logic, which can be used with impunity against those evidently malevolent opponents who refuse to accept the objective, unconditioned truth of the authorities passed on by teachers.

Second, intellectual work, particularly for those of us who have made it our careers, is laced with violence directed at ourselves and at others. In fact, I believe that many of us pursue intellectual power in part as a defensive response to the physical and emotional violence we experience early in our lives. In a workshop I attended, Michael Kaufman asked a group of men to think of an instance of violence experienced at the hands of another male.[19] I thought of the time in the junior-high locker room when Jack Bradshaw, who was three years older and fifteen pounds heavier than I, deliberately reached over and ripped my gym shirt in front of all the other boys. I stood there shamefaced and angry, but did nothing.

Then Kaufman asked us how we compensated for our sense of powerlessness in that situation. I realized then, for the first time, that one of the reasons I quit sports in high school and focused on academic achievement was not only to get ahead, like Ralph and Augustine, but also to defend myself from bullies like Jack Bradshaw. However, I found, to my chagrin, that there is also a lot of intimidation, fear, aggression, lack of empathy, anxiety about pecking order, and rhetorical polemics against the "enemy" in my profession of choice.

Third, this kind of education is the medium for the "cultural invasion" of the student by the teacher. Freire calls this an "antidialogical" educational method because it does not engender a dialogue between two subjects, but rather insists on a monologue by the teacher because of the permanent subject–object relationship in which the teacher stands to the student. By considering the student an object that is absolutely ignorant, the teacher justifies her or his existence. This is the "banking concept" of education. The students are depositories; the teacher is the depositor. Many of us have experienced this educational method.

There are values implicit or explicit in the contents of the deposits that the teacher, or the teacher's teachers, chose to abstract from reality, with all of the values, ideological commitments, biases, and prejudices that led to the choices. The student becomes the compliant receptacle not only for the contents, but also for those values, commitments, biases, and prejudices that shaped the original abstraction. It is the inculcation of these values that Freire calls "cultural invasion."

So, with what kind of values are we culturally invaded? I read very few things about or by a woman, an African-American, an identified gay man or lesbian, or a Jew all during high school and college. I have a dim memory of reading Emily Dickinson and Langston Hughes in American Literature, and I read a few biographies of black sports figures (Willie Mays and Muhammed Ali), but that was about it. I never heard of Elizabeth Cady Stanton, Virginia Woolf, Zora Neale Hurston, W. E. B. Du Bois, and Marcus Garvey. I didn't know that Alexander the Great, King James I, Walt Whitman, and James Dean may have been gay and that Susan B. Anthony and Willa Cather were lesbians. Nor was much mention made of Albert Einstein and Barbra Streisand being Jewish.

When I got to graduate school, we had a strong women's studies program, but although I was sympathetic to the "women's movement" because of the damage I had seen sexism do to my mother, sister, wife, and other women I knew, I never took a women's studies course. Nor did I take a course dealing specifically with issues related to African-American or gay and lesbian religious experience.

The reasons are several. First, such courses were electives and not yet part of the required curriculum. Second, I and many guys like me assumed, wrongly, that these were "special interest" courses relevant only to the persons whose experiences were the subject of the study. Third, it was clear to me that these courses were not going to get me ahead and might well hinder me in that goal. And, like Augustine and Ralph, one of the reasons I was in graduate school was to get ahead; that has to do with class background.

I was raised in what Paul King, Kent Maynard, and David Woodyard have termed the "middle-sector" fraction of the "laboring class."[20] That is, rather than being one of the "laboring sector" or "working poor," my father worked as a manager for a small company, standing between the workers on the one side and the owners on the other. He, and our family, experienced the economic position shared by all fragments of the laboring class—work for and dependence on others—and the economic instability and lack of economic self-determination or real power that come with it. Consequently, his goal, and mine, for my education was for me to move up into what Barbara and John Ehrenreich have called the "professional-managerial class," because we both believed that that would give me more economic stability and autonomy.[21] The options were first, medicine, and then either the ministry or an academic career.

This upward mobility depended on success in undergraduate and graduate education, which required submission to the process I have described and appropriation of the values of my teachers and the institutions I attended.[22] From many, but not all, of my teachers, I received the implicit or explicit message that courses dealing with gender and race were the special interest of women and African-Americans and were of marginal importance to the "real scholar," that is, guys like them. The message was that if I wanted to be taken seriously and succeed, I would avoid spending my time on things like that. Success was identified with mastering the authorities, and women, African-Americans, gays and lesbians, and Jews were not considered authorities. In fact, I felt that if I did spend time reading work by and about these people and working on issues that they were raising, I would be penalized.

One of the things I want to point out here is that there continued to be, even for a highly educated man like me, a lack of information and understanding about people different from me. Not much occurred in my educational experience to counter whatever misinformation I had gotten about others in the way of stereotypes.

RELATIONALITY

What if we live up to these masculine norms; what will be the effects on our relationships? What if we always try to appear physically strong, powerful, hard and emotionally silent, disciplined, and controlled? What if we develop a public persona that is at odds with or misrepresents aspects of ourselves? What if, because of our competitiveness, we don't play very much, are goal-oriented, and conform to many of those whom we believe we need to beat? What if we express ourselves sexually in ways that are aggressive, extremely "penis-centered," somewhat compulsive, and fearful of closeness to other men? What if we beat other people over the head with our logic, ignore the ways our "truth" is conditioned by where we are sitting, refuse to listen to the way things look from other people's perspectives, and think and act on the basis of stereotypes that often justify, or rationalize, other people's mistreatment?

Well, we will find it hard to get close to many people. And when we find ourselves in this kind of isolation, how are we, as men, supposed to act? Well, cool, unemotional, and controlled as if all this were our idea. "No, this is the way I want it; I don't need that; really, I am okay." Cultural images like James Bond, Napoleon Solo, James West, and many of the characters played by John Wayne and Clint Eastwood model this for us.

SEXUALITY

Following the period of the segregation of the sexes comes puberty and the onset of adolescence. As Kreiner points out, this is the time of junior-high dances—where the boys stand on one side of the room and the girls on the other. Having been conditioned to develop only certain aspects of ourselves labeled as "masculine," we look at girls, who have been conditioned to develop certain other aspects of themselves labeled as "feminine," and we don't seem to have anything in common with them—the "opposite" sex. They look like some strange, frightening creature. And what is the one point of contact—the one common activity? Sex!

What is a boy called if he is not "getting any" from the girls? Depending on the place and generation, he is called a "homo," "queer," or "fag." So the escalating levels of emotional and physical violence are repeated at this stage as well. If a boy is not "getting any," or at least not pretending to, he can be targeted for ridicule, humiliation, and physical violence. If he doesn't ridicule boys who don't treat girls this way, he can be targeted. If he doesn't ridicule boys who don't ridicule boys who don't treat girls this way, he can be targeted. Again, often there is no place to hide.

In this stage of masculine socialization, we see the psychosocial roots of the objectification, genitalization, and compulsiveness of male sexuality, homophobia, and compulsory heterosexuality.[23] These are technical terms for some very important dynamics in the lives of men, so I want to explain them.

Note the language of sex here—"getting any"; getting any what? Well, the names are legion and usually have to do with some food, animal, or body part: honey, sugar, sweetie; fox, chick, bitch; piece of ass, cunt, and pussy. The point is that sex is viewed in objectified terms; women are not seen as human persons but as objects of desire. Desire for what? A desire to "score" or "get off," that is, a desire to have intercourse with the goal of ejaculation or orgasm (the two are usually not distinguished). So, the genitals become the focus of male sexuality. Sexual feelings are drained out of the body and located almost exclusively in the penis. Sexuality and genital sexuality are one and the same. Again, if a boy does not treat girls in this objectified, alienating way, or at least pretend to, he is disciplined by the threat and reality of emotional or physical violence. This is not new; Saint Augustine says of his adolescent years: "I used to pretend that I had done things I had not done at all, because I was afraid that innocence would be taken for cowardice and chastity for weakness."[24]

Note also the terms by which this objectified sexuality is enforced— homo, fag, queer. These are names given to boys who also express their closeness to other boys either emotionally or physically and are targeted for it. In other words, a boy's affections and sexual desire must be directed only at girls or he will be the target of emotional or physical violence. This produces two other dynamics in the lives of boys and men: homophobia—the fear of emotional and physical/sexual closeness to other men—and compulsory heterosexuality—the necessity of mating with a woman to be a real man.[25] An extension of this necessity is heterosexism—the mistreatment of those who do not mate with someone of the other sex.

When I ask men how we are supposed to be sexually, they often say active, expert, and initiators. That is, we are supposed actively to take the initiative in a sexual encounter and be expert in what we do. Otherwise we are called a fag, homo, or queer. One of our problems is that much of what we learn about sex is in the locker room from our friends and in magazines, and a lot of the information is either wrong or distorted. Unless we take a course in human sexuality later or actively seek better information in some other way, we carry this misinformation with us for the rest of our lives—much to the chagrin of our partners.

And with whom are we to have sex? Only with women, not with men. And for men like me, only with women of our own race and class; not with women of color or women of a lower class—unless, of course, we pay for it or do not bring any emotional attachment to it. That is, there are women you marry and there are other women with whom you just have sex. This is the madonna–whore distinction that many of us make as a result of this kind of socialization and conditioning.

For example, a man recently reported that when he was an adolescent he had an argument with his father about a racist remark at the dinner table. The boy did not appreciate it and told his father so. There ensued a heated discussion in which the boy contested the racial stereotypes put forward by his father. As he left the room, his father blurted out, "If you ever bring a black girl in this house—that's it!" The man says now that he cannot remember his father ever threatening him, except this one time. In therapy, he recently discovered that, although he can remember the names of a number of black guys in his high school, he cannot remember the name of one black girl. That is no accident. In his home, it was clear that developing a deeply intimate relationship with an African-American woman was out of bounds. The same is often true of women from a lower socioeconomic background. Although casual sexual dalliances may be tolerated, a man is expected to marry someone who can contribute to his upward mobility. In the book and film *Love Story*, Oliver Barrett's father threatened to disown him if he carried through on his intention to marry Jennifer Caliveri, the daughter of a baker.

In my early years, the people from whom I learned the most about romantic relationships with women were James Bond, Napoleon Solo (the man from U.N.C.L.E.), and James West (from the TV show "The Wild, Wild West"). These guys seemed always to perform well, win, and get the woman or women. And there were lots of them to be gotten—usually a new one or more in each episode; they just seemed to be available and often in some sort of distress. I was never sure whether the heroes got the woman because they performed well or because they were handsome, so both seemed important. The sex scenes were not explicit in those days, but they were very spontaneous and I never saw a hint of concern about or provision for contraception or protection from sexually transmitted disease. And what kind of women did they get? Most often, they were of European descent and conformed to the predominant image of beauty of the time—slender, stacked, but soft. Occasionally the "sex interest" was Asian or Native American, but I do not remember even one episode of these particular shows where she was African-American. As for socioeconomic status, that didn't matter too much, because none of these guys ever got married or even developed a relationship that lasted longer than one episode.

Dysfunction in the Masculine Role

Underneath the facade of competence, expertise, and power, Ralph felt isolated, worn out, exploited by "rich money," helpless, and at a loss as to what to do about any of it. In short, he did not think he was very successful as a human being.

The problem is that success, defined as "making good money for a long time," does not provide for everything—some of the most important things— that we and our families need and want—things like having a sense that you matter to another person and that he or she matters to you and spending time with that person, yourself, and the One in whose presence "we live and move and have our being" (Acts 17:28). Often, the pursuit of security, at least the way Ralph and many of us do it, is in conflict with these other deeply felt needs and desires that we and others have.

The way Ralph learned to cope with his worry about succeeding was to "play the system." Playing the system involved engaging in competition and developing a capacity for delayed gratification. He began to compare himself with his peers with whom he found himself in competition for the rewards of the system. It's not enough to go to a university; one has to go to a good university. It's not enough to go to a good university; one has to go to a good professional school. It is not enough to graduate from a good professional school; one must also land a job with a top firm. It is not enough to land the job; one must also make junior partner. It is not enough . . . well, you get the picture. In order to fully secure yourself and your family, you must gain the respect of others—those with whom and for whom you work, as well as those nameless others who might be looking on. You do this by doing more things better than others with whom you compete.

Joseph Pleck and James O'Neill have pointed out that certain contradictory elements are inherent in male sex-roles. That is, if one lives fully in the masculine role, he will inevitably encounter frustration and difficulty.[26]

For example, someone who is in control, powerful, and competitive is considered masculine; however, achievement is often hindered by competitiveness. In his insightful book *No Contest,* Alfie Kohn points out that competition often has deleterious effects on the competitor. If "winning is not everything, it is the only thing," then there is always next year or the next opponent. Even after winning the Super Bowl, a writer observed that Tom Landry, coach of the Dallas Cowboys, never took off "his mask of fear." You never really finish proving that you are the best at whatever you are doing. This sets up a performance anxiety and compulsiveness around performance.

Operating out of a competitive mode can also lead us to believe that we are not the source or in control of what happens to us. Ironically, if we must win to feel good about ourselves, we put our self-esteem, at least partly, in the hands of our opponent. This, too, encourages an external locus of control and results in anxiety. Finally, since competitions are so often structured to allow only one winner, most of us lose more often than we win. In spite of claims that all of this builds character, the public shame and humiliation that often accompany losing can decrease self-esteem.[27]

Even if we win, the result can adversely affect our relationships with other people. We may feel guilty that we made other people lose, or we may fear that they will become hostile toward us.[28] Either way, this doesn't make for good, intimate relationships with others, particularly with one's boyhood friends, among whom one so often learns to compete.

I remember that a group of my friends used to play basketball in my neighborhood every afternoon in the fall. I was always matched up against Don, a friend who was about my height. I would occasionally say things to him like, "I can score anytime I want to; I can score at will on you." It was the kind of dominance that was discussed and prized by my sports heroes on TV. Needless to say, I never got very close to Don. Ralph didn't seem to be close to any of the men with whom he competed during his schooling, at work, or even in the men's group.

I admire some of the things I have seen in the lives of my boyhood athletic heroes like Willie Mays and Johnny Unitas, but I am not certain that competition itself produced them or was even necessary for their expression. Not long ago, I had a spirited argument with a physician friend whose dedication, discipline, and expertise I respect. He argued long and hard for the "naturalness" of competition and its necessary function in producing excellence. I am still not convinced; in fact, my sense is that much of competition is a form of antisocial aggression. As I have said, competitive modes of activity often result in low self-esteem and alienated personal relationships. In addition, Kohn points out that they encourage: (1) a product orientation—the antithesis of play, which is process-oriented; (2) either/or thinking, which pits one person, group, or idea against another; and (3) conformity—to beat someone else, you have to be doing what they are doing.[29] I have never forgotten the advice my mentor, George H. Williams, offered one day as we considered yet one more conflict in the history of Christianity, "Choose well your enemies, for in the end you will become like them." I might paraphrase that in this context, "Choose well your competitors, for in the end you will become like them." By the way, my physician friend and I ended our discussion by agreeing that, perhaps, what we both could affirm is some kind of "mutually enhanced excellence," rather than a competitive situation where one person wins and one or more others lose.

One area in which Ralph and many of us encounter difficulty and frustration has to do with our focus on achievement and success. This focus, which at times can become an obsession, often has two damaging results: compulsive work habits and the neglect of relationships.

Even if we do more things better than most other people, we can never, ever finally rest. Success is often situational; there is always more to do. There is always another goal to be accomplished or another rung on the ladder to be climbed before we have arrived and have the respect we need to be really effective and, therefore, really secure. Superiors hardly ever say, "Well done, good and faithful servant." Rather, the message is more likely to be something like, "Yes, you did that, but what about this?" The effect of this kind of conditioning is similar to that of a greyhound on a dog track. There, the trainers use a mechanical rabbit to motivate the dogs. When they chase the rabbit, it always stays just out of reach; they never quite catch it. No matter how hard they run, they never quite reach the goal. Only after they have performed are they fed and watered.

It seems to me that compulsive work habits are similarly inscribed in the bodies of many men. We never quite reach the goal; it is always moved a little farther out of reach; the production goals always increase, they never decrease. In other words, many of us, like Ralph, never get the respect we seek, because those from whom we seek it keep moving the rabbit. And we never experience the gratification for which we have worked so long and hard. We become so adept at delayed gratification that we forget, or perhaps never know, what it is we want. As my friend said to me, "Most guys never know what they want." And as my clergy friend said, "I wish I were passionate about something."

And what's happening as we chase the rabbit? Well, often we are losing contact with the very ones for whom we are convinced we are working so hard. When our self-esteem is held captive by our jobs, it is very difficult to "find" time to relate intimately with anyone, even those closest to us. In fact, when we are in an obsessive work pattern, time for anything else except some kind of immediate gratification or compensation cannot be "found." We simply do not have very much attention for anyone or anything else. No matter how much we try to convince ourselves and others that we are doing this because we "love" them, it doesn't feel that way to them, or to us, if we think about it very much. So, it's better not to think about it.

CONCLUSION

The net result of these definitions of success and the masculine conditioning that prepares us for it is often a state of frenetic enervation. In addition to devoting the best forty to seventy hours of the week to our jobs or careers, many of us have family responsibilities and commitments that demand whatever time and energy we can muster to give them. Some of us who attend church have committees, boards, and church education classes that claim any time and attention we might have left. For many of us, these are often competing demands that at times threaten to fragment our lives, or even tear them apart. The following diagram illustrates aspects of what I call the public, responsible self many of us have developed. It is the self that is in many ways constituted by the responsibilities we have in various public aspects of our lives.

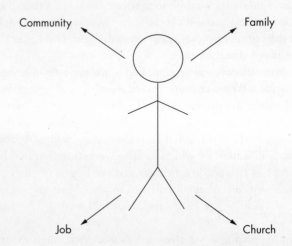

Community   Family

Job   Church

For many of us, our lifework, our purpose is defined by the sum of the vectors. That is, the meaning of our lives is the sum of all our commitments. The problem is that these commitments are often pulling in contradictory directions. Success at work often means failure with the family; success with the family often means failure, or at least the loss of the competitive edge, at work. How can we find time to work both in the community and at church? The various demands on us are often conflicting and fragmenting. Many of us do not sense a center that organizes the many commitments and responsibilities we have. We don't feel drawn into more and more meaningful work and deeper and more satisfying relationships. We feel stuck. Many of us have lost a center and live lives that are too often externally focused and lack deep levels of both meaning and pleasure.

Underneath the facade of competence, expertise, and power, Ralph felt isolated, worn out, exploited by "rich money," helpless, and at a loss as to what to do about any of it. He was a well-trained, efficient warrior who in his alienation and isolation had lost his way. There is a part of many of us that is highly disciplined, focused, task-oriented, and able to accomplish much; but, because of our physical, psychic, and emotional numbness, what we accomplish can sometimes be less than productive or even counterproductive to what we and others really need and want. So, we can end up fulfilling our responsibilities in distorted, even irresponsible, ways.

Like Ralph, what we often show to the world is a facade of competence, expertise, and power—our public self, that magnificent warrior. What we often hide is the frustration, confusion, resentment, and desperation—our private, separative self, that lonely guy. We often have a strong investment in the management of our public images—an investment that requires a great deal of work and constitutes yet another drain of vital energies.

So, many of us identify with Ralph's fragmenting busyness and sometimes wonder what happened.

Has Anyone Seen the Boy?

Has anyone seen the boy who used to come here?
Round-faced trouble-maker, quick to find a joke,
slow to be serious, red shirt,
perfect coordination, sly, strong, muscled,
with things always in his pocket: reed flute
worn pick, polished and ready for his Talent
you know that one.
Have you heard stories about him?
Pharaoh and the whole Egyptian world
collapsed for such a Joseph.
I'd gladly spend years getting word
of him, even third or fourth hand.

RUMI *(version by Coleman Barks and John Moyne)*

Chapter Two

Desperate Lovers:
The Private, Separative Self

I did everything I was supposed to do for forty years, did it better than almost any other man I know, and I lost everyone I love in the process, including myself.

Ralph

I realize I don't need God; I've already got one—women.

Male friend

While we show the world a facade of competence, expertise, and power, there is another, often private part of us that seeks expression. It is the part of us that yearns for significant, intimate connection with other people, other creatures, and other things. According to Saint Augustine, this is the uniquely human part of us, for God created us in and for relationships. However, the responsibilities of public offices often require us to suppress that deep desire for connection with our own bodies and with others. And too much of the masculine conditioning that prepares us to fulfill those offices instills in us a sense that we can and ought to live separately and apart from others.[1] Many of us, like Ralph, feel isolated from others. That isolation often leads, as it did for him, to a sense of powerlessness.

One of the reasons for that is that many of the institutions we are trained to lead are infected with various diseases that break connections between and among people and cut us off from one another. It is reasonable to expect, then, that our preparation to lead those institutions would inculcate in us such divisive attitudes and practices as sexism, homophobia/heterosexism, racism, ethnocentrism, and classism. In this section, I want to explore some of the ways that masculine conditioning can instill attitudes and behaviors that serve to cut us off from significant connections to others and produces within us a "desperate lover."

SEXISM

As we saw in chapter 1, when we are boys, if we exhibit behavior or feelings that are labeled "feminine," we are often hurt. If we walk, talk, throw, or do almost anything else like a girl, we get called things like sissy, girl, baby, and pussy and may be targeted for other forms of abuse if we don't change our behavior. We learn that being girlish is not a good thing to be; it is not a valuable thing to be. We, therefore, internalize the devaluation of those characteristics that have been labeled feminine and, by extension, also devalue women. Woman stuff is simply not as good as man stuff; women are not as good as men.

After a certain age, even hanging around girls makes you suspect; you may not be all boy. Just being close to girls can make you a target for abuse. Unless, of course, you are getting close to them in order to be sexual. That's okay. In fact, as we have seen, if you don't do that after a certain age, you can become suspect—a fag, a queer, a homo. It is no wonder that many of us have such ambivalent feelings toward women. We want and need them desperately but fear real closeness with them.

It is easy, then, for us to internalize stereotypes about women (i.e., they are hysterical, emotional, nonrational, weak) that have historically rationalized their exclusion from significant roles in our public life and institutions. We may even see their continued exclusion as part of our duty as officers of those institutions.

HOMOPHOBIA

Many of us also have feelings about closeness to other men—mostly fear. We can also be labeled fag, queer, or homo and targeted for verbal or physical abuse if we express an interest in being emotionally or physically close to other boys. So, our desires and needs to be close to other males come to have fear and shame attached to them. In addition, since desire for closeness with males is associated more "properly" with women, that desire is seen as "feminine" and triggers also the fear (femiphobia) and devaluation of the feminine I discussed above.

The result for many of us is a profound fear of closeness with other men. This, I think, is the root meaning of homophobia—fear of the same. That is, we come to be afraid of getting close to those human beings most like us—other men. Often homophobia is defined as the fear of homosexuality or of homosexuals. There is certainly that component to it, but I am beginning to believe that the more fundamental fear is our fear of closeness to other men. It is, given the experiences of many of us, an understandable fear, but it is very destructive to us and to others. I think that, because of this fear, many of us deal with our human desire to be close to other men by repressing it as bad. We can then project that forbidden desire onto those men that we perceive to be acting on it—gay men or other men who want to be close to us. We might then participate in the targeting of gay men or "effeminate" men for verbal, emotional, or physical abuse. Or we might stand by and do nothing when we see it happen. Or we might reject the overtures of men who we perceive want to be emotionally or physically closer to us than we find comfortable. We can then justify this mistreatment by internalizing untrue stereotypes about gay men provided by the larger culture—homosexuals are not normal or natural; gays are oversexed; they prey on young boys; they are not family-oriented; they are effeminate.

Because of our fear, we accept the distortion of our own humanity (the repression of our desire to be close to other men) and participate in the mistreatment of others. We may even come to see that mistreatment as part of the responsibility of an office that we hold.

White Racism

One of the effects of racism in our country, particularly in the South, is the continued segregation of whites from blacks in housing; many of us simply don't live close together.[2] For many men who perhaps have found ourselves in close proximity with African-Americans, our desire for relationships with them has met with verbal censure ("nigger-lover") or even threats; recall the man I mentioned in chapter 1 whose father threatened him with physical punishment or emotional abandonment when as a boy he argued against the mistreatment of African-Americans. The result is that our human desire for closeness with people of color, and particularly African-Americans, comes to be associated with fear. African-Americans might have been treated as different and undesirable by significant people in our lives—people on whom our lives and well-being depended. We often resist accepting this mistreatment for as long as we can; the man to whom I referred in chapter 1 developed a love for rhythm and blues and filled the house with the Motown sound throughout his adolescence.

Eventually, however, many of us come to accept the mistreatment and disrespect directed at African-Americans in our society and the isolation from them that results. We then internalize stereotypes about African-Americans—they are less intelligent, more violent, less industrious, less responsible parents—that allow us better to accept their mistreatment and our isolation from them. In addition, we often develop feelings of embarrassment ("I don't know how to talk with a black person"), fear ("The black part of town is violent and dangerous"; "They have been treated badly and don't want to be friends with me and probably want to hurt me if they get the chance"), and resentment ("It's not fair that they are getting preferential treatment in hiring"). This misinformation and our unpleasant feelings increase the forces that isolate us from African-Americans and perpetuate the mistreatment and disrespect they experience.

Similar dynamics are involved in other forms of racism or ethnocentrism, like anti-Semitism. Many of us have had experiences in which Jews were demeaned by significant persons in our lives. We might have heard jokes implying Jewish greediness, or disparaging or misinformed comments about Jewish life and culture, or sermons about the legalistic scribes and Pharisees who, it was claimed, were responsible for Jesus' death. The worst messages we got were that these people are very strange and somehow dangerous; the best messages we got may have led to an ignorant indifference. The result was either antagonism or obliviousness to the historical mistreatment directed at Jewish people.

Classism

Many guys like me from the "middle sector" of the "laboring class" are also trying to climb into higher management or the professional-managerial class. We have often internalized a number of messages about people in classes both below and above us.

Because we believe our economic security depends on our rising out of the "working sector (of the laboring class)," we strive, through education, networking, and any other means possible, to "work smart, not hard." That is, many of us aspire to avoid working with our hands. In fact, we are enlisted to supervise and manage those who work with their hands (the laboring sector and working poor). Many of us believe the myth that a free market rewards industrious workers and works to benefit all of society.[3] Therefore, we, like Ralph, narrow our focus, eliminate distractions, and work very hard to succeed. Fearing that we could fall back into the working sector or even to the level of the working poor, we often distance ourselves from persons in those groups. To help us in maintaining that distance and in managing them, we can internalize stereotypes about them. For example, we might believe that men in the working sector or among the working poor are dumb, brawny, macho, sexist, and violent—beliefs that are not conducive to our being close to these men.

Many of us middle-sector guys hope that we will climb into the professional-managerial class and then, perhaps, into the owning class. The problem is that the class of people owning the means of production is véry, very small. In fact, 60 percent of productive assets are owned by 1 percent of the population.[4] In other words, our chances of entering that class are slim indeed. Our frustration with our "structural powerlessness" leads us to two responses. We may think ourselves to be lazy, insufficiently smart, or otherwise flawed. Or we may think of persons in the owning class as elitist, unfeeling, greedy, and oblivious to the economic plight of others. Either way, we also don't get very close to persons above us in the class pecking order.

As I said in chapter 1, if we try to live up to many of the masculine norms I have described, we will find it very difficult to get close to other people—in fact, most people. When these kinds of sexist, homophobic/heterosexist, racist, and classist dynamics are added to our masculine conditioning, that difficulty increases dramatically.

I have developed a visual image of what this kind of socialization and conditioning does to men:

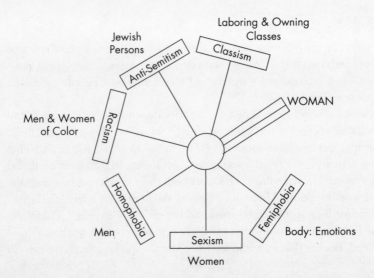

If we visualize a man's life as a circle that, at birth, has many emotional, physical, intellectual, and spiritual connections, real and potential, to other beings, human and otherwise, we might see this kind of masculine socialization and conditioning as a systematic cutting or blocking of those connective ties. Because of the production of femiphobia, aspects of a man that are labeled "feminine" are often split off and repressed or projected out onto other people, with the result that we are cut off from significant aspects of our selves. Because of the violence and threats of violence and resulting misogyny, a man's ability to develop mutually nourishing connections with women is severely damaged. Because of the production of homophobia, his ability to develop connections to other men, including gay men, and to lesbians and bisexual persons is similarly damaged. Because of the production of racist attitudes and behaviors, a man's ability to develop close and mutually nourishing relationships with people of color is greatly diminished. Because of anti-Semitic thoughts and behaviors, closeness to Jewish and Arab people is difficult. Because of classist attitudes, myths, and behaviors, he is isolated from many of those below, above, and beside him in the economic hierarchy.

Do you get the picture? It isn't pretty. We are systematically cut off from most of the human relationships that alone can make us most fully what we are—human.

When we think about the ways we are restricted by these dynamics in our relational lives, it seems that our one legitimate means for connection—our one source for the fulfillment of our needs and desires for meaningful emotional, intellectual, and physical connection in the world—is the woman in our lives. This primary, I am tempted to say sole, relationship is represented by the rectangular box; often this relationship contains most of what connects a man to the world.

WOMAN

We come, then, to channel most of our needs for intimacy into this one box, into this one relationship. Many of us learn to do that first with our mothers and then transfer those dependencies and expectations to our wives, lovers, partners. An image I use for our dependency on the one, or primary, woman in our lives is that of a head of hair, each strand of which is, at birth, attached to the ceiling above us, representing real or potential relationships or connections to other human beings, the earth, and earth creatures.[5] We are suspended by a strong attachment of each of the hairs of our head. As we proceed through childhood and adolescence and experience the violent socialization and conditioning processes described in chapter 1, our hairs, or attachments, are systematically cut. That is, through the installation of sexism we begin to be cut off from women; through the installation of homophobia, we are cut off from other men; through the installation of racism, we are cut off from people of other races and ethnic groups. So we are left with this one slender attachment to reality, or the human community—one woman; we are left hanging by a thread.[6] I call this our "monorelational psychic structure"; it is almost as if our psyches, or souls, are related significantly and intimately in just one relationship—a wife, significant other, or partner.

It is a terrifying predicament in which to find ourselves. That is why our relationships to our mothers and wives, or significant others, loom so large in many of our psyches. Our radical emotional, psychological, and physical dependence on her grants her, both in reality and in our heads, a great deal of power over us. According to Sam Keen, one of the secrets many of us self-styled independent men never tell is how much of our lives is focused on one woman—whether she is the first one in our lives (our mothers) or the most recent (our wives, significant others, or partners). He calls this figure WOMAN, because she becomes to us more of a "larger-than-life shadowy female figure" who "inhabit[s] our imaginations, inform[s] our emotions, and indirectly give[s] shape to many of our actions" than a real flesh-and-blood woman.

> She is the center around which our lives circle. WOMAN is the mysterious ground of our being that we cannot penetrate. She is the audience before whom the dramas of our lives are played out. She is the judge who pronounces us guilty or innocent. She is the Garden of Eden from which we are exiled and the paradise for which our bodies long. She is the goddess who can grant us salvation and the frigid mother who denies us. She has a mythic power over us. She is at once terrifying and fascinating.[7]

What is the nature of this relationship on which we depend for so much of our human need to be close and connected with human beings and the earth? In the image I have used here, what is the nature of that one thread on which many of us depend to connect us to the world and maintain our sanity? What is the nature of our relationship to WOMAN and to the real women in our lives? How do they and their femininity—the patterns of thinking, feeling, and behaving to which they have been socialized and conditioned as women in our society—shape our lives and our sense of ourselves? How do we and our masculinity shape their lives and their sense of themselves?

The Gender Dance: Complementarity and the Roots of Mutual Alienation

A major difficulty we encounter with this primary relationship is that, since our partner is woman, it is infected with the sexism many of us internalize as we grow up. It is also fraught with the mutually diminishing dynamics of what I call the "gender polarization" of our culture. I have developed a chart that focuses on the content of the gender roles in our society that inform the lives of many men and women who are more or less like me.[8]

The chart is labeled the "Polarization of Gender Roles" because our society has tended to overemphasize the differences between women and men. Those differences are then often used to maintain power imbalances between us. Columns 3 and 6 contain descriptions of how women and men, respectively, are supposed to be or act in each of the four areas covered by the chart—physical and emotional life, sexuality, intellectual life, and relationships (column 1). Columns 2 ("Female Enforcers") and 7 ("Male Enforcers") contain the names used to ridicule or humiliate those of each sex who do not act according to the prescribed expectations. The dynamics represented in columns 6 and 7 have already been discussed in chapter 1.

What is described here is called the "Gender Dance" because the roles are complementary and symbiotic. Men and the way we act influence significantly the way women act; that is, masculinity has a great deal to do with the shape of femininity. Conversely, women and the way they act influence significantly the way men act; femininity has a great deal to do with the shape of masculinity. Column 4 ("Men's Experience of Femininity") contains descriptions of the way men feel when they encounter the way some women act out stereotypical feminine behavior in the various areas of life. Column 5 ("Women's Experience of Masculinity") contains descriptions of the way women feel when they encounter the way some men act out stereotypical masculine behavior. What we find is that the stereotypical behaviors lead us to engage in a mutually alienating dance.

It is important to remember, first, that what is contained on the chart does not characterize men's and women's created natures—what is most fundamentally true and possible for us—but describes the behaviors and characteristics we exhibit because of the damage that has been done to us both. I will say more about that in chapter 4.

Second, since this book is primarily about men, I will focus on the impact that this kind of femininity has in the lives of men and not as much on the devastating effects it has on women. That profoundly destructive impact has been described and analyzed quite well by many women.[9] In describing the

POLARIZATION OF GENDER ROLES: THE GENDER DANCE

AREAS	Female Enforcers	Femininity (Private)	Men's Experience of Femininity	Women's Experience of Masculinity	Masculinity (Public)	Male Enforcers
Physical/ Emotional	"tomboy" "dyke" "butch"	soft weak inept helpless	attractive burden unequal protective responsible [overfunction]	attractive intimidated afraid inadequate powerless resentful	hard strong erect tall powerful silent controlled	"wimp" "sissy" "wuss" "pussy" "girl"
Sexual	"easy" "slut" "loose"	passive indirect seductive	attractive excited teased humiliated frustrated	attractive fear repulsion	active expert initiate	"fag" "homo" "queer"
Intellectual	"bitch" "uppity"	dumb subordinate	attractive gratifying superior boring distrustful frustrated	grateful intimidated bored	smart expert right decisive	"loser"
Relational	"cold" "selfish" "old maid" "loser" "bitch"	expert nurturing available	gratitude relief manipulated inadequate smothered resentful anger	needed unequal burdened protective responsible [overfunction]	controlled silent cool unemotional	"hen-pecked" "pussy whipped"
Column 1	2	3	4	5	6	7

negative impact that femininity has on men, I do not blame women for what has been done to them to produce these feminine ways of thinking, feeling, and acting.[10] However, it is important for us to look intently at those feminine ways and their impact on us as men.

By focusing on columns 3 and 6, we can see that the masculine and feminine gender roles are constructed in such a way that the traits of each are the polar opposites of the other. Of course, these characteristics are not entirely true for any one person, but they represent stereotypical expectations for the two sexes of this particular ethnic group and class. There have been changes to these expectations in the last thirty years—changes influenced by the women's movement and the nascent men's movement. I will deal with those changes and their effects on us men later in this chapter. Right now, I want to look at men's relationships to women as those relationships are influenced by these stereotypical role expectations, because they inform some level of the psyches of even those among us who believe that we are liberated from them.

I will organize this discussion of the gender dance between men and women as it affects specific areas of our lives, that is, the physical, sexual, intellectual, and relational (column 1), by describing first the feminine expectations of women's behavior (column 3) and how that behavior is installed in women by (1) other women acting out of the feminine mode (column 2) and (2) men, or women's experience of men, acting out of the dominative masculine mode (column 5). Then I will discuss the effects on men of relating to women acting out of the feminine mode (column 4).

Occasionally, I will also say something about the way these stereotypical, or traditional, expectations have changed for women in the last thirty years and the effects the changes have had on men. For many of us men, these changes, while liberating and welcomed by parts of us, have also led to increased confusion and strain. Further, many of the changes have not yet taken deep root in the thoughts, feelings, and behaviors of most women, so that we often find ourselves in a strong gender "undertow" that drags us back into the old dance.[11]

OUR PHYSICAL LIVES

Physically, a woman is expected to be soft and weak; in things related to physical, economic, or mechanical functioning, she is supposed to be inept or helpless (column 3). If she is not and she is past puberty, she is often ridiculed as a "tomboy" or a "dyke" (column 2). Consequently, men in relationships with women shaped by this kind of femininity are often asked implicitly or explicitly to take care of them and to protect them. Thus, our experience of femininity reinforces our masculine imperatives to be strong, hard, capable, and providing.

In the physical area of our lives, we experience confusion on our part and ambivalence on the part of women. Men, asked how they experience women who implicitly or explicitly ask them to protect them and provide for them, respond in two ways. Sometimes men find this kind of demeanor or behavior attractive; it makes us feel good about our own strength. We feel good about being needed and, therefore, more secure in our relationships with such women. But we also experience women's weakness and helplessness as a burden. It is tiresome to do things for someone that she could and should do for herself. There can also follow resentment about the unequal responsibilities we men carry for the economic security and physical safety of the women in our lives and for our families. Sometimes we, like Ralph, feel trapped in jobs because we carry too much of the financial burden for our wives and families.

Women's ambivalence about our strength, hardness, and provision adds to our confusion. When asked how they experience this aspect of men, women respond in two ways: it is attractive (power is the ultimate aphrodisiac), and it is intimidating and makes women feel afraid, inadequate, powerless, and resentful. So, the message we often get is that we should be strong, but not too strong; threatening, but not too threatening.

The change in sex roles in recent years has helped some but has also added to our confusion and resentment. We can be criticized for offering unsolicited help such as opening a door for a woman or offering other forms of physical assistance. But some women want that sort of treatment; others say they don't want it but seem to expect it; still others say they don't want it and don't. Men, on average, are still somewhat stronger than women; part of that is biological, but part owes to the fact that too many women, even modern women, continue to neglect the development of physical strength, particularly upper-body strength, because of the internalized messages about feminine style and beauty. It is difficult for many of us to figure out what to do and not do.

With respect to financial provision, women have entered the public work force in greater numbers and in greater degrees than ever before. But it is still the case that some women expect more freedom to decide how much they work in the home and how much they work outside the home. That leaves men with an unequal share of the burden for financial provision, while women shoulder an unfair burden for child care and household maintenance. Because "Ginny's income was only part-time" and "she was aching to travel a bit," Ralph felt the need to keep climbing the ladder. They had probably made an implicit or explicit deal that she would stay home with the children and he would continue to work full-time. Guys like Ralph can feel trapped in their jobs, while women often feel trapped at home.

In this area of our lives, the conflicts and strains we experience can be very frustrating. We are both attracted to and angered by women's softness and physical weakness. Women have some of the opportunities afforded by the military without the responsibilities of being subject to the draft and, until recently, combat duty. We find it difficult to express our physical strength in ways that neither make us feel guilty and ashamed nor impervious to how that expression may intimidate or frighten others. It is difficult to find ways of doing our share of providing for financial security without taking responsibility for more than our share and, thus, enabling the underfunctioning of our partners in this area.

OUR SEXUALITY

Traditionally, women have been socialized to be sexually passive (column 3) or, at least, to appear so. Said another way, they are expected to be clear and decisive about what they don't want sexually, but not about what they do want. If they take an active role in defining what they want, they are often censured as "easy," "loose," and "slut" (column 2) by other women, as well as by men. In addition, if a woman is direct about her sexuality, she loses her bargaining power. After all, why should he "buy the cow, if he gets the milk free"?

When I have asked men how they experience women's passivity around sexuality, they tend to give two different kinds of answers. One answer is that they find it erotic; it turns them on. The other answer is that they experience this kind of passive, or indirect, behavior as frustrating. That is, there is a kind of false advertising going on. The indirect sexual initiatives, or flirting, in which many women engage are intended to encourage the man to take direct, or overt, sexual initiative. This is, in turn, often met by the woman's braking action. She decides how "far he gets" or to what degree the physical intimacy will proceed. So, the dynamics of the gender dance around sexuality have the woman retreating and the man pursuing. It is in this way that men's experience of femininity reinforces their hyperactive masculine sexual behavior.

Men, in contrast, are supposed to be active; we are to take the initiative; and we could add here, we are supposed to be experts, to know what we are doing. The problem is that few of us ever had anyone explain to us in a sensible, respectful way what sexuality is about. So, we get what information we have about human anatomy, sexual response, and the possible meanings of sexuality from whatever sources we can—older boys, magazines and other publications (*National Geographic, Playboy,* the Sears, Roebuck catalog), movies, and books—and try things out. Much of what we learn is not very helpful.

And we are supposed to take the initiative, but we can't be too aggressive about it. We are to approach her, ask her out, pay for the date, and then initiate physical, sexual contact. Warren Farrell has identified 150 steps of progressing sexual intimacy from hand-holding to genital intercourse. Who is supposed to initiate each of these steps? We are. When? When she is ready. How do we know that? Well, we know either by omniscience or by listening to her verbal or, more frequently, her nonverbal cues. What is her role? She has been told that she is the gatekeeper; she determines how far the sexual intimacy goes. She says no; we say yes. So, we are busy trying to decide what to do next and she is trying to decide what not to do next. Neither of us is probably very present to the other, and sex therefore becomes increasingly impersonal. If we play out the stereotypical role expectations, we are constantly pursuing and she is constantly putting on the brakes. We are perpetually faced with the risk of rejection at the threshold of every step—all 150 of them!

Our self-esteem rides on every decision or nondecision she makes. When a man pursues and a woman retreats, it is humiliating. Why do we want her more than she wants us? What is wrong with us—with our sexual desire? Consequently, we experience a great deal of shame around sexual desire. The whole gender dance in the area of sexuality is humiliating and degrading for men. I believe that the "dating game" produces a great deal of resentment and anger in men toward women. The tragedy is that we are attracted to and at the same time humiliated by women's sexual passivity. As long as the gender dance is accepted as "normal" or the outgrowth of men's and women's natures, men will not feel that it is legitimate to resent these dynamics and express their anger directly in order to change them. That resentment and anger are often expressed in other, indirect ways through men's controlling behavior, which can ultimately manifest itself in physical or sexual assault.

We could walk away until she takes the initiative herself and bears some of the risks involved, but many of us are so dependent on what we think we need from this "other half" that that is difficult; we need her too much to walk away. Another strategy is what Farrell calls "railroad sex." We go as quickly as we can from step 1 to step 150 to reduce the time of possible rejection and the attendant pain. In addition, some of us reduce the pain and humiliation by pushing the whole situation away from our emotional lives. We objectify, or "thingify," her—fox, beaver, honey, pussy, cunt—and ourselves—rod, thing, tool—and turn the whole thing into a game—scoring. We are the hunters; she is the hunted. If we play out the role expectations to their extremes—women are totally passive and men are totally active—the result is rape. This is the tragic result of our having eroticized women's sexual passivity and men's sexual aggressiveness.

Women's responses to our sexual behavior and attitudes compound our confusion and frustration. It seems that we get mixed messages from them about what they want from us sexually. Some women, or other women at some times, seem to be turned on by our active, even aggressive sexual overtures. In fact, with them, if we don't come on strong enough, they seem hurt or believe that we are not interested in them. When asked how they experience men's hyperactive sexual behavior, women have responded by saying both of these things: it intrigues them, and it causes fear and repulsion. We find ourselves in a no-win situation. We are to be active without being aggressive.

In playing out these roles, we do not experience what we really desire. Do we find what we are looking for in a relationship with a woman? No. What we really want is to know another person and to be known by them. Mariana Valverde has said that these twin desires constitute the erotic.[12] Erotic tension, then, inheres in our wanting to know and be known. Can an object know you back? No. So, this objectifying strategy is doomed to failure—it will necessarily dissolve erotic tension and frustrate our deepest sexual desire.

It is ironic that the very things that are defined as sexy in this stereotypical paradigm—women's passivity and men's activity—are the behaviors and attitudes that frustrate and poison sexual relationships between men and women. That may be one of the reasons that there are so few healthy, mutually enhancing heterosexual sexual relationships; the way we do them is mutually diminishing.

I think that the objectifying aspects of this kind of sexuality contribute to the compulsiveness many of us men experience in our sexuality. We keep trying to get what we want in an objectified and alienating context, which by definition will not deliver it. This frustration and resulting compulsiveness are engendered, fostered, and encouraged by pornography. Pornography promises what it cannot deliver—satisfying, fulfilling sexual experiences—and it contributes to our difficulty in finding that fulfillment with women. The kinds of representations we find of women there make it very difficult for us to be happy with the real women in our lives.

Our Intellectual Lives

Intellectually, a woman is supposed to be dumb, or at least subordinate to the men to whom she relates.[13] After all, the way to be interesting is to be interested—in him and what he thinks, of course. If she is not, she risks driving men away from her and is called "uppity" or a "bitch." I once asked the women in one of my classes, "What happens if you show how smart you are in class?" The response: "You are alone on Friday night!"

Again, there are two ways in which men tend to react to this aspect of femininity. At times, this feminine behavior is appealing, as it reinforces our sense of superiority and activates our paternalistic caretaking. This reaction is part of the reason women feel compelled to keep up a pretense of intellectual inferiority. At other times, it might be experienced by men as either boring or infuriatingly disingenuous. We want and need to know what women really think; when, because of this disability, they can't or won't tell us, it is very frustrating.

Our experience of women reinforces our masculine sense that we must be smart, expert, and confident. So, we often project that image and talk a bit more—sometimes quite a bit more—than we listen. Women experience this tendency in us as comforting, but mostly boring. Again, there is a tragic irony here. If both sexes live out these stereotypical tendencies in our intellectual lives, we find each other terribly boring!

Our Relational Lives

Relationally, a woman is expected to nurture, maintain, mediate conflicts in, and subordinate her own interests and desires to those of others in relationships. She is required to be a "relationship master" or else she is "cold," "selfish," or simply a "bitch." If she is of age and is not in or making progress toward a significant, primary relationship with a man, she is a "loser," "old maid," or "dyke." She must become adept at reading the moods of the man in her life, interpreting his emotional needs, and fulfilling them. She must provide that "unending supply of motherly solicitude," as Catherine Keller calls it, in order to prop up the fragile male ego and hold her man.[14] If she is not "doing" relationships in this way and is not significantly connected to a man, she has been conditioned to view herself as relatively worthless. I believe that the damage this does to women's self-esteem contributes to a life subject to "compulsive relational fantasies."[15] That is, to bolster her self-esteem, a woman fantasizes about a perfect heterosexual, primary relationship. When she gets into a relationship with a man, she tends to dream or fantasize about the future of the relationship and how she wants it to be. The man often senses that there is a script in her head and tries to figure out his part so that he plays it correctly. The reason he does this is because his outlets for intimate relationships and human connections are so restricted that when he does connect with a woman in this way, he is so desperate for her attention and intimate contact that he will do just about anything to assure it.

The man doesn't play the role perfectly, however, and he resents playing it; so he often retaliates passively-aggressively. Why? Because he senses at some level that she is not relating to him—the real him—but to some projection of her own need for a "good" or "successful" relationship. He is a "relationship object" to her, not a real person. In other words, he senses on some level that she is not seeing him, but some projection—some ideal relational partner. That kind of objectification (like his sexual objectification of her) is very alienating and leads to a great deal of anger and resentment in men.[16]

So, how do men experience women's "relationship mastery"? Again, there are alternating, or sometimes ambivalent, responses. One set of responses is gratitude, relief, and attraction; the other includes intimidation, feelings of being manipulated, suffocation, mistrust, and anger. It feels good to have someone else take responsibility for our emotional and relational lives—to tell us what we are feeling, or should be feeling, and what we should do with those feelings; to be our emotional interpreter for others by writing the Christmas cards, planning the dinner parties, and facilitating relational exchanges between us and our friends and, even, our family members.

But these same things can feel terrible. If we perceive that our moods and emotions are constantly being monitored and actions planned to alter or affect them, we feel invaded, assaulted, and manipulated. It is experienced as intimidating and suffocating and leads to both fear and anger—fear and anger that our emotional boundaries have been and will be transgressed without our permission. The net effect of our experience of much of femininity can be a further reinforcement of our emotional and relational isolation, as we move away from the woman, or women, in our lives in self-protective silence.

So, the dynamics of the gender dance around male-female relationships has the woman pursuing and the man retreating. To paraphrase Maggie Scarf, referring to the emotional aspects of relationships, "The woman wants more intimacy and the man flees from that; she runs after, but not quite fast enough to catch him, and he flees but not quite fast enough to get away."[17] We run in a mutually frustrating and alienating race that neither sex ever feels is satisfying. In many ways, this relational race is the mirror image of the sexual one. In the sexual race, the man is the pursuer and the woman, the pursued; consequently, it is humiliating and degrading to him and frightening to her. In the relational race, the woman is the pursuer and the man, the pursued; it is humiliating and degrading to her and frightening to him.

ORIGINS OF THE GENDER DANCE

Two insightful theorists, Nancy Chodorow and Dorothy Dinnerstein, locate the origins and ground of this mutually distorting, complementary gender dance in the dynamics of the isolated nuclear family. There the mother is often the primary caregiver in early childhood and the father is physically or emotionally absent during this crucial developmental period. Because many of us are raised with a woman as our primary caregiver, Dinnerstein believes, we are emotionally predisposed to accept, even demand, these complementary, mutually destructive gender roles that have women wielding almost absolute power in the lives of children and men ruling in the public sphere.

Dinnerstein believes that we, as infants, experience a "primitive joy" of timeless, sensual, seemingly omnipotent unity with our surroundings.[18] Two facts of ordinary human existence interrupt this unity and experience of joy and lead to preverbal rage and resentment. First, as we grow we begin to realize that our bodies are limited and do not have the power to get or accomplish all that we want. That is, our flesh is not only a vehicle but also a "saboteur" of our pleasure. We suffer the loss of both the primitive joy of timeless unity and our seeming omnipotence. There is, then, a growing rage at and resentment of our own flesh. Second, we begin to realize that another flesh and intentionality distinct from our own—our mother's—mediates both the pleasure of sensual fulfillment and the pain of sensual deprivation; she controls the commerce of our bodies—what goes into them and what comes out of them. This recognition of distinction from the mother leads to our first experience of the loss of unity and the pain of helplessness, vulnerability, and isolation. Our desire for pleasure and aversion of pain subject us to the will of the mother and lead us to a resentment of the vehicle of her control—flesh, ours and hers. So, our resentment of the flesh gets linked to our mothers, because they are our primary caregivers.

At a later stage of cognitive development, we are able to conceive of a time when we were not here and of a time when we will not be here, that is, the world without us. In our imaginations, we encounter death for the first time. The thought of this assault on our illusion of omnipotence and the ultimate deprivation of fleshly pleasures restimulates the pain of our earliest experiences of loss, vulnerability, isolation, and fear of abandonment—the same pain and fear that are linked to the mother. This is how, in Dinnerstein's view, our enormously emotionally charged sense of mortality gets associated with our mothers and women generally.

To avoid the pain and fear associated with our sense of mortality, we often distance ourselves from the flesh, or body—the perceived source of the negative feelings—repress its desires, and identify it with the mother. She becomes the target, or scapegoat, for our split-off, projected feelings of rage at the limits of our bodies and fear of our increasingly repressed desires and of our mortality. So, woman carries both the burden of the attractiveness, indeed sacredness, of those early, oceanic desires and the shame resulting from our need to repress and deny them. She is, in Dinnerstein's words, the "dirty Goddess," subject to both adoration and revulsion. The father, who is not as present, physically or psychically, carries our projected needs for distance from and perspective on the body. The mother represents immanence and connection; the father represents transcendence and separation. According to both Dinnerstein and Chodorow, these dynamics are the earliest roots, in both women and men, of misogyny and of male superiority.

Because our mother controls the commerce of our body-selves and hers is the first intentionality we encounter—an encounter that takes place before our own sense of subjectivity is clearly established—she is the "earliest and profoundest archetype of absolute power." Her will becomes both feared and hated, because it is imposed by an omnipotence that violates our own "voluntariness." She controls life and death and has the power to foster or forbid our growth toward autonomy. She also seems to be omniscient, because our earliest failures are often things she told us not to do. She is the first witness to both our failures and our successes and thus, in our struggles with her, holds the power to crush our pride by reminding us of our earliest humiliations or to leave us to an empty victory by withholding her attention. In short, she has the power to bestow or withhold happiness.[19]

One result of our mother's omnipotence is misogyny—the hatred of women generally. Because it reminds us of our own, we have contempt for her fleshly mortality. We are furious at her autonomy, with which she seems to thwart ours. She seems malevolent and, therefore, untrustworthy; we are thus outraged when we meet her in any position of worldly authority. Since we need her for our own growth, however, we assume she exists as a material resource for us—a resource that must be harnessed and controlled lest it continue to exercise power over us.[20]

Another result of our felt sense of our mother's omnipotence is submission to male domination in the public realm. In comparison to our mother's authority and power in the home and in our personal, emotional lives, our father's authority looks like a reasonable refuge, so we transfer our almost complete dependence and submission to him and to male authority. As we, men and women, rush to male domination, what we seek is not an escape from freedom but a refuge from what we experience as female tyranny. So, Dinnerstein concludes that male domination has been for us an inexorable emotional necessity and will continue to be as long as women in our society are the primary caregivers in early childhood.[21]

In the sexual aspects of our lives, the mother-child bond can also be debilitating. Chodorow argues that in middle-class, American, father-absent, nuclear families, a wife is "as much in need of a husband as the son is of a father."[22] That need may express itself in physical/sexual or emotional ways or both. For example, according to Chodorow, a mother may confuse her relationship to her infant son with a sexualized relationship to him as a male. The consequence is that she may push him out of his pre-Oedipal relationship to her into a heavily sexualized relationship when he has not yet resolved early issues of individuation and the establishment of ego boundaries. In other words, it is possible that she might have erogenously stimulating experiences with her son, though unconscious to or denied by her. These kinds of experiences can push him into a very frightening, nonmutual sexual situation, before he has the ego strength to deal with it. This early experience of sexual violation may be one of the reasons that some men split off emotional intimacy from sex; it is a way of coping with the fear of an overwhelming sexual, female presence.

Kenneth Adams has described similar dynamics when the attention of a parent to a child is not sexual but emotional.[23] He calls this kind of attention "covert incest," that is, when a parent makes a child a surrogate partner. In cases where the adult marriages of the parents are not healthy and needs for dependency, intimacy, and emotional support go unmet, parents can turn to their children to supply those needs. The child is often idealized or put on a pedestal and feels a certain privilege in the relationship. The cost of such attention, however, is a lost childhood. Many adult survivors of covert incest find themselves unavailable for intimacy, because of the repeated violation of their boundaries by the opposite-sex parent. In the case of boys, they feel both hostility toward their fathers as competitors and, later, anger for their not having protected them from their mothers. Some survivors, fueled by rage and shame, act out in sexually addictive behavior that objectifies women, as they feel objectified by their mothers. Others have difficulty being comfortable with their bodies and sexuality and find themselves sexually shut down.

In Dinnerstein's view, if we do not outgrow our tendency to project our split-off feelings of love and anger toward the flesh onto women and to project our need for transcending the flesh onto men, we will continue in a soul sickness that is killing our earth and ourselves as a species.[24] This means that we must stop projecting our ambivalent feelings about our bodies onto our mothers and our need for body-denying autonomy and transcendence onto our fathers and learn to integrate those feelings and needs in ourselves. We must see our mothers and fathers not only as parents who have, mostly unconsciously, hurt us, but also as female and male human beings who themselves have been hurt.

The effects of these dynamics and feelings on our relationships to women are profound. According to Dinnerstein, we seek each other out because of the complementarity of our emotional strengths and weaknesses, but we are acutely aware of each other's childishness.

RELATIONSHIPS WITH PARTNERS

This complementary socialization and the resultant symbiotic relationships can be mutually disabling. To summarize, it might be said that this socialization to stereotypical feminine and masculine behavior disempowers women in tasks and functions related to the public sphere and empowers them in the private sphere, while it empowers men in the public sphere and disempowers them in the private. In the categories of the chart, we might say that men's overfunctioning in the sexual, physical, and intellectual areas enables women's underfunctioning, while women's overfunctioning in the relational area enables men's underfunctioning. In other words, if women and men follow these prescribed roles, the message they receive from our culture and the message they internalize is that they are really only one-half of a person and that they need another half to be whole or complete. They need someone else to do for them what they believe they cannot do for themselves. Women need men to do the public things, and men need women to do the private things. It looks like this:

WOMAN			MAN	
Private	Public		Private	Public
1/2	1/2		1/2	1/2

1

The diagram depicts what I think this socialization does to women and men. The polarized definitions of what men should be like and what women should be like come in and split the psyches of real women and men. With men, the definition of masculinity convinces us that we are only one-half of a person: that we can function fairly successfully at work but not at home or with our friends. Consequently, I have shaded the other half of us that relates to functioning in the private sphere (e.g., experiencing, reflecting on, and articulating our feelings). We, as men, feel that we are fragmented, crippled, inadequate human beings without a woman in our lives to do for us what we do not believe we can do for ourselves. Therefore, we must mate or pair with someone of the "opposite" sex in order to be a whole human being. We do not believe that we have those capabilities, so we look for them in another person. We look for them in a woman because we have been conditioned—for many of us, in our relationships to our mothers—to find them there.

Women are doing the same thing. Their psyches have been split by the expectations of femininity. Internally, they find it hard to believe that they can care for themselves physically and economically, so they look for someone to do that for them. Externally, they continue to be confronted by significant obstacles in their pursuit of economic independence. They believe that they cannot be whole, fully functioning, worthful human beings alone, so they too must complete themselves by finding their other half.

All of this lies beneath what we usually call "romantic love," which I am beginning to believe is an oxymoron. What we usually call romance may well mutually foster men's and women's disabilities and distort our humanity; therefore, it has nothing at all to do with love. In fact, it is very destructive for both men and women.

Let's take a closer look at what might be happening in the "romantic" and mysterious bonding with an opposite. It seems to me that what we are doing in such bonding is finding our other half; the equation looks like this:

$$1/2 + 1/2 = 1$$

But, if I am correct in assuming that we men come into the world with the potential to develop capacities for intimacy, emotional disclosure, and relationship maintenance and that women come into the world with the potential to develop capacities for powerful intellectual and physical work, as well as for active sexual fulfillment, then a more accurate diagram of what is taking place are the equations.

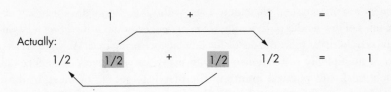

That is, the fact that we are really, potentially whole persons in ourselves is covered up and repressed by the damage that is done by the feminine and masculine socialization and conditioning processes. So, we think that we do not possess the capacities that we believe the "other" possesses (indicated by the shaded areas). In reality, we do; we just think we don't. What really happens when we pair with an "opposite" is that rather than finding our other half, we actually give away half of ourselves (i.e., the shaded half) into the keeping of the other person. For men, we give women responsibility for our emotional lives, for our bodies (nutrition), and for most, if not all, of our relationships and ask that they care for them in a way that will ensure our happiness. If they do not do what we want with what we give them—and it is impossible that they can or will—we resent them. We find that to have any sense of happiness or self-determination we must exercise control over them, because they have control of half of our selves. What we have here is a fusion of identities through a blurring of personal boundaries, not the intimacy we seek. So, there begins a kind of guerrilla warfare by which we attempt to manipulate, control, or otherwise affect the other person in such a way that our happiness will be assured—that we will be whole, complete human beings. The consequence is that both we and they are diminished in the bonding 1 + 1 = 1. One person plus one person equals *one* person—not even two persons!

Why are we diminished? The reason is that we have done something very inhuman to ourselves and to our partners—we have turned ourselves and them into objects of our projected needs, not full, whole human beings. Given our complementary and symbiotic socializations, women and men objectify each other. For us men, women are the objects of our genitalized sexual fantasies (whores) or the custodians of our emotional and relational lives (madonnas). And for women, we are the objects of their relational fantasies, which include not only chivalrous physical and financial provision but also emotional tenderness and exclusive romantic devotion.

In other words, the one relationship in which we attempt to get many, if not all, of our intimacy needs met too often contains the seeds for frustration, anger, resentment, and alienation. Even without the mutually alienating dynamics of the gender polarization we experience in our culture, one relationship could never meet the needs for intimacy we bring to it. We were created for a multiplicity of relationships with many, varying levels of intellectual, emotional, and physical intimacy. To attempt to get all, or most, of those needs met in one relationship is foolhardy, destructive (to us and to our partners), and downright idolatrous.

A man once told me that he went to the Far East to find God. He was in the midst of some wrenching relational dynamics with women. He had been in a primary relationship with a woman, and she wanted to move toward a permanent commitment. He was unsure whether he was ready for that and became sexual with another woman. He felt pulled in different directions and very confused. He decided to take a moratorium and go east to find himself and God. When he got there and was alone and began to sort through the emotional issues and dynamics that had led to his confusion, he came to a startling discovery. He said that, though he went to find God, he discovered that he didn't need God, because he already had one—women!

He spoke truth for more than just himself. In a sense, he did have an unconscious god—the "dirty Goddess," as Dinnerstein would argue—and one about which he felt intensely ambivalent. He also probably had a conscious god—a transcendent, omnipotent, omniscient, Father god—which served to counterbalance the threat he felt from his unconscious female god. All of which means that he was cut off from any real sense of God.

So, we are cut off not only from significant aspects of ourselves and from others, but also from real intimacy with God.

Desperation

Masculine socialization and conditioning produce within us a desperate situation. Since we view the open expression of emotions as feminine, we develop only a limited ability to recognize and express them. This greatly obstructs our human need for intimacy. Because we view touching and sensuality as feminine and sex more as something we do than as something that is done to and for us, we experience a very limited range of sensual and sexual feelings.[25] Many of us are, in fact, touch-deprived. Add to this the ways we are cut off from others because of sexist, homophobic, racist, anti-Semitic, and classist attitudes and behaviors and we find ourselves in desperate need of love, which we can often look for in some wrong places and in some pretty unhealthy ways.

Another image for the intensity of our need for intimacy and the way it is often directed at one woman is that of a river. Our needs for intimacy correspond to the strong current of a river like the Mississippi. Our masculine socialization puts a dam in the river and provides one small floodgate in the middle. Can you imagine the water pressure as it comes through the floodgate? Often, as I have said, our desire for intimacy is channeled into genital sexuality. In mixed-gender groups, I often ask women if they have experienced that tremendous pressure coming at them—that is, men's enormous desire for intimacy in the form of sexual contact. Many nod affirmatively with various expressions of concern, sadness, resentment, and anger on their faces. I think this is one of the roots of sexual violence against women, from persistent sexual pressure, to date and acquaintance rape, to stranger rape. It is behind some men's difficulty in keeping appropriate sexual boundaries with women, and men, in professional relationships.

In fact, the acting out of the desperate lovers within us can threaten to undo much or all of what our lonely warriors have worked so hard to secure for ourselves and others. The examples of this are legion. O. J. Simpson is one. Jimmy Swaggert is another.

A few years ago a radio reporter called and asked me to comment on the public revelation that evangelist Jimmy Swaggert had been involved with a prostitute. By the leading questions she asked, I think she expected me to denounce the hypocrisy of this self-righteous fundamentalist preacher. Instead, I said that there was an interesting question here, "Why would a man risk his reputation, and in this case the career, and even vocation, to which he had devoted his entire adult life, for such a fleeting rush of sexual excitement?" My thought now is that for Jimmy Swaggert, as for many of us men, his work in his public office did not include enough of his desire for excitement and pleasure and his sex life did not include enough of his sense of justice and his desire for connection. He is not alone among his brothers. Many of us experience this same kind of desperation, though we may not all express it in the same way.

THE DREAM

He dreamed of
an open window.
A vagina, said
his psychiatrist.
Your divorce, said

his mistress.
Suicide, said
an ominous voice within him.
It means you should close the window
or you'll catch cold, said
his mother.
His wife said
nothing.
He dared not tell her
such a
dangerous dream.

FELIX POLLAK

Chapter Three

A House Divided:
The Punishment of Adam

I did everything I was supposed to do for forty years, did it better than almost any other man I know, and I lost everyone I love in the process, including myself. . . . In some ways, I feel I could handle all that, too. But look at me—paid more than any two of you guys put together, supposedly one of the top decision-makers in the country, and when it comes to my own home, my own life, I don't even know how to begin.

RALPH

I do not understand my own actions. For I do not do what I want, but I do the very thing I hate. (Romans 7:15)

SAINT PAUL

But we enjoyed playing games and were punished for them by men who played games themselves. However, grown-up games are known as "business," and even though boys' games are much the same, they are punished for them by their elders. No one pities either the boys or the men, though surely we deserved pity.

SAINT AUGUSTINE, *Confessions*

WHAT I HAVE SAID so far is that much of masculine socialization and conditioning produces in us two kinds of identities, or selves—a lonely warrior and a desperate lover. The lonely warrior is highly trained, disciplined, expert at delayed gratification, and works hard to provide for and protect his family. He also is externally focused on the approval of others and, consequently, expends a fair amount of time and energy on managing his public image and hiding aspects of himself that would not meet with approval. He is often pulled in different directions by conflicting demands and expectations that lead to fatigue and enervation. In addition, he hasn't got many people to talk to about any of this.

The desperate lover yearns for connection and intimacy with others on many levels but finds that desire thwarted and frustrated. The demands of the offices he fills afford little opportunity to develop mutually satisfying relationships. He finds himself isolated by sexist, heterosexist, racist, and classist dynamics in and around him. The result is either a withering state of alienation or an explosive, compulsive drive to connect with others and with aspects of himself; often that drive takes forms that are destructive to him and to others with whom he is trying to connect.

These two identities, or selves, I believe are false selves that produce a great deal of physical, emotional, psychological, and spiritual strain in our lives and in our relationships to others. Unexpressed emotions and uncared-for bodies lead to pain and stress, which in turn may cause acute and chronic illnesses and lowered life expectancies.

In addition, it is very disconcerting to be criticized for the way we carry out our public responsibilities. When individuals or groups seeking liberation object that these public offices, which are ostensibly carried out for their benefit, may well do them more harm than good, many of the men who hold them have difficulty hearing this criticism and responding to it. We accurately sense that we sacrifice a great deal to fill these roles through which we believe we are discharging our social responsibility to our neighbors. When the neighbor criticizes these roles as, in fact, socially irresponsible, we can become angry or confused. The criticism is threatening on several levels. It may lead us to question whether the enormous sacrifice has been worth it; it may lead us to question our fundamental sense of identity and worth as human beings; or it may challenge our faith, that is, our trust in and loyalty to the God we believe sanctions this identity and requires this sacrifice.

So, to the extent that we live out our lives as lonely warriors and desperate lovers, we find ourselves alienated from significant parts of ourselves and from others for whom we believe we sacrifice so much out of our love for them.

We also experience a tension within ourselves. As I have pointed out, the imperatives of the offices seem to run counter to many of our personal needs for connection and intimacy. And our resulting drive to connect with parts of ourselves and others can have devastating effects on our careers.

There seems to be a struggle between these identities and some of our deepest longings. We can, like Ralph, wake up one day and realize that we have worked as hard as we can, doing what we have been told we should, doing it better than many other people we know, and yet, we find that we have become somebody we don't even like. In addition, we might not know any better than he where to begin finding our way out of this mess.

The apostle Paul describes the effects of sin as a war that goes on inside us. Speaking of his own experience, Paul says,

> But I am of the flesh, sold into slavery under sin. I do not understand my own actions. For I do not do what I want, but I do the very thing I hate. . . . For I delight in the law of God in my inmost self, but I see in my members, another law at war with the law of my mind, making me captive to the law of sin that dwells in my members.
> (ROMANS 7:14–23)

In other words, Paul experienced a tension, or strain, within himself. He had an "inmost self" that somehow knew the law of God—the good—but another part of him—the sin that dwelled in his members—led him to do evil, or that which he did not want to do. It is this sin that dwelled in his members that Paul calls the "flesh" (*sarx* in Greek). He does not mean that his body was evil; it had been created by God and awaited redemption. When Paul speaks of his fleshly body, he uses the Greek word *soma*. Rather, flesh for him is a term that contrasts with the Spirit: "But you [Christians] are not in the flesh; you are in the Spirit, since the Spirit of God dwells in you" (Romans 8:9). Flesh refers to a state of being alienated from the Spirit of God and, by extension, from aspects of one's inmost self and from others.

I believe that, for many men, "living according to the flesh" is living according to the imperatives of these dual identities—the lonely warrior and the desperate lover—that seem to compel us to do things that at some level we know to be counterproductive and even destructive to our health and wholeness and that of others. Ralph, like Paul and many of us, seemed to be careening out of control—"sold under sin"—unable to do the very things he wanted to do and doing the very things he didn't want to do. We, like Ralph and Paul, many times do not understand our own actions. How could we have worked so hard to become somebody we don't even like? How did we lose so many people we care about? How did we get on the wrong side of so many barricades?

The Distortion of Men's Characters

My sense is that much of the masculine socialization and conditioning I have described significantly disconnects men from others and aspects of ourselves and installs profound isolation patterns, which are held in place by deep and pervasive fears—fears of violence for noncompliance and fears of our perceived inadequacies being exposed. The effect for many of us is a distorted, or deformed, character. To illustrate that, I want to introduce some conceptual tools I have found helpful in beginning "to understand my own actions." The first involves a distinction between men's maleness and our masculinity; the second involves a distinction between an immature masculinity and a mature masculinity.

As human beings, men are created in the image of God and have inherent capacities for justice, strength, intelligence, and compassionate connection. These capacities are part of the image of God within us, or what Paul called the "inmost self." Ethicist Judith Kay points to a distinction Saint Thomas Aquinas makes between what she calls our first and second natures.[1] The first nature is this image of God, which though marred by original sin, has the potential to grow into maturity or to grow into immature expressions. I will refer to these capacities and their potential as our "inmost self," our first nature, or our human maleness.

The second nature is that nature in which the potentialities of our first nature are actualized—in virtues and vices, or habits of thinking, feeling, and acting.[2] So, for us men, our masculinity is an expression of our inherent capacities. Mature masculinity reflects the virtuous fruition of those God-given capacities for justice, strength, intelligence, and compassionate connection. Immature masculinity manifests distortions of that image of God in us. Much of the masculine conditioning I have thus far described produces immature masculinity and distorts our characters as men.

When we think about who we are and what we do, it is useful to keep this distinction in mind. That behavior and those patterns of thinking and feeling are not necessarily who we essentially are or what we might have become; they are what we have become because of those factors that have shaped our lives and the choices we have made. Our second natures are also not the way we have to remain. Based on the continued, though muted, existence of our first natures and the possibility of experiencing different extrinsic social dynamics, we can change; we can make other choices.

Let's take a closer look at the image of God in men, or men's first natures. I have come to affirm these four capacities—justice, strength, intelligence, and compassionate connection—as a part of the image of God in us because of a convergence of a variety of sources, including contemporary psychological theory and historical theological traditions.[3] Here, I do not wish to argue for the existence of these capacities but simply to assume them. I encourage you to try them on, think through some of their implications, and see if they make sense to you. I want to give a brief description of each of these capacities and then discuss ways in which they are distorted by the masculine norms I have described.

First, men are inherently just or fair. That is, we have an innate sense of justice. Early in life we rage if unfair things are done to us and to others; we have to unlearn this righteous indignation. If we had not unlearned it, there would be a lot more rage evidenced today concerning what we are doing to each other and to our world. It is this part of us that knows on some level that others are mistreated because of, for example, sexist and racist attitudes and behaviors. We also sense that we men are mistreated, and that is why we have trouble completely agreeing with those who would see us only as the oppressor without acknowledging the ways in which we have been mistreated.[4]

Second, we are inherently strong and powerful. By strength and power I do not mean coercive power that violates the boundaries and physical, emotional, and intellectual integrity of another person. Rather, I mean the ability to act decisively, effectively, and in cooperation with others for one's own good and for the good of others. That includes defending one's own and others' appropriate boundaries. A recent example of this was the courageous action by four African-Americans during the riots that were sparked in Los Angeles after a jury acquitted white policemen of brutally beating Rodney King during an arrest. These people came to the aid of a badly beaten white truck driver and drove him and his truck to safety in the midst of ongoing violence. This demonstrates that there is an inherent power by which one can act outside of the self- and other-destructive patterns of behavior, thoughts, and emotions of one's second nature.[5]

Third, men are inherently flexible and intelligent—brilliant, in fact. In spite of the fact that we are surrounded by a lot of rationalizing and mystification, particularly about mistreatment and oppression, we can, at times, think clearly about ourselves, others, and our world. This doesn't mean that we come into the world able to do differential equations. We need the right conditions, nurturing support, good information, and instruction, but if those are provided, the capacity becomes an ability. Because of the continuing existence of that inherent intelligence, we are able, though in a limited way, to think creatively and clearly.[6]

Fourth, we are inherently compassionate creatures who are connected on many levels—physically, sexually, emotionally, psychologically, and intellectually—to our world. Little children crawl in our laps and explore every aspect of our being with their hands, their eyes, their minds, their hearts—with everything they have at their disposal.[7] They embarrass us, because they have not yet learned what we have long since internalized—we are not supposed to be so connected to others and to the world. This connection brings with it a sense of compassion; we feel some of what others feel if we are connected to them. Although there is much in our experience that obstructs our connection with others and isolates us from other people and other things, we maintain a sense of and desire for connection, as well as a deep co-feeling with others.[8] Ralph somehow knew that he was deeply alienated from others and from himself.

Let me say a couple of things about this image of God, or first nature, as I have described it. First, I believe that what I have said is true of both men and women. Women have the same inherent capacities, although they, generally, have quite different opportunities and constraints. This is not to say that women and men are not different. We are, but my sense is that those differences have been exaggerated and distorted to justify unjust power relations between us. It seems more useful, at this particular point in our evolution and interaction, to focus on those things that we have in common.[9]

Second, I find persuasive Robert Moore and Douglas Gillette's contention that each of these capacities is inextricably linked to the others. For example, you can't be just without being compassionately connected; you can't be just without strength and the intelligence to know how and when to use that strength; you can't be intelligent without connection with others; you can't be compassionately connected without justness; and so on.[10]

Based on these assumptions, then, the intention of God for us is that we find ourselves in a vibrant, rightly ordered community with others; acting powerfully in concert with them; thinking clearly about ourselves, others, and the earth; and feeling and loving deeply God, ourselves, and others, as well as the earth and its creatures. In other words, we should find ourselves in a mutually enhancing web of life.[11]

Unfortunately, these inherent capacities are distorted and stunted by the dynamics of sexism, heterosexism, racism, and classism. These dynamics and our internalization of them produce a second nature in us, part of which is characterized by behaviors, feelings, and thoughts that are self- and other-destructive. They constitute an immature masculinity.

The distortions show up in lots of different ways. Moore and Gillette observe that immature, or distorted, masculinity causes the archetypes—transpersonal elements that structure the unconscious—to be expressed in what they call "bi-polar shadow sides."[12] In the language of this book, we can oscillate between contradictory expressions of our inherent capacities. For example, a distorted sense of justice might manifest itself in tyrannical or passive behavior; distorted strength can be expressed in sadistic or masochistic behaviors; distorted intelligence can be either manipulative or naive; and a distorted capacity for connection can lead to addictive or depressive behaviors.

On retreats, I ask men what they don't like and what they do like about men and write the results on two sheets of newsprint.[13] Recently, on the sheet labeled "Don't Like About Men," I recorded:

pretense, wear masks	shaming	controlling
goal-oriented	competitive	non-emotional
obsessive-compulsive	shut-down	don't relate well
women-centered	nonspiritual	arrogant
sexually compulsive	caretaking (financially)	violent
passive	know-it-alls	stupid
glorify violence	physically abusive	judging
verbally abusive	insensitive	cold
unimaginative	dishonest	hen-pecked
self-destructive	pleasers	timid
weak	domineering	dissembling
fawning	abuse power	

These negative male attitudes and behaviors can be sorted out according to Moore and Gillette's schema of distorted masculine archetypes, or, in my language, capacities. In the following paragraphs, I will suggest, with the aid of Moore and Gillette's schema, ways in which masculine socialization and conditioning distort those capacities that are a part of the image of God in us. I believe that our socialization to masculine roles radically disconnects us from others and aspects of ourselves and thus most significantly damages our capacity for compassionate connection. Therefore, I will treat the capacities in a different order than I have so far presented them.

COMPASSIONATE CONNECTION

To be a man in our society is to have a wounded capacity for connection. From almost every direction, we are assaulted with relational dynamics and

pressures that cut us off from other persons, other things, and significant aspects of ourselves—particularly our bodies and our emotions. To be a "man"
we must separate—from girls, gays, African-Americans, lower-class people,
Jews, and others. In order to survive the violence directed at us and to maintain a sense of worth and value, we must get used to being alone. The one relationship by which we are connected (mother/wife/partner) is fraught with
difficulties. Because we are expected both to provide for and to protect others, we find it necessary to discipline and subdue our bodies to do what is required for our survival and for our self-esteem. The diagram in chapter 2
(page 48) illustrates that in pretty stark terms.

So, what happens to our inherent capacity for compassion and connection in all of this? We often compulsively direct our desire for emotional and
physical connection to substances, projects, or objectified relationships, or
we might sink into an enervated state of isolated depression. Or we might do
both alternately:

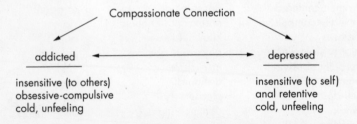

Many of us, then, swing between an anxious, obsessive-compulsive pursuit of altered states and feelings of boredom, shame, and isolation. Perhaps
it is not so much that we are addicted to substances, things, or relationships
as that we are addicted to not feeling. It seems to me that is what the polar
manifestations have in common.

Ralph had made a mark for himself but had lost everyone he cared about
in the process, including himself. What are the effects of giving up everyone
and everything in the process of making a mark for ourselves? Well, sometimes we don't think too clearly, act very justly, or defend the right things.

INTELLIGENCE

A man with a distorted intelligence might use it to manipulate or coerce others or he might remain studiously naive about things he would rather not
have to deal with. Or he might oscillate between these two.

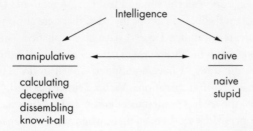

Because of our training to be economic and military warriors, we often use our intelligence to master situations and solve problems. The imperative to figure things out and make them work often means that we stay with the concrete and rigorously employ our left-brain capacities to the task at hand. Because of the disconnection we experience from other people, we grow up learning very little about what life is like for women, African-Americans, gay men and lesbians, people of different classes, and Jews. We often lack accurate information about others and internalize many inaccurate stereotypes. In addition, we often don't know what we don't know about others.

The effects of this split on us and others can be profoundly destructive. The split many men experience because of our masculine socialization and conditioning can lock us into what Joseph Campbell calls the concrete level of reality—the level of practical living and technical manipulation. We focus on doing things for the right reasons. We don't often step back and ask ourselves why we do them or why we came to believe what we believe to be right—what Campbell calls the psychological level of reality. And we don't often enough experience the transforming power of an intuitive insight or vision that comes through a story—Campbell's mythological level.

Edward Farley offers a provocative analysis of four ways of understanding the world (hermeneutical modes): Mode 1—left-brain, critical reason; Mode 2—intuitive, unitive reason; Mode 3—gleaning wisdom from historical traditions; and Mode 4—a praxis analysis of the way power relations affect our understanding. Although Mode 1 has been privileged in the university, seminary, and church, all four modes must be used in order to have accurate, authentic knowledge of the world.[14] I think masculine norms lock us into Mode 1, with occasional reference to Mode 3.

One result is that many of us have impoverished imaginations. I have found that my imagination is most often employed in objectifying myself and my life and thinking about the past—measuring myself to see if I have lived up to those expectations—or in thinking about the future and trying to imagine ways that I can get done all the things I feel I must get done. Of course, I almost always end up feeling bad about the past: there are always more things I could have done, more things I could have accomplished. And I almost always feel anxious about the future: there never seems to be enough time to do, and do well, all the things I have committed myself to do. This is an awful waste and misuse of our imaginations. Victor Seidler has said, "The rationalism which social theory has tended to build on and retain is itself at the basis of many of the problems we face, as men, when we try to change."[15] When Ralph realized that he was "paid more than any two of you guys put together, supposedly one of the top decision-makers in the country, and when it comes to my own home, my own life, I don't even know how to begin," he became angry. Good for him; he should be.

Again, it seems to me that many of us men use our technical, left-brain reason in the service of what we are asked to do—keep the barbarians away from the gates, or keep order in an otherwise chaotic world. We, and others, see that exercise as virtuous, but often it is not, because our reason is not always used in the service of justice.

Justness/Fairness

Because our masculine socialization and conditioning disconnect us from others and aspects of ourselves and mystify our intelligence, our sense of justice is also distorted. We might act in ways that ignore the dignity and sovereignty of others or we might fail to act when others do:

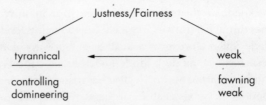

Beginning with the feminist insight that all knowledge is "body mediated," ethicist Beverly Harrison affirms that moral knowledge is "rooted in our sensuality" and that the power to act on the basis of that knowledge is "rooted in feeling." Consequently, she argues that "if we are not perceptive in discerning our feelings, or if we do not know what we feel, we cannot be effective moral agents." If she is right, and I think she is, one wonders how effective men can be as moral agents when we have been socialized and conditioned to fill public offices by restricting our emotionality and sexuality. Harrison believes that "a major source of rising moral insensitivity derives from being out-of-touch with our bodies."[16] How can we feel the pain of our own mistreatment and the mistreatment of others if we have repressed our feelings? How can we see other people and groups of people clearly if we are physically isolated and emotionally disconnected from many of them? How can we see and understand unjust power relations between people and groups of people if our reason is disembodied and we resolutely refuse to analyze those power relations?

Earlier, I mentioned Farley's belief that Mode 1 has been privileged in the university, the seminary, and the church and the other modes have been marginalized. I think the church he is referring to is the white church. James Cone believes that American/white theology is racist because it "identifies theology as dispassionate analysis of 'the tradition,' unrelated to the sufferings of the oppressed."[17] To the degree that white churches (Protestant and Catholic) have been dominated by men, they too have absolutized modes of understanding that have distorted reality. If we white Christians used our right brains to think about the ways we are in reality connected to and interdependent with people of color; to imagine and feel what it is like to be objectified and economically, politically, and culturally discriminated against because of our skin color and continent of ancestry; if we analyzed the power relations that have led to this oppression and our own isolation; and if we moved out of our isolation, we would rage at the theology and practices of white churches that either rationalize and sacralize or, at least, leave unchallenged racist attitudes, behaviors, and practices in ourselves and other Christians.

Our socialization and conditioning take us, not only out of our bodies, but also out of our centered selves. We become externally focused. I have found that asking a man what he wants to do is a pretty cruel thing to do. Most of us don't know. Our lives are structured by the requirements of our jobs, the commitments at church or in our communities, and the desires and needs of our wives and children. We are frequently pulled apart and fragmented by conflicting demands and, unfortunately, there is often not a deciding center—there is no one home—to adjudicate those demands.

Strength

Robert Bly has said that one of the purposes of the Warrior is to defend boundaries—to exercise the capacity to say no. Because of our isolation, misinformation, and mystification, and our distorted sense of justice, we men can spend too much of our time defending the wrong barricades—saying no to the wrong things—and leaving the right ones unprotected—not saying yes to the right things. The result is that we either use our strength, or power, in aggressive, bullying ways that harm other people or turn the same destructiveness on ourselves. We feel angry, vengeful, competitive, and ambitious and act out in what Miedzian calls antisocial aggression or even destructive violence. Or we feel insecure, inadequate, scared, and shameful and aim that aggression or violence toward aspects of ourselves or simply do not, with constructive aggression, defend ourselves and others from the antisocial aggression and violence that continue to be recycled. Rather than a safer, more secure place, the world becomes a scarier, more dangerous place for others and for us.

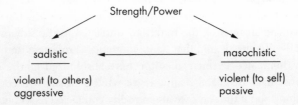

The only people Ralph loved in the world were Ginny and his two sons, yet he spent probably sixty of the best hours of his week at the law firm "kowtowing to rich money," rather than using his considerable intellectual ability and discipline in the service of those who needed them most. He was, however, doing what most of the people around him—his father, his uncle, his peers, and even Ginny—expected him to do. One of the things Ralph needed to learn was how to say no to parts of what his father, uncle, peers, and wife wanted from him and how to say yes to the people he loved, to the people whose needs he could have served with his ability, and to his own desire for more meaningful, pleasurable work and deeply satisfying relationships.

THE PUNISHMENT OF ADAM

So, we have shorter life expectancies than women, increased animosity aimed at us from those we believe we sacrificially serve, dislike from other men, and compulsions to act in ways even we don't like. As Augustine said in his *Confessions,* "No one pities either the boys or the men, though surely we deserve pity." Indeed, we do. Martin Luther saw some of the effects of these masculine norms that lead to this alienation and our shorter life expectancies as a punishment for, or consequence of, sin.[18] Interpreting the Fall narrative in Genesis, he observed:

But his [Adam's] position is burdened with a definite punishment. . . . [It is Adam's responsibility] to be a husband; to till the soil or do some other work by which children and wife are supported; to rule the home, the family, cities, kingdoms; to instruct and bring up the people of the household and others with a view to godliness and good manners. But these very important duties . . . cannot be carried on without the utmost difficulties, as is shown by examples all around us.[19]

In other words, Luther saw the "masculine" requirements of economic provision and exclusive patriarchal rule as men's tragic lot in life. These requirements were, in his view, not a privilege but a punishment for sin.

Said another way, this kind of self-sacrifice, economic provision, and coercive control is a manifestation of human sin, not God's intention for us in creation. In Luther's view, the results of these onerous duties were twofold: (1) the earth endured a curse (Romans 8:20), which made men's work exceedingly more difficult, and (2) adducing the much higher life expectancy of the patriarchs, Luther claimed that "the body was healthier then than it is now."

With respect to male–female relations, Luther believed that in creation, women and men were equal and that women had equal access and responsibility for public institutions. However, as a result of Eve's disbelief and, then, disobedience, she was "punished" by being subjected to her husband: "Your desire shall be for your husband, and he shall rule over you" (Genesis 3:16). The result of this, according to Luther, is that women understandably resent the power they lost in the Fall and use whatever means they can to wrest what power they can from men, including and most especially their husbands:

On the woman obedience to her husband was imposed, but how difficult it is to bring this very condition about![20]

Luther says that women, at best, will mumble against their husbands and, at worst, will engage in a kind of guerrilla warfare against them. It seems to me that he had a pretty good sense of the ways in which the gender dance can be mutually alienating in the most intimate of relationships. Luther understood the source of the antagonism between women and men, locating it in what we would today call sexism—the rule of men over women.

The flip side of economic provision and protection is rule. In order to do the first, we must have the second. It is clear that this is oppressive to women; the first and second waves of the women's movement continue to explore and demonstrate the dire effects of oppressive domination on women.

Men also, because of human sin—men's and women's—are in a very difficult situation. We might even say that men are in an oppressive situation. I hesitate, though, to use the term *oppression* for our situation for a number of reasons. First, for many of us men, it has either scary or negative connotations or both. When the word is used, men often come off on the short end of the stick; that is, we are almost always identified as the oppressor standing in an exploitative relationship to another person or group that is identified as the oppressed. We are pretty much at the top of the oppression pyramid. We can be targeted as the universal bad guys and often don't know what, if anything, we can do to change that situation. I think this targeting brings up for many of us painful feelings associated with earlier targeting for ridicule, humiliation, and abuse. We reexperience the earlier feelings of powerlessness, humiliation, and shame and want to do everything we can to get out of the painful spotlight. My sense is that this is why many of us reply to the various movements for liberation with defensiveness and ridicule attempts at changing oppressive relationships of power as victim-glorifying "political correctness."

Second, claiming that men are oppressed can and has been used to divert attention from the mistreatment of the targets of other forms of oppression (e.g., sexism, heterosexism, racism, classism, and anti-Semitism) with the effect that men, particularly men like me, do not examine carefully those forms of oppression with the intention of resisting them. If we all are in pain and oppressed, then no one group (read: men) can be held responsible and we go on doing what we can't help doing. The result of making such a claim without the intention of and commitment to resisting other forms of oppression is an acquiescence to the inevitability of all forms of oppression, including one's own, and a resignation to living in one's distorted second nature, by which we continue to mistreat others and ourselves. So, claiming to be a victim of oppression without analyzing how that mistreatment is related to other forms of oppression and committing oneself to resisting it and them helps no one.

I am beginning to believe, however, that unless men like me come to terms with the ways we are mistreated as boys and adults, we will not be recruited in large numbers to efforts aimed at ending those other forms of oppression. If we are to come to terms with some of what we find ourselves doing to others and to ourselves and what is done to us, we must look at the large, socially structured dynamics of oppression. Therefore, I want to frame what I will say later about the distortion of men's characters by a discussion of the dynamics of oppression.

The Dynamics of Oppression

In the last thirty years, significant work has been done on understanding the dynamics of oppression and liberation. Insights have emerged from various perspectives as people have analyzed the dynamics and effects of sexism, racism, classism, heterosexism, and anti-Semitism. Paulo Freire's *Pedagogy of the Oppressed*[21] has served many as a theoretical foundation on which to build liberation theory and practice.

Two concepts—internalized oppression and internalized domination—have emerged that help us better understand the overall dynamics of oppression and victimization and address these questions. Judith Kay defines oppression as the systematic mistreatment of one group by another group for the perceived benefit of another group or society as a whole.[22] She says further that the primary form of that mistreatment is disrespect. Internalized oppression describes the way victims adopt as their own the oppressor's false opinion of them. For example, when someone who loves another (or says he or she does) treats that person unjustly, cognitive dissonance is produced in the mind of the victim. The victim might think, "That person loves me, but he [or she] is hurting me; how can this be?" Though one sees, or senses, the unjustness of what has been done, one is often dependent upon the emotional, psychological, financial, or physical support of the person or persons perpetrating the injustice. Since one's own physical or emotional survival may depend on the good graces of the perpetrator, the victim finds himself or herself in a dilemma. To solve the dilemma, reason supplies a third proposition: "I must deserve it." Then the contradiction is resolved. The problem is that this conclusion is not true. So, the victims have resolved their cognitive dissonance by internalizing a false image, or stereotype (if it is a systemic oppression), of themselves that rationalizes their own mistreatment. This image or stereotype is often provided by the oppressor group through the process of socialization (see chapter 1). For example, victims of childhood sexual abuse, even as adults, continue to believe that they were "bad" and thus responsible for what the perpetrator did; when they do so, their self-esteem plummets and recovery is made much more difficult. Historically, many women have had to rationalize their unjust exclusion from public offices, such as the ministry and government service, by internalizing stereotypes about themselves (e.g., women are "naturally" less rational and more emotional [hysterical] than men) that justify this disrespectful treatment.

Internalized domination has to do with others or even aspects of oneself. Someone one knows and respects hurts or mistreats someone else unjustly and one says to oneself, "How can this be? Those people are, or that person is, innocent, but they have hurt them unjustly." Again, there is cognitive dissonance and the dilemma of being dependent on the perpetrator of an unjust action. Now we supply a third proposition about "them," which is, "They must deserve it." So, we internalize the stereotypes about them that the oppressor group uses to rationalize the unjust treatment.[23] Returning to the examples I gave above, the perpetrator of childhood sexual abuse may believe that the child acted seductively or, in the case of "covert incest," that the child is responsible for meeting the adult's intimacy needs. Also, because of our "outrage" at meeting a woman in a public place of authority (Dinnerstein), many of us men have internalized those stereotypes about women's excessive emotionality and incompetence that justify their exclusion from those public roles.

So, what happens in an oppressive situation is that victims are often forced to internalize a false, or distorted, view of themselves as a coping mechanism or survival technique; the problem is that they then collude in the perpetuation of their own oppression, because they come to believe that it is justified—they deserve it. This is what Freire calls the "cultural invasion" of the victim by the oppressor; the victim is forced to internalize the definitions and values of the oppressor in order to survive. Victims then play "host" to the oppressor and can mistreat others of their group because they hold the same distorted view of them. Victims of childhood sexual abuse can become perpetrators; some women put up the most difficult obstacles other women face in moving into positions of public power and responsibility.

A member of an oppressor group can participate in the unjust treatment of victims because he or she has been socialized and conditioned, often through the threat of violence for noncompliance, to internalize distorted views of the oppressed group. So, the members of the oppressed group and the members of the oppressor group not only lack accurate information about themselves and others, but also have internalized misinformation about themselves and others. Again, the second natures of members of oppressed and oppressor groups are shaped by cultural processes of socialization, as well as by psychological conditioning processes that are in some cases driven by large-scale, socially structured oppression. Those processes instill in us certain rigid, inflexible, reflexive behaviors, thoughts, and feelings.

I think these insights can help us men understand some of the things we don't like about ourselves and other men. Many of those things are a result of our collusion in the unjust treatment of others (i.e., our internalized domination patterns) and in the mistreatment we have experienced (i.e., our internalized oppression).

THE MISTREATMENT OF MEN: MEN'S OPPRESSION

Paulo Freire believes that liberation of oppressed and oppressor is the work of the oppressed, to be accomplished through conscientization—a process that includes the organizing of groups for the analysis of oppressive situations and the creation of new cultural alternatives to the old oppressive attitudes, behaviors, relationships, and institutions. I believe that this is precisely the kind of activity men like me and, indeed, all men need to be involved in for the liberation of ourselves and of our society. We need to begin to look at the particular forms our own mistreatment takes and how they are linked to other forms of oppression. I believe that this is the kind of work necessary for the redemption and salvation of men, women, children, and the earth.

THE PECULIAR FORMS OF THE OPPRESSION OF MEN

Men, as men, are systematically oppressed, or mistreated, not by another particular group (women, children, etc.), but by society as a whole. The mistreatment takes at least four forms. First, men are exclusively required to sacrifice our lives in the protection of others (e.g., conscription for military service). Second, men are required to carry heavy responsibilities (e.g., financial and institutional), leading to grim overwork and significantly reduced life expectancies.[24] Third, men are inhibited from expressing our emotions, including our emotional responses to the above mistreatment and responsibilities. Fourth, men are otherwise objectified, or stereotyped, in our society as inherently violent, emotionally constipated, relationally incompetent, and sexually compulsive.

It seems to me that the third form of mistreatment is required by the imperatives of the first two. If one is going to be responsible for the physical and economic well-being of others, or if one is going to fight a war, whether it be military or economic, it is best to repress one's emotions, lest one's enemy or competitor gain an advantage by one's vulnerability. The final objectification or stereotyping of men may be seen as internalized domination attitudes and behaviors of members of society as a whole—stereotypes that rationalize, or justify, men's mistreatment. If men are inherently violent, they ought to fight the wars; they are the ones who start them. If men cannot express their emotions, they can be expected not to.

Many men internalize these stereotypes about ourselves and, thereby, come to accept the mistreatment that comes our way. In fact, many of us not only see the requirements of manhood as appropriate, but also defend them as our duty under God. According to Freire, if the oppressed don't see the oppression, they cannot liberate themselves or their oppressors. Our obliviousness as men to our own oppression obstructs us from seeing that of others and from doing very much about any of it.

Not only do we men internalize stereotypes that justify our mistreatment, but also, as I have said above, we are conditioned to internalize racist, heterosexist, anti-Semitic, and classist stereotypes that justify the mistreatment of others. That is, we manifest attitudinal, thought, and behavior patterns of internalized domination.

My sense is that these two things—our internalized oppression and our internalized domination—are linked. Therefore, if we begin to deal effectively with one, we will deal effectively with the other. Perhaps the best place to start is to tap into the justifiable rage many of us feel about our mistreatment and then trace out the ways in which that is linked to the mistreatment of others. In order to stop objectifying others (women, gay men and lesbians, African-Americans, working-class and owning-class persons, and Jews), we must realize and feel the pain of and rage at our having been objectified. We will then see that we must stop objectifying ourselves (internalized oppression). When we do that, we can empathize with the objectification of others (internalized domination), see the links between theirs and ours, and become real allies in opposing those forms of oppression that hurt them and us.

The Genesis story used by Luther can help us here. Part of what the story of Adam and Eve discloses is the attempt by the Hebrew people to explain how things came to be the way they are. How did women become subject to men? How did Israel become a patriarchal people? Well, the story is an explanation of that. We might look at the narrative not as a prescriptive account of the way God wants it, but as a descriptive account of the way it came to be for both men and women. Patriarchy was never God's intention, but a manifestation, or consequence, of human sin. The rule of men and the disastrous effects it has on women and men are a result of rebellion against God and God's intended order.[25] Implicit in this reading is that the author(s) of the story, like Luther, had a sense that something was wrong here and needed an explanation.

Since this dominating role for men, with its ill effects, is a result of the Fall, we might expect Luther to go on to say that Christ puts an end to that dominating role and those ill effects and restores the equality that was God's intention in creation. Although Luther expects that this domination-subjection pattern will be done away with in the next world, he thinks it will continue in this world. Here, we see Luther's pessimistic doctrine of humanity. He believes that the effects of sin are so great that in this life all we can attain is the hope of salvation, not much of its actuality. So, the hierarchical institutions— the church, the family, and the state—and men's dominating role in them will continue until Jesus' return.

Unfortunately, too much of Christian thinking has maintained the oppressive, dominating hierarchies and has, thus, served to encourage men to "live according to the flesh" and not "according to the Spirit" (Romans 8:13).

CHRISTIAN THEOLOGY IN AN OBJECTIFIED PARADIGM

My claim here is not that Christianity, as such, has done that or must do that or that Christianity is inherently antithetical to men's psychic and spiritual growth and health; in fact, I believe just the opposite. Rather, I believe that many men have been hurt by internalizing interpretations of Christianity that have been distorted by the structures of oppression I have sketched up to this point (sexism, heterosexism, racism, classism, anti-Semitism, and the oppression of men). In the language of the New Testament, the good news of Jesus, the Christ, has been, particularly since the time of Constantine, distorted by the "principalities and powers" of this world. They have shaped interpretations of Christianity in an "objectified paradigm."

By objectified paradigm I mean a framework for understanding the world in which one person is ever the subject and the other person, or group, is ever the object of the first person's knowledge or action.[26] Because human beings have a profound need to know and be known by others, we can be satisfied and most fully human only when we stand in a dual relation to others. We must be the active subject of knowledge about them and the receptive object of their knowledge about us:

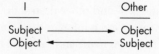

The problem in oppressive situations is that one group attempts to affect another group, or individual members of that group, without being affected by them. There is an attempt by members of the oppressor group to freeze members of the oppressed group exclusively in the role of object (S→O). In other words, members of oppressed groups are *objectified* by members of oppressor groups. There is an attempt to rob them of their inherent dignity as human subjects and their ability to affect others. I call *domination* this attempt to affect others without being affected by them, or to stand exclusively in a subject→object relation. This attempt to dominate others leads to a zero-sum understanding of power in this paradigm. That is the belief that there is only so much power in the world to go around and if someone has more, someone else has less. So, we are essentially competitors for power, or influence (to impose our will or to protect ourselves).

The form of masculinity I have been describing in this book is a socialization and conditioning to domination. Men are expected, even required, to try to affect others without being adversely affected by them. Christianity, interpreted in a model that assumes objectification, not only requires this kind of domination by men, but also sanctifies it. I give here a brief sketch of some major Christian doctrines as seen in such a paradigm.

God is seen as the ultimate Subject, or Affecter, who is not affected by anyone or anything else. Aquinas said that God is *actus purus,* pure act, with no potentiality. That is, God is ever what he is and does not become; he is not acted upon. Thus, he is absolute (literally: all relations that might affect him are absolved) and transcends, or is completely other than (*totaliter aliter* in medieval scholastic terms), everything else. God's other attributes follow from this view. God is omnipotent, meaning that he has ultimate power to affect everything and everyone.[27] And God is omniscient, knowing all things, with no need of input from anyone or anything else.

I say "he" because, in this paradigm, God is masculine—in fact, hypermasculine. Men are supposed to be in control, or dominant; God is omnipotent. Men are supposed to be experts; God is omniscient. Men are supposed to restrict their emotionality and sexuality; God is impassible.

If one takes H. Richard Niebuhr's definition of God as one's center of value, one could argue that this view of God leads to a "cult of masculinity," at the center of which is a hypermasculine image of God.[28] Rather than healing men of the strains and self- and other-destructiveness inherent in many masculine norms, this view of God reinforces them. In traditional theological terms, this view of God leads not to life and salvation but to death and perdition. To explore how that works, I will refer to the effects on men of several of the doctrines I discussed earlier.

In this paradigm, God is believed to have ordained an order to things— an order that is hierarchical. For example, the author of the Letter to the Ephesians advises:

> Wives, be subject to your husbands, as to the Lord. For the husband is the head of the wife as Christ is the head of the church. . . .

Children, obey your parents in the Lord, for this is right. . . . Slaves, be obedient to those who are your earthly masters, with fear and trembling, in singleness of heart, as to Christ; . . . Masters, do the same to them, and forbear threatening, knowing that he who is both their Master and yours is in heaven, and that there is no partiality with him.
 . (EPHESIANS 5:22–6:9)

When we add other aspects of the world to this hierarchy, what we get looks like this:

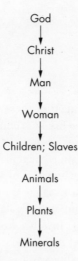

God
↓
Christ
↓
Man
↓
Woman
↓
Children; Slaves
↓
Animals
↓
Plants
↓
Minerals

Those at the top of the hierarchy affect those underneath them without being affected by them. That is, the top members "objectify" the lower members. There is a unilateral flow of action or influence; that is why the arrows point in only one direction.

Justice, in this paradigm, is understood as the maintenance of this God-ordained, hierarchical order. Authority, which comes from the Latin word *auctoritas,* meaning power, is the coercive means by which this order is maintained. Authority is viewed as coming from the top down, which legitimates the unidirectional nature of the influence of those higher up the hierarchy on those lower down.

If we were to add the other objectified relationships shaped by the "principalities and powers," the hierarchy would look like this:

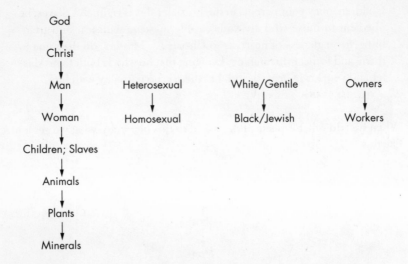

And justice is construed as maintaining these oppressive hierarchies.

Sin, in this paradigm, is the refusal to submit oneself to this ordering. For example, for a woman, it is to refuse to submit to the rule of men; sin is the rejection of sexism. For a man, sin is the refusal to take his place in this hierarchy and carry out his ruling function of keeping everyone else in their places. Said another way, sin for a man is the refusal to fill public offices in a dominating way and the rejection of the dual masculine identity of the lonely warrior and the desperate lover. In other words, sin is the attempt to integrate one's soul and body.

The doctrine of Christ's saving work is, then, seen in this context. Because human beings stepped out of the order ordained by God, or disobeyed God, we have incurred a debt and must pay a penalty for this disobedience. Since God does nothing more justly than uphold his order, he must exact a price for that disobedience. That price, as he ordained it (Genesis 2:17), was death. But, according to some readings of Saint Anselm of Canterbury, it would be unfitting if God, after having created human beings, simply allowed us to go to ruin without doing anything about it; it would show weakness in an omnipotent God. In addition, the dishonor we did to our Infinite Creator God is greater than anything finite creatures can redress. So, though human beings incurred the debt, or penalty, of sin, we cannot pay it. What is needed is a God-man, who because of his humanity can experience death, but because of his divinity can overcome it. That God-man was Jesus, the Christ— God's only-begotten Son. Christ undid our disobedience by his obedient submission to death—the just penalty imposed by God—on our behalf. In the resurrection he wins a victory over death. By doing so, he pays our penalty and shares with us his victory over death.[29]

If we have faith in Christ we are forgiven and redeemed (bought back) from death. We then step back into our proper place in God's order by accepting Christ, not only as Savior, but as Lord of our lives. We submit to his authority and express our love to others by becoming a conduit of his authority to others below us in God's order.

Grace in the dominating, or objectified, paradigm enables the man to deal with the strains consequent to the masculine role without changing the role. For example, grace gives men the ability to limit their yearning for intimacy and sexual/sensual expressions to one woman in the context of marriage and to endure the ensuing isolation and powerlessness; to dominate women, children, and the earth without abusing them; and to neglect or even punish their bodies and still believe that those same bodies are temples of God.

Love is understood to be selfless service in maintaining this order for the good of all. "[Love] does not insist on its own way; ... [love] bears all things, believes all things, hopes all things, and endures all things" (1 Corinthians 13:5–7). For men, love is the acceptance of the dual identity— the tight control of our own emotionality and sexuality and of others through public offices.[30] Spirituality becomes any discipline or practice that enables us to imitate Christ's selfless love in submitting to God's hierarchy of obedience.

DOMINATIVE MASCULINE MEN AND KENOTIC MASCULINE MEN

I believe that this kind of theology both reflects and shapes the distortion of our characters as men.[31] As an illustration of that, I will look at the two predominant responses—defensive denial and guilty silence—that men in the church have given to women's objection to their objectification and exclusion from positions of leadership.

DOMINATIVE MASCULINITY AND DEFENSIVE DENIAL

In 1984 the Southern Baptist Convention, the largest Protestant denomination in America, passed a resolution excluding "women from pastoral leadership . . . to preserve a submission God requires because the man was first in creation and the woman was first in the Edenic fall." Brought to the floor by an all-male committee, the resolution makes clear how such questions are to be determined—*not* by "modern cultural, sociological, and ecclesiastical trends or by emotional factors" but by "the final authority of Scripture." It is this "final authority" that also attests to "God's delegated order of authority (God the head of Christ, Christ the head of man, man the head of woman)."[32] A motion made to extend the time for discussion of the resolution to ten minutes failed—a refusal to listen to the voices of those who opposed the resolution.

In the Roman Catholic church, the Vatican, on the basis of the 1976 *Inter Insigniores* document, claims that since God in Christ determined the specific nature of the sacramental sign, the church has no right or authority to change it and admit women to the priestly order. The argument then runs: since sacramental signification requires a natural resemblance between the sign and thing signified; and since the priest, in the specific and unique act of presiding at the Eucharist is a sign; and since Christ was and remains a man, therefore it is fitting that priestly ordination be reserved to men. The reason that God chose to incarnate God's Word in a male is a mystery beyond the competence of the "human sciences"; it is simply a fact of God's revealed will to which the church (read: the church hierarchy) humbly submits. Since the church has received "charge and control" of the priesthood, the pastoral office is "not granted by people's spontaneous choice . . . ; it is the laying on of hands and the prayer of the successors of the Apostles which guarantee God's choice." One cannot give oneself access to it; the priestly vocation "cannot be reduced to a mere personal attraction, which can remain purely subjective."[33] It must be given to males by the exclusively male hierarchy, which listens not to the human heart or mind but to the immutable will of God, and to which the laity must humbly submit.

In both of these responses, there is a denial that the church and its authoritative structures are harmful to women, much less to men, and an unwillingness to listen to evidence that suggests otherwise. To the contrary, the hierarchical structure must be good for all involved, including women; it is the will of God. In both, an exclusively male authority structure is speaking without listening. In fact, any listening to human voices is ruled out because that would violate the immutable voice of God, the integrity of which the authority structure must protect. For many of the "conservative" men of the Southern Baptist Convention, the source is an inerrant Bible that contains the unassailable pronouncement of a perfect, omniscient Supersubject who needs no input from human beings. In fact, one must ignore the human mind and heart, that is, "modern cultural and sociological trends," as well as "emotional factors." For the Vatican, God's mysterious will is revealed in the

Scriptures and protected by the male successors of the apostles—protected from "personal attraction" and "pure subjectivity." In both cases, the authoritative transmission of truth is unidirectional—from the top down. An implicit assumption seems to be that, though the authoritative structures are not harmful to women, women would be harmful to those structures.

It seems to me that these men tend to work out of internalized domination patterns and therefore manifest active distortions of our inherent capacities— tyranny, sadism, manipulation, addiction. Because God requires order-keeping and is the ultimate Order-keeper himself, our behavior has to be controlling, domineering, and judgmental. We must be aggressive, even to the point of violence, because people's selfishness is so deeply rooted and resistant to change. If we are calculating and manipulative, it is because so many people have been misled and are confused about the proper order of things. And we find ourselves, because of all this, a bit obsessive-compulsive about our very important work and other things that might compensate us for the energy we expend and the pleasures we forgo in those quite strenuous tasks. We believe that this behavior does not stem from our sinful selfishness, but rather from our selfless love. Obedience is the cardinal Christian virtue, and we preach it to others and to ourselves.

KENOTIC MASCULINITY AND GUILTY SILENCE

There have been, however, church bodies that have listened to the voices and criticisms of women but have been slow to speak, that is, to root out sexism or share institutional power with women.

The American Baptist Convention, the liberal Protestant counterpart to the Southern Baptists, passed a "Resolution on Increased Opportunities for Women" in 1969—a resolution brought to the floor by a committee chaired by a woman. More important, the ABC General Board adopted a "Resolution on the Empowerment of Women" in 1977 that called for a reversal of the declining number of positions held by professionally trained women on the city, state, regional, and national staffs.[34] However, although modest progress was made during the decade 1971–81 on the basic professional and middle-management levels, there was "a net decrease of one woman and a net increase of four men on the National Staff." In 1981 no women served on the National Executive Council or on the Regional Executive Ministers Councils—the most important decision-making groups in the ABC.[35]

The National Conference of Catholic Bishops, considered by many to be more cognizant than the Vatican of the negative effects of sexism, published the First Draft of "A Pastoral Response to Women's Concerns for Church and Society" in 1988. Having conducted hearings for groups within the church representing "voices of alienation," the conference recognized the existence of sexism in both society and the church and rejected "actions by which women have been undervalued, subordinated, made objects of suspicion, condemnation, condescension, or simply ignored." Consequently, it declared its intention "to ensure that women are empowered to take part in positions of authority and leadership in church life in a wide range of situations and ministries." The bishops balked, however, at extending the equality of women and men to priestly ordination. Distinguishing the "priesthood of the faithful" from the ministerial priesthood, the conference excluded women from the latter, citing *Inter Insigniores,* which had declared that this exclusion "witnesses to the mind of Christ." Noting that some Catholic scholars had not found the arguments of *Inter Insigniores* persuasive, the bishops encouraged further study of the matter. However, the purpose of such study seemed simply "to place in proper light the Church's consistent practice."[36] This purpose was made clearer in the Second Draft of the Pastoral, which more explicitly endorsed the church's prohibition of contraception and women's ordination and "took a position closer to that of Pope John Paul II, who has said that debate is closed on the matters."[37] While the Second Draft called for thorough study of the possibility of ordaining women as deacons to "be undertaken and brought to completion soon," the Third Draft calls only for "continuing dialogue and reflection" on the meaning of ministry. The Fourth Draft insists that such reflection "proceeds with an objectivity and serenity whose necessary context is respect for the authority of the magisterium of the Church."[38]

In both of these responses, predominantly, if not exclusively, male authority structures are listening to the "voices of alienation" and seem repentant about sexism; they may even use gender-inclusive language when referring to human beings (though few of us do when referring to God) and criticize those dominative masculine men who do not. As we have seen, however, many of these men are either strangely quiet as to what positive, constructive steps ought to be taken in response to them or, when such steps are defined, quite reluctant to take them.

It seems to me that internalized oppression patterns are prominent in these men's lives and therefore they manifest the passive distortions of our inherent capacities—weakness, masochism, naïveté, depression. Because we have listened, we are acutely aware that we have "sinned and fallen short of the glory of God" (i.e., we are inherently violent, emotionally constipated, relationally incompetent, and sexually compulsive). Consequently, our feelings of insecurity and shame lead us to cultivate the approval of women by actively repressing those shameful parts of ourselves that we believe have led to women's oppression and pain. We might fail to challenge the unhealthy feminine patterns in the woman we are close to, seek her forgiveness by compulsively disclosing or confessing faults, overfunction by taking responsibility for her pain and healing, and/or live for long periods in sexless relationships. This leaves many of us pretty frustrated and confused and emotionally shut down.

We too believe that we are doing these things because of our selfless love for women; we are not like all those other selfish men who hurt women. The cardinal virtue for us is a self-emptying. We believe that we have a lot of bad stuff inside us and that, in order to be okay, we need to empty ourselves of it. The Greek word for empty is *kenosis*. That is why I call this form of Christian masculinity kenotic masculinity.

I call us SURGes—screwed-up religious guys. As you can probably tell from what I have said so far about my own life, these are the patterns of feeling and behaving that have most characterized my life. I developed the term *SURG* from a conversation with a man much like me. We did not identify with a lot of what was being criticized about men; we did not feel we were particularly coercive, insensitive, and oppressive toward women. One reason is that, having grown up in Christian homes and churches, we had been taught that this kind of mistreatment of women was wrong and we felt bad when we did it. That part was right, but we ended up pretty confused and not very happy. Consequently, though we abhor sexism, we seem reluctant to take significant steps toward the inclusion of women in the structures of power as they now exist, or to work actively for new, more mutual structures.

I believe the reason for this is that many "liberal" men are changing, to the extent that we do, for what we believe to be the good of our neighbor, in this case women, and do not see that change is also necessary for our own well-being. That is, we are still acting as self-sacrificing officeholders, whose ostensible "listening" does not affect the performance of our offices as much as we believe and publicly profess. Whatever change there may be is expressed in our personal relationships but seldom is manifest in the transformation of our public offices. We are still acting out of a deeply divided self, whose dominative patterns continue to be reflected in the institutions in which we participate.

It seems to me that both the dominative masculine men and the kenotic masculine men have some things right and other things wrong. Dominative masculine men often take pride in themselves as men and rightly see and value the sacrifices they make to do what they think is right. They also appreciate the depth and pervasiveness of what is wrong in the world and do not think that it will easily be overcome. They express their concern for connection with others through the discharge of their responsibilities, so they often act decisively. They don't always see, however, that their pride is sometimes misguided—that some of what they are proud of and what bonds them are second-nature patterns that are destructive to themselves and others. So, these men tend not to see clearly their mistreatment of others or victims of oppression generally. Consequently, they tend to exacerbate the oppression by ignoring the subjectivity and sovereignty of others in the name of order, or a hierarchical notion of justice. They are often unconscious of the fact that these ways of thinking and acting, rather than connecting them, disconnect them from other people.

Kenotic masculine men are sensitive to the effects of their actions on others. They tend to be able to see somewhat more clearly the fact that women are hurt by sexism and, to take another example, that African-Americans are hurt by racism. In other words, they can recognize victims of oppression and realize that the enforcement of a hierarchical order is simplistic and often redoubles the mistreatment of people. However, they don't often see the ways in which they themselves have been victimized to produce the oppressive patterns of thought, feeling, and behavior, nor the ways in which those patterns make them less human. For example, they don't often distinguish maleness, their own or others', from masculinity or the fact that they are white from their whiteness. Because they fail to distinguish their and others' first natures from their second natures, they have more compassion for other victims, but little for themselves and others most like them. Without this intellectual and emotional clarity, they often find themselves without a positive vision to replace the destructiveness they see and, consequently, are paralyzed in inaction.

Saint Augustine said that, as human beings, our ethical responsibility to one another is twofold—we are to harm no one and to help whomever we can. Because of the distortions to our character, we men find fulfilling this responsibility difficult. Dominative masculine men tend to try to help others, but are often oblivious to the harm we inflict in the ways we do it. That is, because of a distorted sense of justice and naïveté about oppression, we sometimes defend the wrong barricades. Dominative masculine men tend to identify the body and members of oppressed groups, as well as disloyal members of oppressor groups, as the problem at which we must direct our warrior energy. Kenotic masculine men tend to try to avoid harming others but find ourselves unable to do enough to help decisively where we might. Because of our shame and its concomitants—emotional and psychological powerlessness—our sense of justice and our clarity about the ways our mistreatment is connected to others' are impaired. So, kenotic masculine men tend to identify their own deepest desires and dominative masculine men as the problem against which we need to direct our warrior energy.

Unfortunately, we don't learn very much from each other, nor help each other recover from the socialization and violent conditioning that have led to much of our self- and other-destructive thoughts, feelings, and behavior. In fact, we often end up reinforcing that violent conditioning by targeting each other for ridicule, humiliation, and, if not physical, at least rhetorical violence. My sense is that we split off aspects of ourselves about which we carry shame, project that shame onto the other group of men, and then criticize them. Dominative masculine men ridicule kenotic masculine men for being weak, naive, unfair, and pandering to "special-interest groups." Kenotic masculine men ridicule dominative masculine men for being tyrannical, authoritarian, violent, and "out of touch." We must stop this. Instead, we must begin to use our God-given capacities for justice, strength, intelligence, and compassion to work cooperatively in analyzing and resisting what is producing these patterns in both of us.

HEALING

I am not a mechanism, an assembly of various sections.
And it is not because the mechanism is working wrongly, that I am ill.
I am ill because of wounds to the soul, to the deep emotional self
and the wounds to the soul take a long, long time, only time can help
and patience, and a certain difficult repentance,
long, difficult repentance, realization of life's mistake, and the freeing
    of oneself
from the endless repetition of the mistake
which mankind at large has chosen to sanctify.

D. H. LAWRENCE

PART TWO

The Love of God and the
Men We Long to Be

Chapter Four

"A New Creation": The Call to a Center and Over the Barricades

I hope at least the following will endure: my trust in the people, and my faith in men and women, and in the creation of a world in which it will be easier to love.

PAULO FREIRE, *Pedagogy of the Oppressed*

So if anyone is in Christ, there is a new creation: everything old has passed away; see, everything has become new! All this is from God, who reconciled us to himself through Christ, and has given us the ministry of reconciliation. (2 Corinthians 5:17)

SAINT PAUL

THE LONELY WARRIOR and desperate lover are false selves, or the "old creature" in Paul's language, that distort the image of God in us and lead to the kinds of dynamics I have described in part 1. These are deadly, but God calls us to life and healing. For those of us who are Christians, we have experienced that call in Christ.

In this chapter, I want to talk about that call by sketching an alternative interpretation of Christianity in a mutual paradigm.

As I have said, H. Richard Niebuhr, influenced by Saint Augustine, identified the term *God* with the center of value in a person's or a culture's life.[1] Faith he defined as one's loyalty, or commitment, to that center of value. For him, there are no atheists; we all have a "god," a center of value—something or someone to whom we are loyal; something that makes life worth living; something that gets us up in the morning. The question is what, or who, is it? Whatever or whoever it is will determine for us how we think we should live our lives—what we ought to do and not do; what we should value and what we should take to be valueless. Niebuhr goes on to define henotheism as faith in something that is finite; it might be a person, a cause, or a group of people. Our center of value might be our spouse; capitalism or socialism; our nation, our church, or our family. Polytheism characterizes a person who has not one, but several or many centers of value, all of which compete for that person's commitment, time, and loyalty.

Using Niebuhr's definitions, we might say that the men afflicted by the kind of masculinity I've been describing alternate between a polytheistic faith and an idolatrous, henotheistic faith. The lonely warrior finds himself torn between sometimes conflicting value centers—his family, his career, his community, and, perhaps, his church. He might measure his own worth by the evaluations of those holding each of those sets of expectations and, most often, find himself wanting. Or, in his isolation, he might find himself clutching tightly to the one woman in his life and judge himself solely in terms of her expectations, desires, or needs and his ability to stay in relation to her. To do that he might sacrifice other relationships, his sense of his own dignity, or even his vocation, if he has one. If Carter Heyward is right in saying that God is our "power in relation,"[2] what I have described as our "monorelational psychic structure" (that is, our fixation on the one woman in our lives) is idolatrous. And so it is. Remember the man who went to the Far East to discover God only to realize that he already had one in women?

None of these "gods" satisfy our deepest longings for communion with God, with aspects of ourselves, and with others. As Saint Augustine said, "Our hearts are restless until they find their rest in You [God]." And so they are. Underneath all of this stuff—the dominating habits of thinking, feeling, and acting that we mistake for our selves—lies our "inmost self" that yearns for God. God, that delighted and delightful Good, draws us, through our passion, delight, or bliss, to communion and satisfies our deep spiritual longing for a just world and life-giving connections to others.

We can experience that call in Christ. Well into Jesus' ministry, James and John came to him and said:

> "Teacher, we want you to do for us whatever we ask of you." And he said to them, "What is it you want me to do for you?" And they said to him, "Grant us to sit, one at your right hand and one at your left, in

your glory." But Jesus said to them, "You do not know what you are asking. Are you able to drink the cup that I drink, or be baptized with the baptism that I am baptized with?" They replied, "We are able." Then Jesus said to them, "The cup that I drink you will drink; and with the baptism with which I am baptized, you will be baptized; but to sit at my right hand or at my left is not mine to grant, but it is for those for whom it has been prepared."

When the ten heard this, they began to be angry with James and John. So Jesus called them and said to them, "You know that among the Gentiles those whom they recognize as their rulers lord it over them, and their great ones are tyrants over them. But it is not so among you; but whoever wishes to become great among you must be your servant, and whoever wishes to be first among you must be slave of all. For the Son of Man came not to be served but to serve, and to give his life a ransom for many."

(MARK 10:35-45)

It seems to me that the image of Jesus presented in the Gospel of Mark explicitly rejects modes of thinking, feeling, and acting that are produced by an understanding of the world and religious duty from the perspective of an objectified paradigm. For him, there is no place for "lording it over others"; for domination; for freezing others in the role of object and robbing them of their subjectivity. That is the way of those outside the family of God, or in his vocabulary, the Gentiles. Rather, those who would follow Jesus will make themselves vulnerable; that is, they will be willing to be affected by others. As is often the case in the Gospel of Mark, Jesus turns the hierarchy, which others believe to be God-ordained, upside down. The greatest shall be last, and the last shall be greatest.

According to the author of the Gospel, this is what got Jesus into so much trouble with some of the male officeholders—both religious and civil—of his day.[3] He implicitly and explicitly challenged the way some of them did what they did, and it was hard for them to hear. By challenging what they did, he also challenged their understanding of themselves; that was hard for them to take—as it is for many of us.

Jesus invited people to participate in what he called the "kingdom of God"—or put another way, the justice of God.[4] This is an order, or justice, that is free of objectification and domination. The problem is that many of us have had and continue to have difficulty envisioning and embracing a world in which everyone is treated as a sovereign person and everything is treated with respect.

CHRISTIAN THEOLOGY IN A MUTUAL PARADIGM

As I have said, I believe, following Augustine, that human beings have been created with an inherent desire to love, or to know and be known. Human beings' first natures, or "inmost selves," are inherently relational; we and other human beings, earth creatures, and nonanimate beings are interdependent. Paul saw the Christian community as "many parts, yet one body"; therefore, one part cannot say to the other, "I have no need of you" (1 Corinthians 12:20–21).

In a mutual paradigm,[5] there is an implicit assumption about power. Contrary to the objectified paradigm, in which there is a competitive, zero-sum notion of power (i.e., there is only so much power to go around, so if I have more, you have less), the assumption in the mutual paradigm is that power increases as it is shared. The authentic mode of human relating is, then, cooperation, not competition.

For the fruition of our truest natures and the fulfillment of the desire to love and be loved, we must stand in a dual relation with others; we must be the subject of knowledge about them and the object of their knowledge. This second aspect of our loving is what Beverly Harrison calls vulnerability—the willingness to be deeply affected by another. Mutuality is, then, the state of relation in which one affects and is affected by others. In that state, there are authentic, deeply human dependency needs; the human self is enhanced, not diminished, by mutual or right relation with others and with split-off aspects of oneself.[6] An important aspect of the self that has been split off in many men is the bodily—including the emotional and sexual—aspects of ourselves. In this paradigm, the self is seen not simply as a disembodied soul but as a body-self, which Beverly Harrison calls "sensuous centers of self-direction and relationship."[7]

Sin, in this paradigm, is seen both as acts that are performed and as a state of being. Moreover, it has a social as well as a personal dimension.

If we were created to be interdependent and to share freely what we have with others and gratefully receive from and be affected by them, sin is a state of isolation from God, aspects of ourselves, and others that results from objectification. If our and others' lives are such that we cannot say to anyone, "I need thee not," then sin is objectification—the freezing of another or parts of oneself as an object in the attempt to keep them from affecting us. In effect, then, sin is saying to God, aspects of oneself, and/or others, "I need thee not." It fractures the interdependent web of life intended by God. I will return to our isolation from God later. Here I want to focus on how sin is manifested in our own lives and in our relationships to others.

Acts of sin, then, include attempts both to split off aspects of ourselves and to treat others as though they do not matter—by actively harming them, by remaining passive when they are harmed by others, or simply by ignoring them and continuing in our ignorance. To think of ourselves as "having" a body that has bad, distracting desires and uncontrollable emotions is sinful. Not that our desires, because of the ways our lovers have been distorted, are always healthy, but repressing such desires and not analyzing why they are being expressed in destructive ways is blaming the victim—in this case our bodies—and does not contribute to their transformation. It is sinful to treat others as if they don't matter by excluding them from significant participation in economic systems (e.g., discrimination against African-Americans in home-mortgage lending and the "glass ceiling" encountered by professional women), government employment (e.g., ban on gay men and lesbians in the military), and religious institutions (e.g., resistance to the ordination of women, gays, and lesbians) or by inequitably requiring of them high-risk services that, in effect, render them expendable (e.g., the exclusive conscription of men for military service).

Jesus consistently opposed the objectification of aspects of the self and of others, that is, the labeling of others for the purpose of dismissing them or excluding them from significant participation in human communities. Religious leaders brought a woman caught in adultery before Jesus, not because they were concerned about her or the sanctity of marriage, but in order to find a way to justify silencing him (John 7:53–8:11). They said that the law of Moses commanded them to stone her; Jesus' response was to challenge the men's sin that had led them to bring her before him: "Let anyone among you who is without sin be the first to throw a stone at her." We might understand him to be saying, "Why do you try to exclude her and not yourselves? Would you want to be treated that way?" To the woman he said, "Neither do I condemn you; go, and do not sin again." That is, "Have more respect for yourself and others than this; go and deal with whatever it is that led you to this destructive behavior." Paul, too, repudiated the labeling of others for the purpose of dismissing them: "As many of you as were baptized into Christ have clothed yourselves with Christ. There is no longer Jew or Greek, there is no longer slave or free, there is no longer male or female; for all of you are one in Christ Jesus" (Galatians 3:28).

The effect of these sinful acts is a state of alienation within the sinners and between the sinners and the ones sinned against. By splitting off aspects of ourselves, we live in a state of internal division and alienation. By repressing and denying an authentic capacity of ourselves, we find that it is not eradicated but often expresses itself in compulsive and destructive ways—the bipolar behaviors (tyrant–weakling, etc.). By making other people objects, we live in a state of external division and isolation. People do not like being treated as objects, no matter how much they may acquiesce to their own objectification. And because they don't, they end up not liking or wanting to be around those that treat them disrespectfully. The result is alienation and isolation. Both sinners and those sinned against are made less human and less powerful by the objectification. Because of the alienation, isolation, dislike, and disempowerment, we feel less secure and more afraid; that is, we experience increased anxiety. This insecurity and fear usually compel us to try to secure ourselves by protecting ourselves from being adversely affected by others. So, again, we treat them like objects to keep them from affecting us, and the cycle begins all over again. By trying to make ourselves invulnerable, we make ourselves more vulnerable, and there seems to be no way to stop it. It seems to be a never-ending, vicious cycle.

We end up denying that our own created capacities and those of other persons and nonhuman beings are necessary for our well-being. In fact, we become so mystified that we believe they constitute obstructions to our well-being. Sin, then, is a denial and rejection of our essential, interdependent, relational nature. It is an attempt to live in ways that we were never intended to live. And in those attempts, we die. As the story says, "You shall not eat of the fruit of the tree that is in the middle of the garden, nor shall you touch it, or you shall die" (Genesis 3:3).

Sin, then, has a personal and a social component. We split off aspects of ourselves and then find ourselves subject to compulsions that we can't seem to stop. We push people away from us by treating them disrespectfully, find ourselves anxious and afraid, and compulsively continue to do that which produced the anxiety and fear. Again, we find ourselves in the position Paul describes, "I do not understand my own actions. For I do not do what I want, but I do the very thing I hate" (Romans 7:15). It is as though something else has a hold of us; something is compelling us to act in ways that, on one level of our consciousness, we know are not right. So, sin is something we do and are responsible for, but also something that is bigger than us and seems, at times, to control us.

The early Christians had a sense of a malevolent force, or forces, in the world that included but was larger than what human beings intended individually or even collectively. The writer of Ephesians says:

> For our struggle is not against enemies of blood and flesh, but against the rulers, against the authorities, against the cosmic powers of this present darkness, against the spiritual forces of evil in the heavenly places.
>
> (EPHESIANS 6:12)

The sense was that God had created certain structures in the world that were to order the world (Colossians 1:16) and that those "rulers," "authorities," and "cosmic powers" had, through sin, fallen. Therefore, they are rulers of "this present darkness." In other words, there was something, or some things, abroad in the world and experience of these early Christians that seemed enormously powerful and destructive of human life.[8]

Since the Enlightenment, many of us Western Christians have had difficulty with this kind of language in the New Testament and from other early writers. As Rudolf Bultmann asked a generation ago, what can we, who flip a switch to turn on a light, make of this talk of spiritual forces, cosmic powers, demons, and Satan?[9] René Descartes claimed that there are two kinds of things in the world, mind and extended matter. What are demons, rulers, spiritual forces, and cosmic powers? Do they have any meaningful ontological status? Anyway, for many of us this language reflects a mythological worldview and three-story cosmology (hell, earth, heaven) that are no longer intellectually meaningful.

However, a number of contemporary Christian writers have reappropriated the language of "principalities and powers" as meaningful and helpful in describing the enormity and pervasiveness of structures of oppression that fracture the web of human and nonhuman interdependence and distort humanity.[10] Marjorie Suchocki, in a feminist reappropriation of the doctrine of original sin, has called this aspect of sin "structures of consciousness which bode to our ill-being."[11] Among the structures to which she refers are sexism, homophobia/heterosexism, racism, anti-Semitism, and classism.

Another notable example of this reappropriation is Walter Wink's recent three-volume study of the "powers."[12] He argues that those early Christians, when they talked about principalities and powers, "were discerning the actual spirituality at the center of the political, economic, and cultural institutions of their day."[13] The "heavenly" rulers and cosmic powers can be seen as the internal aspect of the "earthly," or external, structures and institutions that order our society. The principalities and powers refer to what we might call the corporate culture, or collective personality, that pervades such institutions as businesses, schools, governments, and families.[14] To the degree that the corporate cultures of our institutions are infected with oppressive (e.g., sexist, heterosexist, racist, anti-Semitic, and classist) dynamics and relationships, then we might say that these institutions, which determine much of the material, emotional, and psychological bases of our lives, are indeed "spiritual hosts of wickedness."

Wink, following many other New Testament scholars, points out that the words translated "world" (*kosmos*) and "flesh" (*sarx*) in the New Testament often refer not to the earth and the body as they were created by God, but rather to the distortions of creation as a result of sin, or objectification. The writer of the Gospel of John says, "He [the Word] was in the world [*kosmos*], and the world [*kosmos*] was made through him, yet the world knew him not" (John 1:10). Later, Jesus said to religious leaders, "You are from below, I am from above; you are of this world [*kosmos*], I am not of this world [*kosmos*]" (John 8:23). Since the world was made through the Word, it like everything else is good (Genesis 1:9ff.). Therefore, Jesus, or the Gospel writer, is not referring to the material world but to the distortions caused by the Fall. From his perspective, Wink suggests that a better translation of *kosmos* would be "system." That is, the *kosmos* referred to in these passages is not the earth, as created by God, but the interlocking dynamics of particular corporate cultures, or collective personalities, that affect our lives in destructive ways. So, reread, the Gospel writer is affirming that the Word, through which the ordering structures were made, came into the systems (as they became after the Fall), and the systems did not recognize that Word. And Jesus is saying to those particular religious leaders, "You are of this system, I am not of this system." Read this way, Jesus is not some ethereal, "otherworldly" spirit-being who opposed and transcended the physical body, but rather a concrete human being who opposed systems of objectification and oppression, embodied in institutions, that distort this world and these physical bodies. He is not antiworld, but antiestablishment, to the degree that those establishments distort our humanity.

As I have noted before, the word *sarx,* usually translated "flesh," must similarly be understood to refer, not to the physical body as a body, which in creation is good and after the Fall awaits redemption, but to the distortions of creation as a result of sin, or objectification.[15] Again, Paul asserts, "if you live according to the flesh [*kata sarx*] you will die, but if by the Spirit you put to death the deeds of the body you will live" (Romans 8:13). Placed in the paradigm and terms I have been using, Paul can be understood to say, "If you are pervaded with these habits of domination and objectification, you are dying; but if by the Spirit you refuse to participate in these oppressive dynamics and treat others and yourself respectfully, you will live." In other words, *sarx,* or flesh, can be seen to refer to those aspects of our second natures that are a distortion of our first-nature capacities, or "inmost selves."

One of the things many people have come to see in this postmodern period is the degree to which we are not isolated, completely autonomous individuals but are shaped by the language, customs, and patterns of relationships of the communities in which we are nurtured.[16] Consequently, we are in a better position to appreciate the impact that social forces have on us. Marjorie Suchocki's notion of original sin as "structures of consciousness which bode to our ill-being" is helpful here. Rather than seeing sin as something that is transmitted personally through the sexual intercourse between one's parents (Augustine), she suggests that it is passed on through the social structures of consciousness that shape our institutional and, therefore, personal lives. Rather than a sexually transmitted disease, we might see original sin as a socially transmitted disease.[17]

Though sin is passed on through social structures and dynamics, it is not just something "out there" in our institutions and social life; it is in us too. That is, we assent to these dominating and objectified ways of acting. Why do we do that; why do we consent to treat ourselves and others in these destructive ways? I have suggested we do so, in part, to survive. We aren't stupid; we rightly perceive that a great deal of destructive energy will be directed at us if we do not comply. But where did the first inclination to act in such ways originate? In the human heart? In the "principalities and powers"? In the institutions? These are very difficult questions; they are perennial theological questions. The answer is yes, sin originated in all of them, yet not in any one of them altogether. There is mystery here. That is why we have religious stories, or myths; they describe in multilayered narrative form something of the way things came to be. And they prevent us from blaming evil exclusively on humanity, or on spiritual powers, or on institutions.[18]

So, sin is not just a socially transmitted disease; it is also in us. One of the reasons for emphasizing here sin's social character is that, by focusing so much on sin's personal character and tying it so closely to a privatized notion of sexuality, we haven't paid sufficient attention to the social dimension and the ways in which oppressive social dynamics have distorted our whole lives as well as our sexuality. Consequently, we have too often been mystified about both what can be done about oppression and about distorted and destructive expressions of our sexuality. Sin is mysterious, but we, others, and the earth are ill served by our prematurely surrendering our intelligence to its mystery when there are important things we can know and do about it.[19]

We have a personal, volitional choice, and that choice has been profoundly conditioned by oppressive dynamics and forces. But that also means that there can be a personal, volitional choice not to participate in these destructive dynamics. How is that possible, though, when we feel so powerless?

We do so by the grace of God; we are saved by grace, through faith. Grace can be understood as that gift or gifts that facilitate the healing of our body-selves and our relationships with others and with God.

Grace comes to us both in creation and in redemption. The grace of creation is that gift of life given in creation with all its beauty and potential. One way of thinking about the grace of creation, or the grace of nature, is that it is that "inmost self," or first nature, with its capacities. Though distorted by sin—original and actual—those capacities remain in us and with us. So, we can see general grace as that inherent awareness of justice that senses the wrongness of these dominative relationships and oppressive structures. Or, we might see it as that inherent strength by which we resist these structures for as long as we can and oppose them in large and small ways. Or we might see it as that inherent intelligence by which we see through the mystifications and rationalizations for the mistreatment of others and know more than we can always live into. Or it might be that strong desire in us for significant, intimate connections that draws us toward God and just relationships with others.

The grace of redemption is grace that comes to us personally and historically, by means of particular events and persons. For many Christians, God is believed to have acted historically and particularly in Jesus, the Christ. That is, redemptive grace was given by means of the incarnation, the life and ministry of Jesus, his suffering and death, and his resurrection and continuing presence in the world. For men like me, redemptive grace heals the painful rending of our psyches and bodies and is that which enables us to step over the barricades that isolate us and hurt others. We cannot stand against these "principalities and powers" alone; we are who we are because of the communities of which we have been a part. What kind of communities empower us to act in new and different ways? What makes it possible to overcome the fear that seems to compel our collusion in our own and others' mistreatment?

These questions have to do with what has traditionally been called in Christian theology the "work of Christ," or that which Christ did to save us, redeem us, transform us. The language one uses depends on what it is that one thinks Christ did. Interestingly, while there have been official dogmatic statements concerning God's nature and Christ's nature, there has never been such a definitive statement concerning the work of Christ. That may seem odd, because whatever it is that Christ did is at the center of the Christian tradition. One might say that it is the fundamental mystery of the Christian faith.

There have been, however, many theories concerning Christ's work throughout Christian history. The theories usually focus on scriptural passages, employ metaphors, and reflect the cultural context and concerns of the persons developing them. The theories might be categorized under two headings—objective theories and subjective theories. Some theories assert that Christ affected or transformed objective reality (e.g., Christ conquered the devil, ransomed us from the devil, paid a debt to God, or brought healing to us). Other theories affirm that Christ affected or transformed subjective reality (e.g., Christ enlightened us or demonstrated God's love for us). It seems to me that many of the theories might be clustered around two models—a juridical model and a medicinal model. The juridical model stresses the transcendence (otherness) of God, God's rights, human wrongdoing, the imputation of guilt or innocence, and recompense. The medicinal model emphasizes God's immanence (withness), God's generosity, human sickness, the impartation of righteousness or justice, and healing. My sense is that our masculine socialization and conditioning to separateness predispose many men toward the juridical model. Since many of our pastors and theologians have been men, this model has historically predominated in teaching and preaching, particularly in the Western church, since Constantine.

I believe that the many metaphors and these two models contain useful insights for revealing aspects of the central mystery of the Christian faith. I think, however, that the medicinal model has been underrepresented in our theological thinking, speaking, and writing and that it contributes insights that are particularly important to men at this historical moment. I offer here, then, an interpretation of the work of Christ that builds primarily on the medicinal model, incorporating aspects of the juridical model, and addresses both objective and subjective realities—that is, external and internal dimensions of the world.

In a mutual paradigm, Christ can be seen as one who, himself, opposed and exposed these dehumanizing "powers" (Colossians 2:15), preached good news to the poor, proclaimed release to the captives and recovery of sight to the blind, set at liberty those who were oppressed, and proclaimed the acceptable year of the Lord (Luke 4:18–19). It was this liberation that constituted the "good news of the kingdom of God" (Luke 8:1). As I said before, in the Gospel accounts, Jesus persistently challenges the orders of domination he encountered: the rich over the poor; Jews over Samaritans and Gentiles; family members over outsiders; men over women; adults over children; and the well over the sick. To those who listened and who sought to follow him, Jesus said, in effect, that these categories and relations of power obtain among the Gentiles, but in the coming kingdom of God, "it shall not be so among you." His vision of the kingdom, or realm, of God is one of mutuality; we are invited to be friends, not servants (John 15:14–15). As far as we know, Jesus was not married; he had no one significant other, but rather a network of intimates. He stood against the principalities and powers that get in the way of our developing significant, intimate, trusting relationships with other people like and unlike us—sexism, ethnocentrism, religious imperialism and isolationism, classism, adultism. Jesus insisted on close, fully human relationships. And all are invited to participate; Jesus reached out to people who had been objectified and robbed of their dignity as persons. He treated them as subjects and was willing to be affected by them. The righteousness of God is the justice of God, that is, an ordering in which the dignity, subjectivity, and sovereignty of each person is respected and protected.

It was this vision and these actions that seem to have drawn the ire of some public officers (religious and civil) and led to his death.[20] In the Gospel of John, he tells his disciples:

> If the world [dominating system] hates you, be aware that it hated me before it hated you. If you belonged to the world [dominating system], the world would love you as its own. Because you do not belong to the world [dominating system], but I have chosen you out of the world—therefore the world [dominating system] hates you. . . . If they persecuted me, they will persecute you. . . . If I had not done among them the works that no one else did, they would not have sin. But now they have seen and hated both me and my Father.[21]
>
> (JOHN 15:18ff.)

Jesus, in the view of this Gospel writer, exposed the "world," or dominating system, for what it was—an enemy of God. He died not to assuage God's anger or restore God's honor; rather, Jesus died because of his passionate, divine commitment to the dignity and inclusion of all persons in the realm of God.[22] The result is that, in the words of Paul, Christ sets us and the creation "free from [our] bondage to decay" (Romans 8:21).

Is it possible that what was transcendent about Jesus was precisely his humanness? That is, he insisted on resisting those things that separate us and isolate us from God, aspects of ourselves, and others. In doing so, he established, nurtured, and maintained a human community that survived his death. This was his power; this was an aspect of the miracle, or power, of his resurrection: alienated individuals were knit into a human community—the body of Christ. Because they had experienced its beauty and transforming power, they would not give up on it. They came to have faith in its strength and were impelled toward reconciliation with others. Is it possible that that same experience and faith are what has kept Christian communities going through thick and thin throughout history? It was not the power of the Constantinian state, but the experience of and belief in a new community that have inspired and empowered us to live in a fully human way.

I say that this is *an* aspect of the miracle of Christ's resurrection, because the new life we experience in this new community—his body—points us beyond even that community in which we experience it. That community, as with every Christian community, embodies Christ's resurrected life only partially. There is an aspect of Christ's resurrection that transcends any particular community or, even, all Christian communities taken together—the Church universal.[23] It is that life that ever draws particular communities and the Church universal toward increasingly inclusive salvation.

It is a salvation, however, that we do not see consummated here and now. We have a sense that there must be something more—something at some future time and, perhaps, in some other place. Just as we do not feel, therefore, that the full reality of Christ is comprehended by the Church or what we experience here, so, too, we cannot quite believe that our own reality and others' can be comprehended by what we know of life here and now. The Apostles' Creed affirms, "I believe in the resurrection of the body and the life everlasting." Who knows what that means? There has been a lot of speculation about it in the history of Christian thought. What seems clear is that "our bodily life . . . is intrinsically part of us and is valued eternally by God, the Cosmic Lover."[24] That is, the valuing of our lives and bodies seems to extend beyond our existence in this time and place.

After Jesus' death and resurrection, his followers found that they had been and were being brought together and transformed into a new community where barricades, including various forms of oppression, were being broken down. They had experienced reconciliation with God, with aspects of themselves, and with one another. I will return to reconciliation with God shortly; here I want to talk a bit about reconciliation with aspects of ourselves and with others.

Athanasius of Alexandria, in his *On the Incarnation*, said that we were brought out of nonexistence into existence by the divine Word. Our lives, then, depended upon the maintenance of our continued participation in the Word. Sin was a turning away from the Word, which because of God's promise (Genesis 2:17) and the nature of things meant our death. Because of sin, says Athanasius, death was wound into our bodies. In Christ, God sent the Word into the world and into a human body. In the crucifixion, death came to do its bidding; however, because of the power of the divine Word, death was blotted out in Christ's body. This is the meaning of the resurrection. Because Jesus' body so participated in the Word, the divine, death was undone, or conquered.[25] In the terms I have been using, Christ brought, enacted, and embodied a countervailing structure of consciousness and mode of being in the world that was life-giving and liberating from the death-dealing structures of consciousness and modes of being that prevailed.

Christ, then, offers to us participation in his body so that in our bodies, psyches, and lives death might also be undone. The Eucharist became one of the primary, concrete means by which we might participate in his body and receive what Ignatius of Antioch called the "medicine of immortality."[26] I think that this emphasis on the Eucharist as the most significant means by which we participate in the new life in Christ was one of the reasons that, historically, the Eucharist became the focus of the liturgical life of the Western church. So, through our participation in the Eucharist, death in our bodies and psyches is undone. The split-off parts of us that go underground only to pop up in destructive ways begin to be healed and integrated into our lives. We begin to become integrated. The lonely warriors can become less lonely and, therefore, more just, and the desperate lovers can become less compulsive and more compassionate. Our actions begin to correspond with our most deeply held convictions.[27]

For other traditions, like the believers' churches, the "medicine of immortality" has often been seen, not solely in the elements of the Eucharist, or Lord's Supper, but in the life of the gathered church—in the congregation of baptized believers. That is, the healing presence of Christ is experienced in the life of the believers as they are being reconciled and transformed by the Spirit of Christ poured out in his death. Through his life, ministry, death, and resurrection, Christ also reconciled us with one another. As the writer of Ephesians (2:14) says, "For [Christ] is our peace, who has made us both one, and has broken down the dividing wall of hostility." The Spirit of Christ is mediated by the community's ordinances and life together (e.g., the Supper, baptism, profession of faith, prayer meetings). That Spirit knits us into respectful and mutually enhancing relationships. They, in turn, evoke and nourish our deepest longings for connection and imbue us with a vision of life without the distortions of sin. Insofar as those ordinances and that life mediate that Spirit and, thereby, foster mutuality, they are sacramental.[28] In other words, we experience communities that begin to actualize the potential of our "inmost selves," or first natures, and give us the courage to face those things in us that we fear. They also empower us to oppose those things in us and in the world that obstruct the flourishing of our lives, the lives of others, and, ultimately, the life of God.

To summarize one view of Christ in this paradigm, he is seen to have established a new community in which a reordering of the world was begun. The reordering overturns nonmutual, hierarchical structures of oppression and establishes a more mutual ordering in which "the first shall be last and the last shall be first." An aspect of the once-for-allness of Christ's work is not that what Christ did remains external, limited in space and time to Palestine two thousand years ago, but that the incarnation initiated the ongoing existence and work of the salvific community, or body of Christ. One is saved by Christ, who has been embodied in the lives of Christians through the successive generations since the resurrection of Christ. Those Christians and those concrete communities that birthed them could be viewed as "a prolongation of the incarnation."[29]

Luther was right: these oppressive structures are a result of, or manifestation of, sin; they were not intended by God in creation. But they are capable of redemption. As Paul said, "The creation itself will be set free from its bondage to decay and obtain the freedom of the glory of the children of God" (Romans 8:21). In the view of the author of the Gospel of John (12:47), Jesus "did not come to judge the world [system], but to save the world [system]." The writer of Colossians (2:15) believed that Christ "disarmed the rulers and authorities and made a public example of them, triumphing over them in it [the cross]." This, I think is important. It is easy, when we get a glimpse of all that stands against us—the pervasiveness and depth of sexism, heterosexism, racism, and classism—to despair, to give up on the institutions and structures of our society and withdraw into safe enclaves. It seems impossible to change anything significantly; it all seems so intractable. And here Luther's caution stands us in good stead. The dynamics are pervasive and deep-rooted. If we ever had an idea that this was going to be easy or that continuous emptying service and social engineering (solutions that kenotic masculine Christian men are wont to adopt) are going to straighten all this out and soon, this realization chastens us.

But we cannot consign our collective lives to hell. When we do, we become what Paulo Freire calls "left-wing sectarians." We isolate ourselves, keep ourselves pure, and, thereby, do not contribute to any significant change at all. No, these structures were good in creation and shall be good again. God is calling us to participate in their redemption.

Our hope continues to be an eschatological hope; that is, what we hope for, we will probably never completely experience in our lifetimes. There is much, inside of us and outside of us, that stands in the way of a restoration of that interdependent web of life intended by God. And because of that interdependent character of all creation, none of us will be completely saved until all of us are saved. So, it is an eschatological hope that, rather than encouraging us to sit and wait for a cataclysm at the end of history or a purely personal transformation at our death, inspires us to "dream dreams and see visions" of that interdependent web of life that calls us to its cocreation. We are drawn by a deep desire for reconciliation to others, to God, and to neglected aspects of ourselves. That yearning within constitutes a calling, or vocation, to participate in the renewal, reconciliation, and transformation of ourselves and our world—internally and externally, personally and socially. As Augustine said, "You made us for yourself and our hearts find no peace until they rest in You."[30]

The "You" he was referring to was, of course, God. The question is, In what kind of God can we find our rest? The kind of God I described in chapter 3? Ultimately, I don't think so. As I have said, I think that conceptualization of an omnipotent, omniscient Being—what amounts to a hypermasculine Supersubject—may give us men some psychic peace by counteracting, or protecting us from, our often unacknowledged sense of the omnipotence of WOMAN. But that notion of an utterly transcendent, absolute, perpetually active God also legitimates the patterns of isolation and domination and the delusory attempts at invulnerability that produce in us much of our performance anxiety and "works righteousness." It is that anxiety and that neurotic striving that is killing us, others, and our earth. This notion of God contributes to that death; we can find no long-lasting rest in that understanding of God.

I believe one of the most debilitating effects of sexism in Western Christianity is the distortion it has caused in the ways we image and think about God. I think that our splitting off of those vulnerable aspects of ourselves as bad, debilitating, or counterproductive to our roles as protectors and providers contributed to the predominance of this image of God as omniscient, omnipotent, and disconnected from us. Those things we feared, including our own bodies, became identified with femininity. This, in turn, became identified with an immanent God, or Goddess—a God with or in us. That which we constructed to deal with our fear—invulnerability—became identified with masculinity; this, in turn, became identified with a transcendent God—a God completely separate from us. We, consequently, tend to emphasize those aspects of God when we find them in the Bible or in tradition.

We highlight male images of God and tend to suppress female images of God.[31]

A perennial issue in the history of theology is how to develop ways of talking about God that integrate both God's transcendence, or distinctiveness, and God's immanence, or withness. The reason for that is that salvation—whether one views that by means of a juridical or a medicinal model—makes no sense without both. If God is completely other and apart from humanity, what good does that do us? If God is completely identified with us, what hope do we have of emerging out of the destruction in which we find ourselves?[32] So, we must find ways of holding the otherness of God together with God's withness—God's transcendence with God's immanence. Without one, the other is distorted. Without God's transcendence, God's immanence becomes petty and idolatrous; our God becomes too small. Without immanence, God's transcendence becomes distant, cold, even cruel.

Because there has been such an overemphasis on the transcendence of God in Western Christianity, I think we are in a historical period where an emphasis on the immanence of God is needed to balance our views. Dietrich Bonhoeffer, a Lutheran pastor and member of the German resistance movement, saw such a need during his imprisonment for his participation in a plot on Hitler's life. Reflecting on the passivity of many German Christians in the face of the horrors of the Nazi regime, he imagined a "world come of age" in which Christians practiced a "religionless" or "this-worldly" Christianity. For ethical reasons, he saw the need for Christians to reject a deus ex machina, or a false notion of a God who steps in when our justice, strength, intelligence, and compassion give out and saves us, in the next or "other" world, from the consequences of our finitude, weakness, and confusion in this one. In contrast, these "religionless" Christians do not engage in escapism or denial; they participate in the "powerlessness of God in the world."[33] They are

> summoned to share in God's suffering at the hands of a godless world. [They] must therefore really live in a godless world, without attempting to gloss over or explain its ungodliness in some religious way or other. [They] must live a "secular" life, and thereby share in God's sufferings. [They] may live a "secular" life. . . . It is not the religious act that makes the Christian, but participation in the sufferings of God in the secular life. That is *metanoia* [conversion]: not in the first place thinking about one's own needs, problems, sins, and fears, but allowing oneself to be caught up into the way of Jesus Christ, into the messianic event.[34]

That is, these "religionless Christians" don't wait for an utterly transcendent God to do something extraordinary to save us from deadly things, like sexism, heterosexism, racism, classism, or the oppression of men; they act.

What Bonhoeffer means by becoming "godless," I think, is to give up that distorted notion of God that has been produced by exaggerating God's distinctiveness, transcendence, or activity and ignoring God's withness, immanence, or vulnerability. It is that notion of an utterly transcendent God that contributes to the distortion of our sense of justice and our own strength. God is just, so we don't have to be; we can remain naive. "He" is strong, so we don't have to be; we can remain passive. This is just one of the ways such a notion of God hurts men and, by extension, others and the earth. It also means, I think, that we must stop splitting off our finitude, mortality, sensuousness, bodiliness, and desire for pleasure and projecting them exclusively onto our mothers, other women, and the Goddess. We need to stop splitting off our need for self-direction, self-definition, and boundary setting and projecting them exclusively onto our fathers, other men, and the Father God. Changing such a notion of God is extremely painful; as I have said, that notion has been very comforting and reassuring.[35] We can, however, take comfort in the fact that God is behind and in the painful process. As H. R. Niebuhr said, God is the "slayer" of all other gods.[36] That is, God is in the process of slaying that distorted notion we have of God. I'll say more about this in chapter 5.

Bonhoeffer believed that in moving out of denial and into honesty—in becoming "more godless"—we draw "nearer to God." God is the "beyond in the midst of our life. . . . The church stands, not at the boundaries where human powers give out, but in the middle of the village."[37] We are called to act out of more mature expressions of our first natures and to participate with others in the cocreation of more just, intelligent, and connected relations. God's power draws us into that maturation and empowers it. As we think more clearly and act more decisively in order to relate more justly, we experience the power of the God whose transcendence is found in the midst of us.

This is the God revealed to us in Christ; this is the God to whom Christ reconciles us. This is a God who is beyond us and within us; a God who is powerful and vulnerable; a God whom we need and who needs us. We need to be reconciled with God—not the distorted image that legitimates oppression, but the real God. The writer of the Gospel of John believed that Jesus provided that reconciliation: "On that day you will know that I [Jesus] am in my Father, and you in me, and I in you" (14:20). In Christ, knowledge of

God is restored to us. We need, therefore, images of God that are less objectified and more mutual. We must stop objectifying God and believing the distorted stereotypes about God that are not true.[38]

Part of what it means, then, to be reconciled with God is to pay attention to images of God that express both God's transcendence and God's immanence. We have historically ascribed one set of human characteristics to men and then associated those with transcendence, and we have ascribed another set of characteristics to women and associated those with immanence. Consequently, since we have emphasized the transcendence of God, we have associated God with masculinity, or maleness. Few Christians, if asked, would say God is male, and many would say that God transcends gender, or sex. Nevertheless, when feminine images or language are used for God, many of us are disturbed. Part of the reason for that discomfort is, I think, because we have so overemphasized God's transcendence that female, or feminine, images suggest to us immanence and, thus, seem inappropriate. Further, because we have split human qualities into polarized masculine and feminine characteristics, and projected only one set onto God, we have a stunted sense of God's fullness. The answer to these difficulties is not to attempt to balance God's transcendence with God's immanence by using both masculine and feminine images. Rather, since men are both active and vulnerable and women are both active and vulnerable, we need to distinguish maleness from distorted notions of masculinity and femaleness from distorted notions of femininity.[39] Consequently, male images and female images can convey both transcendence and immanence, and we need to use both.[40]

One understanding of God, or the center of value, in the mutual paradigm is as the ground of our right, or just, mutual relation, whose nature is love.[41] The trinitarian affirmation of God is that God is a plural, dynamic reality, not a singular, static one.[42] Within God's self, there is giving and receiving, affecting and being affected—mutuality. And there is mutuality between God and human beings. God desires to be known by us. In the Gospel of John (17:3), the author writes, "And this is eternal life, that they know you the only true God, and Jesus Christ whom you have sent." We can know God as God speaks to us through Scripture and tradition, as well as through our own bodies, through the earth, through the lives of women, gay men and lesbians, African-Americans, Jewish people, persons of different classes, and all others.

Authority in this paradigm is not perceived to be the coercive power to keep people in their proper places in a divine hierarchy; rather, it is the openness of one person to be affected by another because one is drawn to that person and trusts him or her. We are most deeply moved toward transformation not by someone's insistence or threats, but by our attraction to aspects of someone's life that we find compelling. In other words, authority is not something exacted from us, but an openness we freely give, because we know that something about that person will enhance our lives, or, in the words of Catherine of Siena, "fatten our souls." We are most deeply formed by our attractions—by our erotic desire to know and be known. As Augustine said, if you want to know who someone is, look at what that person loves; we become like what we love.

In the objectified paradigm, because of the hierarchical valuing of the soul over the body, issues of authority usually focus on the realm of ideas. Which ideas are right; which ideas are wrong? Which ideas serve to uphold the hierarchy; which ideas serve to upset it? So, the term *truth* comes to have a decidedly intellectual connotation. In the mutual paradigm, truth is a more inclusive term. We are attracted to and allow ourselves to be affected by more than people's ideas. We find ourselves attracted to their bodies, to their expressions of their emotional lives, to the just ways in which they live their lives, to the powerful ways they act on what they believe, and to the ways they relate to others. My sense is that our first natures are profoundly attracted to expressions of others' first natures. In fact, I think we are often open to other people's ideas because we find something in these other areas we admire.

Augustine believed truth (*veritas*) was the integration and harmony of the soul and body made possible by our attraction to the supreme Good, or God. For him, it was unreasonable to pursue truth by reason alone and unpleasurable to pursue truth by pleasure alone. Our reason and our bodily pleasure are drawn toward integration and fulfillment by our love of God (*amor dei*).

SEXUALITY, SPIRITUALITY, AND THE LOVE OF GOD

Consequently, there are deep connections between those aspects of ourselves that we have traditionally labeled our souls and those we have referred to as our bodies. When we think of ourselves as body-selves, we see deep connections between our sexuality and our spirituality. Carl Jung once said that when people came to him with a spiritual problem, it often turned out to be a sexual one; and when they came to him with a sexual problem, it often turned out to be a spiritual one.[43]

Consistent with this more body-integrated notion of the self, James Nelson has developed some very helpful definitions of sex, sexuality, and spirituality.[44] Sex is a "biologically-based need which is oriented not only toward procreation but, indeed, toward pleasure and tension release." It is often genitally focused, with an aim toward orgasm. Sexuality is a broader term that includes sex but goes beyond it to refer to the ways we relate bodily to ourselves, God, and others. Since those ways are significantly shaped by the cultural definitions of gender, sexuality can be seen as "our way of being in the world as gendered persons, having male and female biological structures and socially internalized self-understandings of those meanings to us."[45] Sexuality includes our feelings and attitudes about our body-selves and our affectional orientations toward the other sex, the same sex, or both. In addition, sexuality is the "desire for intimacy and communion, both emotionally and physically" and is, therefore, "the physiological and psychological grounding of our capacity to love." In other words, for *homo amans* our sexuality calls us to our full humanity and is "intrinsic to our relationship with God."[46] Spirituality refers to "the ways and patterns by which the person—intellectually, emotionally, and physically—relates to that which is ultimately real and worthful for him or her."

The more violence there is in the world, the more we will fear being vulnerable to or being affected by another. In other words, the more fear there is, the less genuine love; and the less genuine love there is, the less we are fully human and the less God is God. What we need is to prepare the way to make love possible. To do that, we must work toward the material, psychological, emotional, and institutional grounds that make mutuality possible. Paulo Freire believes that resisting oppression in the world and in oneself helps "create a world in which it will be easier to love."[47] What kind of love casts out fear and draws us toward truth? Or, put another way, what kind of love draws us toward psychic and bodily integration and fulfillment?

James Nelson identifies four classic distinctions used when speaking of love:

> Epithymia (or *libido*) is the desire for sexual fulfillment. *Eros* is aspiration and desire for the beloved. *Philia* is mutuality and friendship. And *agape* is freely offered self-giving.[48]

He points out that there has often been a dichotomy, even an opposition, between divine love (*agape*) and human love (*libido, eros,* and *philia*), especially human sexual passion (*libido* and *eros*). Anders Nygren believes that divine love (*agape*) is completely self-giving and unmotivated by its object, while human love is possessive and egocentric.[49] It seems to me that his definitions and the juxtaposition of divine and human love emerge from an objectified paradigm. God affects without being affected, and the human desire to affect and be affected is seen as egocentric. Nelson offers an interpretation that integrates these various aspects of love from what I have called a mutual paradigm. I provide here a synthesis of his insights with some of the terms I have been using.

Libido might be understood as the passionate desire to know another—physically, emotionally, intellectually, and spiritually. *Eros* might be understood to be the desire to be known by another—the desire for communion.[50] *Philia,* or mutuality and friendship, provides the conditions for the fulfillment of both *libido* and *eros.*[51] As Nelson points out,

> a marriage without *libido* and romantic attraction is less than full, at best, and most likely has become a marriage of convenience. But sexual and romantic attraction without genuine friendship is also an invitation to disappointment and distortion.[52]

In other words, without mutuality—the willingness to know and be known—human libidinal and erotic desires are infected with dominative elements that thwart and destroy them. *Agape,* according to Nelson, is not another kind of love but a "transformative quality essential to true expression of any of love's modes." He says that without *agape,* or divine love, the other modes of love "are ultimately self-destructive." *Agape* releases sexual desire, erotic aspiration, and mutuality from "self-centeredness and possessiveness into a relationship that is humanly enriching and creative." It undergirds and transforms other modes of love. Ultimately, he says, "faith knows that agape is gift, and not of our own making."

Given what I have said about the mutual paradigm, the four aspects of love and their relation might be visualized this way:

Subject ——————▶ object (*libido*)
                                        } mutuality (*philia*) } universality (*agape*)
Object ◀—————— subject (*eros*)

The implication is that the kind of love that casts out fear is that which draws us out of the isolation produced by the various forms of external and internal oppression I have described. One of the transforming aspects of *agape* is its universalizing pull. That is, what is ultimately fulfilling for human beings is a mutuality that is not limited to one romantic, dyadic, heterosexual relationship, or even to an isolated, "righteous" community, but rather grows to include all of reality, or as H. R. Niebuhr said, "the whole realm of being." We realize that everything is "worthy of our loving curiosity."[53]

Earlier, I said that Paul believed that each part of Christ's body needed every other part. Catherine of Siena expanded this vision to an interdependence of all human beings. She believed that God wished that human beings should have need of one another and so did not place all the things necessary for human life in one soul. Rather, God placed the "gifts and graces" indifferently, so that "whether [one] will or no, [a human being] cannot help making an act of love."[54] I think it is important to add to Catherine's web of human interdependence our relationship to nonhuman beings. Our own lives depend on our loving others—human and nonhuman.

God is calling us away from those false identities and into wholeness and communion. In other words, God is calling those lonely warriors away from our identifications with those destructive external expectations and deeply into ourselves. And God is calling those desperate lovers out over the barricades of sexism, heterosexism, racism, and classism that alienate us from others, aspects of ourselves, and God. It is the perfect love of God that "casts out fear"—the fear that keeps those identities in place.[55]

THE HOLY LONGING

Tell a wise person, or else keep silent,
Because the massman will mock it right away.
I praise what is truly alive,
what longs to be burned to death.
In the calm water of the love-nights,
where you were begotten, where you have begotten,
a strange feeling comes over you
when you see the silent candle burning.
Now you are no longer caught
in the obsession with darkness,
and a desire for higher love-making
sweeps you upward.
Distance does not make you falter,
now, arriving in magic, flying,
and finally, insane for the light,
you are the butterfly and you are gone.
And so long as you haven't experienced
this: to die and so to grow,
you are only a troubled guest
on the dark earth.

GOETHE *(translated by Robert Bly)*

Chapter Five

Losing Ourselves to Find Ourselves: Faith

You shall love the Lord your God with all your heart, and with all your soul, and with all your strength, and with all your mind; and your neighbor as yourself. (Luke 10:27)

JESUS

Beware of a naked man who offers you his shirt.

AFRICAN PROVERB

When Christ calls a man, he bids him come and die.

DIETRICH BONHOEFFER, *The Cost of Discipleship*

GOD CALLS lonely warriors deep into ourselves—to that inmost self. When we respond to that call, significant parts of us must die; that is, we must give up the attachments we have to many of our public identities and the anxious striving by which we maintain them. To do so involves pain, or grief, but also brings an almost unimaginable richness into our lives.

Using the diagram of the lonely warrior, I want to explore the nature of that call and suggest some of the concrete implications it might have for our lives.

As I said in chapter 1, we are pulled out of ourselves by the often conflicting expectations of the various offices we hold. We come to have a fragmented, or decentered, self. In doing so, we can also develop habits whereby we objectify ourselves. That is, we can treat ourselves as objects; we see ourselves through the eyes of others and judge ourselves to be more or less adequate in fulfilling those expectations. In doing so, we become captive to the

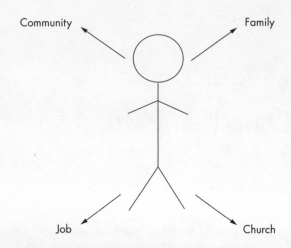

opinions of others. Those opinions are often conflicting; we can never perfectly fulfill all those expectations or please all those people. Consequently,
we inevitably feel shame or guilt or both. So, we end up feeling bad about
ourselves, or shutting down emotionally in order to avoid those negative feelings. Either way, many of us are captive to the opinions of our various
"publics."

The results of this captivity are twofold. First, it causes tremendous stress
in our lives. A great deal of the stress comes from our belief that we need to
defend an identity that is important to us.[1] We spend a lot of energy and time
worrying about how we are perceived; whether we, or others, perceive us as
having lived up to the masculine expectations of the roles we play. As I said
before, many of us focus on the past, evaluating whether we have measured
up, or on the future, worrying either about whether we are going to have time
to get everything done or about being found out as inadequate. In other
words, because of the time we spend judging ourselves or justifying ourselves, we spend very little time in the present.

Second, this self-justification oftentimes leaves us self-absorbed and unable to love ourselves, others, or God. Love requires that we are present, not
off fretting about the past or the future. If we are not present, we cannot love.
If we cannot be present to ourselves, we cannot love ourselves. If we cannot be
present to ourselves, we cannot be present to God or to others and, therefore,
we cannot love them—"Beware of a naked man who offers you his shirt."

A word needs to be said here about "selfishness" and "self-love." Self-love
has come to have very negative connotations in much of Christian teaching

and preaching. That is unfortunate, for us and for those around us. We can't love others unless we love ourselves; but we also cannot love others if we are self-absorbed. I think it is helpful to keep in mind the difference between the two selves—the "inmost self" (first nature) and the distorted self (second nature). Consequently, there are two very different selves to love with very different effects. Loving or being attached to the distortions of our second natures can be narcissistic and alienating; loving our "inmost self" deeply connects us to God and to others.

I take the first, narcissistic kind of "self-love" to be our attachment to the identities I have described—that is, an attachment to those habits of thought, feeling, and acting that are alienating to important parts of ourselves and others. Ralph was so absorbed by "making it" and maintaining his corporate identity as a "serious" lawyer that he distorted his own sense of justice (he "kowtowed to rich money") and lost everyone he loved, including himself— that is, he lost his self-respect and the ability to show compassion to himself. His unthinking attachment to those destructive aspects of his second nature, or the "flesh," alienated himself and others. Therefore, this way of loving oneself—the attachment to destructive aspects of one's second nature—is not properly called self-love at all.

The part of himself that he alienated was his "inmost self," his first nature, or the image of God in him. There was another part of himself that yearned for justice (as opposed to kowtowing to rich money), for strength (to resist the expectations that led him farther and farther from his inmost self), for wisdom (to know what to do about his life), and for connection (with aspects of himself, his wife, and his sons). It was this self that he had neglected, that he had let atrophy. And it was this self that needed his attention and compassion.

Ralph's problem was not that he loved himself too much, but that he did not love himself enough. That is, his attachment to that public identity as a "serious" lawyer was not true self-love at all, but a result of self-loathing. His obsession with it alienated him from his deepest self and distracted him from nurturing that self and allowing it to flourish. It is only in attending to those deepest desires, as they are called out of us by others, and ultimately by God, that we can authentically love ourselves, or love our increasingly authentic selves. An authentic self-love is both called out by others and leads us to others. In it, we become present to ourselves and, thereby, find enough attention to be present to others and to God. It is to that authentic self-love that God calls us.

In other words, in order to love God and our neighbor as our selves, we must lose our selves—those alienating aspects of our second natures. Only then, do we find our selves—that image of God intended in creation. And that takes faith. Dietrich Bonhoeffer said it this way:

> It is only by living completely in this world that one learns to have faith. One must completely abandon any attempt to make something of oneself, whether it be a saint, or a converted sinner, or a churchman (a so-called priestly type!), a righteous man or an unrighteous one, a sick man or a healthy one. By this-worldliness I mean living unreservedly in life's duties, problems, successes and failures, experiences and perplexities. In so doing we throw ourselves completely into the arms of God, taking seriously, not our own sufferings, but those of God in the world—watching with Christ in Gethsemane. That, I think, is faith; that is *metanoia;* and this is how one becomes a man and a Christian. (cf. Jeremiah 45!)[2]

In his view, God, in Christ, cuts across all our attempts at self-justification. We don't have to continually produce something to be okay, to be acceptable. We don't have to uphold any hierarchical, alienating order to be valuable; we don't have to continue to pour all our energies into external projects, monuments, or self-flagellation for our sexism, heterosexism, racism, anti-Semitism, or classism. We have been fearfully and wonderfully made, and Christ came to reconcile us to God, to ourselves, and to others.

To become a man and a Christian, we must abandon our anxious striving—our works righteousness. That is the only way we will be freed from our captivity to embrace the way of Jesus, who stood against those structures of consciousness that split our psyches and divide our human communities and who stood for the dignity, sovereignty, and integrity of every person. It is the only way we can be freed to join and participate in the "kingdom," or new order of things.

But there is the rub—abandoning our identities and our anxious attachments to them. Bonhoeffer calls it *metanoia,* or conversion, and says that it requires faith. He is right. In that conversion, something has to die. As Paul says, "the works of the flesh must be put to death." Habitual ways in which we think, feel, and act must die; we must leave them behind in order to live. Again, Paul says, "We are baptized into [Christ's] death" so that we, too, "can walk in newness of life" (Romans 6:3–4). Said another way, we must be born again—not of flesh and blood, but of the Spirit (John 3:1–7). As with the first birth, there is a great deal of grief—uncertainty, fear, and pain—involved in this death and rebirth; it is this grief with which we have to deal, if we are to heal and experience transformation.

GRIEF AND CONVERSION: "BLESSED ARE THOSE WHO MOURN"

As I have said, I believe that the capacity in men that gets systematically distorted is our deep desire and potential for compassionate connection—our lovers. Traditionally, this capacity has been imaged as the "heart"; Jesus said, "For where your treasure is, there will your heart be also" (Matthew 6:21). For many of us, our hearts have been set on things that have been too small— that have isolated us from the fullness of the connections for which we deeply yearn, that have distorted our sense of justice, that have clouded our thinking behind rationalizations, and that have made us weak when we need to be strong and aggressive when we need to be receptive. That is, we have too often set our hearts on things that "moth and rust consume" and that "thieves [can] break in and steal" (Matthew 6:20). Rita Nakashima Brock has said that many people live in a state of what she calls "brokenheartedness."[3] We adopt a "false self," or the negative aspects of a second nature, which consists of interlocking coping mechanisms by which we protect the wounds we have received to our desire for connection. One of our coping mechanisms is emotional numbness. As Robert Bly has said, when a man is asked how he feels, he often looks down into his chest cavity—the seat of the heart—and shrugs his shoulders; often he simply doesn't see, or feel, anything. For transformation to take place, we need to follow our hearts, but to do that we need to start feeling again. This is very difficult and very scary; there are lots of things we have good reasons not to want to feel. But feel them we must.

Michael Meade says that "we enter the territory of the heart by going into our wounds and reliving them."[4] In order to feel again, we must begin with feeling the pain of our wounds. Three sources of those wounds that he identifies are (1) the hurts suffered in childhood, (2) the blows received in initiatory circumstances, and (3) the losses in life that become the cloaks of the elders.

To illustrate Meade's point about the potential our wounds hold for our healing, I will return to the story of Ralph. As I said in chapter 3, Ralph's inherent capacities suffered distortion under the pressures directed at him and the decisions he made: instead of acting on his sense of justice, he "kowtowed to rich money"; instead of saying no to the pressures of work and his peers, he said no to spending time with his wife and sons; in spite of being "paid more than any two of you" and being "one of the top decision-makers in the country," he, when it came to his own life, did not even know where to begin; and, finally, he lost everyone he had ever cared about, including himself. His attendance at the men's group for six months had led him from the concrete level of reality to the psychological. He began to look at his life and his patterns of thinking, feeling, and acting as just that—patterns. He began to see that they were patterns, or habits, that had historical roots and causes and had led to certain effects; they were not necessarily the way he had to be. He could be different. In other words, he was able to distinguish aspects of his second nature from his first nature. In fact, his first nature was freed in an atmosphere of safety and trust to evaluate those habits and make judgments about them. He could see his disconnection from people he loved and from aspects of himself; he could see how it was that his sense of justice had gotten skewed; he could see how he had failed to protect some of the things he cherished the most; and he could see that in certain respects he couldn't see at all. He could see some of the reasons why he did some of the things he was ashamed of. His intelligence was released to analyze the larger dynamics that shaped his life. Instead of turning his anger inward at himself—which usually leads to enervated depression—he had the opportunity to use his power to express anger at those structures and resist them. He could see his relational isolation and begin to take steps to contradict it.

In fact, his different kind of connection to men seems to have alleviated some of the shame he probably experienced around expressing emotions. In the relative safety of a group of empathic men, Ralph saw and felt things that he had never had the permission or the support to see and feel before, and it was painful. In his story, Ralph mentions wounds he received from the three sources Meade identifies. During his childhood, he was called by his father, "Ralph, who pitched the no-hitter." This, no doubt, was a mixed blessing. His father expressed his admiration for Ralph, but the admiration was tied to something he had done, not for what kind of boy/man he was becoming. Upon entering the period of initiation into manhood, he was told by his uncle (read: ritual elder) that he should give up something he loved in order to be successful. The institutions presiding over his initiation into his profession and, unfortunately, into manhood rewarded him for using his intelligence in manipulative ways, for compliantly and uncritically internalizing their institutional values, and for ignoring larger social-justice concerns. Finally, in adulthood, he suffered the loss of all those whom he loved, including his own first nature. In entering his wounds, he entered his own "broken-heartedness" and a floodgate opened; he cried for the first time in twenty years. The reservoir of suppressed emotion was enormous; one wonders what it had done during those years to sabotage his psychological and physical health.[5]

This confrontation with his grief was a teachable moment for Ralph. Here was a door to his feeling life, to his heart and its distortions. According to Malidoma Some, "pain is the result of a resistance to something new— something toward which an old dispensation is at odds."[6] This was a moment when something new was struggling to be born in Ralph. For something new to be born, however, there must be room for it in the psyche and body. Therefore, the new birth demanded a letting go of old ways of being—of thinking, feeling, and acting.

This letting go and opening to a new way is what Bonhoeffer refers to as *metanoia,* or conversion. This is a helpful way of thinking about what many of us are undergoing.

The Catholic theologian Bernard Lonergan distinguished among three kinds of conversion—moral, intellectual, and religious.[7] It seems to me that these distinctions are helpful in understanding some of the things that happen in men's lives as we are drawn and reach toward wholeness.

Conversion means, literally, to turn about. A conversion is a turning about or a turning around. It involves *metanoia,* a change of mind, and repentance, a change in behavior. Yearning for connection with others leads us to a moral conversion. As we experience and learn to embrace our own finitude and begin to trust God and others in God, we begin to recognize the finitude and vulnerability of others, not as a threat to our own survival and flourishing, but as an invitation and responsibility to become a part of their lives as we invite them to be a part of ours. With a commitment to being close to others, we begin to see and feel what has hurt and is hurting them. We begin to see them not as competitors, but as cherished partners in the cocreation of our common life. We also see the vulnerability and fragility of the earth and earth creatures, not as an opportunity for exploitation in our frightened and wrongheaded attempts to secure ourselves, but as teachers and friends whose flourishing is linked inextricably to our own. We consequently begin to act differently as we step over those barriers that obstruct our connections with others and begin to resist, individually and collectively, those institutional realities and structures of consciousness—internal and external—that harm and distort others and ourselves.

Moral conversions often entail intellectual conversions. We begin to see and understand things differently. I am not convinced that these intellectual revolutions are precipitated by left-brain (Mode 1) argumentation, although they may include them. I recall a poster on the wall of Dr. George Schweitzer, a chemistry professor and my college Sunday school teacher: "Because you have silenced a man does not mean you have converted him." Conversions are not about coercive arguments in which syllogisms are manipulated; they are not evoked by the gesticulations of an immature magician. Rather, they involve a mature lover.

When speaking of an intellectual paradigm shift, Hans Küng observes that "a new model of understanding demands something like a conversion, which cannot be extorted in a purely rational way."[8] Since those articulating the old and new models live in "different worlds" of ideas and language, they often can scarcely understand each other. There is some translation from the old to the new, but persuasion is ultimately a matter of trust; that is, which model copes better with the new problems and at the same time preserves most of the solutions to old problems; which model has a future?

A venerable tradition within Christianity, including figures such as Saint Clement of Alexandria, Saint Augustine of Hippo, and Saint Anselm of Canterbury, asserts that we do not believe because we understand, but that we understand because we believe. Belief in this sense is a "grasp of first principles," which is an act primarily of the will, not the intellect. In the terms I have been using, the lover more than anything determines what first principles, or assumptions, we are going to work from to build our understanding and knowledge. In other words, we are not saved by reason, but reason must be saved.[9]

So, in some ways, our intellectual allegiance to either the objectified paradigm or the mutual paradigm comes down to which of them feeds our souls and particularly our lovers, or our capacity for compassionate connection. Assent to the assumptions of the mutual paradigm involves significant rethinking and changes in the ways we think. For example, we will begin to reevaluate the stereotypes, misinformation, and lack of information we have about other people—people unlike us and like us. We will seek more accurate information about others and ourselves. We will begin to look at things more consciously from various angles of vision, employing our left brains in incisive, critical ways; attending to the unitive, intuitive movement of our intelligence (right brain); listening to the voices of communities of people, like and unlike us, that have gone before us; and analyzing how power relations affect what we and others think and say.[10] When we do this, it will be painful. It is hard to give up habits of thought that, in some ways, have served well our need for protection. It is difficult to reeducate ourselves.

To the degree that our yearning for compassionate connection determines those first principles on which our thinking and understanding rest and leads us to consider the quality of our connections to others, our intellectual and moral conversions are results of religious conversions. The term *religion* comes from the Latin *re,* meaning again, and *ligio,* meaning to tie, as a ligament ties bone to bone. So, religion means to be tied again, or to be tied back; to be bound to something.

What drives the processes of spiritual growth and moral and intellectual conversion is an inherent religious impulse within us—that passionate, restless desire for connection. It is this restless desire that impels us and causes the shifts I have described in the way we understand ourselves, our relationships to others, and our understanding of God. One might say that what is happening is that our notion of God is getting bigger. As it enlarges, so too, in the words of H. R. Niebuhr, does our field of value, and with it, our souls; our first natures will stand for nothing less. Niebuhr says, consequently, that God will stand for nothing less. If reality is such that our souls are restless with gods that are too small and God attracts us inexorably to God's self, then God is the "slayer of all other gods." The nature of reality itself and our own natures demand that we are involved in a series of painful conversions from self- and other-destructive patterns of feeling and acting, from less adequate to more adequate notions of ourselves, others, and God, and from isolationist modes of being and acting.

Having our gods slain is, indeed, a painful process. As our centers of value, our gods organize our lives and our energies. Because the old must give way to the new, there is grief involved in the process of spiritual growth. We must give up aspects of ourselves that, no matter how distorting of our first natures and our relationships, are nevertheless familiar and comfortable.

Meister Eckhart observed that, when one is experiencing what he called the "eternal birth," one cannot always trust one's thoughts and feelings.[11] The reason is that our thoughts and feelings have been conditioned in a fallen world and often make deathly ways of being seem reasonable and normal and feel comfortable and right. As we have seen, our patterns of thinking can rationalize our own and others' mistreatment. Our patterns of feeling can make the right things feel wrong and the wrong things feel right.

For example, if we are in the presence of a man who is mistreating a woman by making a comment that is disrespectful and serves to marginalize her, we might consider interrupting this manifestation of sexism. When we do, we might experience in ourselves fear of ridicule and of our own marginalization. That might be followed by shame at feeling fearful, which in turn might elicit some anger on our part for being thrust into such a situation that generates feelings we would rather not feel and may be afraid of showing. Consequently, there are a lot of feelings that come up; they are all real. They do not all lead us to "truth," as Eckhart would say. Which ones do we pay attention to; on which of these feelings do we act? The shame that shuts us down physically, emotionally, and relationally is real; however, we cannot allow it to continue to control our lives. There are times when we must act even when that acting contradicts conventional wisdom—our own and that of our communities—and, therefore, does not feel right and comfortable.

In acting in these ways, we will sometimes feel that we are losing our minds, coming out of our skins, and losing our very lives. And we are in a sense. We are losing a lot of what we thought we were; that is, we are losing patterns of thinking, feeling, and acting that we mistook for ourselves. We are, in the words of Paul, "dying to ourselves." And there is much authentic grief we need to go through—not around, over, or under, but through.

I have found Elizabeth Kübler-Ross's description of the stages of grief helpful in sorting through what happens to us if we walk through the door of grief into our feeling lives.[12] I give a brief summary of those stages in the hope that it may be helpful as a map for those who journey on this road.

Kübler-Ross is describing a process people go through as they come to terms with the knowledge that they are terminally ill, that is, that they are going to die. She identifies five stages—denial, anger, bargaining, depression, and acceptance—in this process. I think that as we confront or are confronted with the destructiveness of aspects of our second natures as men, we go through a similar kind of process. In our case, we have to come to terms, not with impending physical death, but with an impending *spiritual* death. We realize that there is something in us that is killing us (spiritually and physically) and that, in order to live, it must die. The problem is that, because we have so identified ourselves with these negative aspects of our second natures, when they die, we feel like we die. We are losing our very selves, or that is the way it feels. In fact, what is dying is a configuration of our second natures, but since we don't have a very clear sense of our own first natures that lie under our second natures and we have lived with these patterns of thinking, feeling, and acting for so long, it seems like we are going to lose everything we know about ourselves and think we are.

So, I will describe the five stages Kübler-Ross identifies and apply them to some of what happens to men as we confront and let go of self- and other-destructive aspects of our second natures.

The first stage is one of denial and isolation. A terminally ill patient denies that this can be happening, or she or he simply stays away from those bearing the news. We men respond similarly when confronted with the fact that some of our modes of thinking, feeling, and acting are hurtful to others and to ourselves. The male responses to critiques of sexism that I outlined in chapter 3 are examples of this stage. Men who are in defensive denial protest, "There is nothing wrong with the way things work, and there is nothing wrong with me!" Men who respond with guilty silence move away from the sources of the criticism or from other men in order to avoid dealing with what is being exposed in themselves. Both are in denial. Robert Bly has said that we live in a culture of denial.[13] There is a lot of truth to that. Many of us don't want to look too closely at the enmity between women and men, the disrespectful ways in which gay, lesbian, and bisexual persons are treated, the continued antagonisms between races and classes in our society, and what we are doing to our environment. This is very painful stuff and tells us more about ourselves than we are immediately able to take in. According to Kübler-Ross, that is a normal reaction. We develop defense mechanisms to protect us from things that we are not yet ready to handle. Ralph joined the men's group because his wife forced him to. While he was there, he said he might as well see what these "fags" were up to; there was certainly nothing wrong with him. He remained silent until the deadline imposed by his wife was up.

As we are able to look at whatever it is that signals to us our "dis-ease" or are no longer able to maintain our denial of it, we become angry. Kübler-Ross says that terminal patients experience anger, rage, envy, and resentment from a variety of sources and direct it at almost anything and anyone around them. In this stage, we men might say with Ralph, "Why me? I have done everything I was supposed to do, better than anyone I know, and now you tell me I am killing myself and other people? This is not fair. I did it right!" Our rage also comes from a number of other sources. We might be angry at God for requiring, as far as we can tell, those things that have been so destructive to others and to ourselves; those members of oppressed groups who confront us with our destructive attitudes or behaviors; other men who have bullied us into this kind of behavior; those systems and institutions that required these patterns for success; ourselves for buying into and assenting to the things that are killing us; women for sometimes asking us to do the very things they end up complaining about. Or we may be angry just because we see what we didn't see before and we cannot go back and pretend we don't. We have a lot to be angry about; some of it is productive anger, and some of it is not. We will have to learn how to sort it out; we will need communities of women and men who empower our sense of justice and our intelligence, in order to decide what to do with our anger and the power it generates. We will begin to see that expressing it in unjust, sadistic modes (wife battering, child abuse, violence against other men) or masochistic modes (overwork, substance abuse, compulsive risk-taking) must stop.

Our anger can begin the emotional thaw necessary for our healing. Beverly Harrison argues that anger is a powerful emotion, arising from our bodies, that signals that something is wrong in our relational lives.[14] It, therefore, can energize us to think more clearly about what is wrong and why and to act to correct whatever is unjustly obstructing our connections with others or with aspects of ourselves. In other words, anger is a manifestation of our kings that mobilizes our magicians and warriors to protect our and others' lovers. We must begin to direct that energy at the structures of consciousness and internalized attitudes, feelings, and behaviors that distort others, ourselves, and our perception of God.

In the third stage, people with terminal illnesses often try to bargain with God to postpone the inevitable; if God did not respond to my anger, maybe asking nicely will help. With men coming to terms with the death of negative aspects of our second natures, this may take the form of promising to give up some of our old habits, while trying to hold onto others: "I promise to spend more time with my wife and children, but I can't really change much at work just yet"; "Yes, women have a right to be ordained, but changing the language and forms of the liturgy to be more inclusive of them is just too much; people are not ready for that"; "Yes, my body is the temple of the Holy Spirit, but this particular habit—obsessive, toxic, or alienating as it is—is compensation for the many sacrifices I have to make"; "Yes, black people have a right to be treated fairly, but I don't have time to learn anything about what life is like for them, much less participate in doing something about what hurts them"; or "I will stop telling disrespectful jokes about gays and lesbians, but helping to stop discrimination against them or getting close to another man, gay or heterosexual, is pretty scary." The reason we do this is because we don't yet believe that our lives will go on without at least part of the negative aspects of our second natures. In other words, we want to be delivered from some of the effects of our destructive habits, but not from all of the habits themselves. In his *Confessions,* Augustine tells of a dream he had as he was on the verge of the transformation of his compulsive, objectified sexual behavior. Earlier, Augustine had said that he had prayed, "Give me chastity, but not yet!"—quintessential bargaining. Later, he says that his old habits came to him, tugged on his sleeve, and said, "You will no longer have us around; do you think you can live without us?"[15] Well, no, he didn't think he could, and neither do many of us.

There comes a time when we realize that no amount of denial, anger, or bargaining can stave off the death of what must die. Often it is because it is more painful to remain in the habits than to get rid of them; we realize that we must be released not just from their consequences, but from the habits themselves. We finally want to be free not just from the consequences of sin, but from sin itself. The letting go brings us a tremendous sense of loss, or depression.

Kübler-Ross identifies two kinds of losses people with terminal illnesses grieve in the fourth stage—past losses, leading to reactive depression, and impending losses, leading to preparatory depression. Past losses might include lost jobs, opportunities, abilities, freedoms, or pleasures. Impending losses include the loss of all our objects of love as we anticipate death; everyone and everything we love we will lose. For men, there are similar losses to grieve when we realize that significant portions of who we have thought we are must die. We might grieve the loss of familiar feelings and activities, destructive as they might have been; the loss of closer relationships with friends and family we forfeited as we strove for our professional goals; the loss of health, rest, and pleasure resulting from our fear and works righteousness; the hurts we have caused other people because of our thoughtless participation in oppressive structures and dynamics; the pain we have caused God by our objectification of ourselves, our neighbors, and God. As we look back from this new vantage point, we have much to grieve and we need to find safe places to do so.

We also grieve impending losses. If this part of me dies, I might lose the love of the people closest to me—perhaps it is that part of me that they love and need; I might lose the respect of my peers, my colleagues, my mentors, my supervisors; I might lose my place in the ordering of things that has made sense to me all my life.

These are real concerns and real losses. This depression, I think, is different from the kind of depression that is the polarized unhealthy expressions of our lovers. That depression is caused by being cut off from healthy attachments to others and to aspects of oneself. This depression is caused by being cut off from unhealthy attachments. Eckhart called this kind of detachment *Abgeschiedenheit*—a state of being cut off. We are cut off from unhealthy habits of thinking, feeling, and acting; we are cut off from significant parts of our selves as they have been constituted. A significant part of our social self is dying, and it is, and should be, the cause of much pain and grief. But it is not a pain "which afflicts or dries up the soul, but one which rather fattens her," as Saint Catherine of Siena would say.[16] It is a "dark night of the soul" in which something new is incubating in preparation for birth.[17] Augustine called it a "stern mercy" or an "insanity that makes us sane."[18] It cleans out the old in preparation for the new.

There comes a time when many terminally ill patients accept their impending death with a quiet expectation. During this time, Kübler-Ross says, they often need a gradually increasing amount of sleep; it is like the needs of a newborn baby, but in reverse order. It is not the sleep of avoidance, but "the final rest before the long journey."[19] One might say that the baby rests from the long trip it has taken to get here, and the terminally ill patient rests for the long trip he or she is about to take.

When a man finally accepts that something significant in him must die, he needs rest to prepare for the long journey to new life. Said another way, we need the kind of rest a mother needs as she prepares to give birth to a new person. We must be still and let something happen in us—something that we cannot control or force. This is difficult for many of us, because we have been conditioned to believe that anything of value for us is something we actively do, not something we receive or allow to happen in us. Because we feel deeply in our bodies that most of what has happened to us has been violent and diminishing, it is very scary to open ourselves to a process that is beyond our control. But we must.

Just as with physical birth, this "eternal birth" requires labor, but it is a labor that is directed at ceasing those aspects of our lives that would obstruct what is necessary for the emergence of a new life within us. What labor we do is in conjunction with the process, not obstructive to it. Eckhart says, "[I]f you are to experience this noble birth, you must depart from all the crowds and go back to the starting point, the core [of the soul] out of which you came." We must leave all the activities of the soul—memory, understanding, and will; we must "leave them all: sense perception, imagination, and all that [we] discover in the self or intend to do."[20] That is, we must cease our striving, or works righteousness—that which we have come to believe is our only defense against the violence we have experienced in our lives.

This requires a great deal of warrior energy. Eckhart says that the eternal birth is "impossible without a complete withdrawal of the senses from the [world of] things and great force is required to repress all the agents of the soul and cause them to cease functioning. It takes much strength to gather them all in, and without that strength it cannot be done."[21] As men, our capacities for strong, decisive action are usually directed toward the "world of things" in accomplishing what we intend. To make space for a new birth, we need to act decisively to take a moratorium on the demands and activities that often enervate us and dissipate our energies. In order to allow the birth of a deeply connected self, we may need to, for a time, renegotiate the obligations, responsibilities, commitments, and demands that can decenter and fragment us. Eckhart says that when we enter upon a "true spiritual experience" we are released from the many things to which we have vowed ourselves.

I see now that the painful experiences of leaving the pastoral office and of my divorce served to provide for me the psychic and physical space I needed to undergo this process of grief and rebirth. From the outside, I am sure that it seemed to others that these events marked the death of something good and the birth of something bad. It sometimes seemed that way to me. But I no longer believe that. Rather, I see it as a time when, in Eckhart's words, God kept "on withdrawing, farther and farther away, to arouse the mind's zeal and lure it on to follow and finally grasp the true good that has no cause."[22] That is, my God, or center of value, grew to include realities beyond the church and beyond the family. I sense, as I reconsider the role of a family and the church in my life, that those now have the possibility of being more life-giving to me and me to them. Before, when they were in some ways idols for me, there was less possibility for that.

This is not to say that every man must take a moratorium on family life or church life.[23] That is not the point. Each man has his own road, and each must discern his path and take it. The point is that we may need to take a hard look at the ways we spend our time and energies and be prepared to act decisively when we see that some action is required to free the psychic time and space we need for transformation.

Also, this withdrawal, or renegotiation, is often temporary and does not represent an abdication of responsibility to others. Eckhart says that, when a spiritual experience is over, one should "fulfill the vows appropriate to each passing moment as it comes."[24] This is not an abdication of our sense of justice and decisive action for others; rather, it is a necessary preparation precisely for decisive, just action on behalf of others and oneself. In these kinds of transformative experiences, the healing of our sense of justice makes possible decisive, enduring action for others. Eckhart affirms that "what we plant in the soil of contemplation we shall reap in the harvest of action and thus the purpose of contemplation is achieved."[25] In other words, this kind of healing transformation moves us beyond the postures of defensive denial and guilty silence I described in chapter 3. There is not a polarized dichotomy between personal healing and social transformation or, in theological terms, between evangelism and social ministry. Rather, the withdrawal marks a movement needed for a centered self, which is in turn empowered to relate to others in more just, empowering ways. It is a part of a rhythm in life that affirms that we must be both a centered self and a relational self; we can't have one without the other. Otherwise, we can have an isolated self or a fused self, but neither of those fulfills our humanness.[26]

CLEARING THE WAY WITH MEDITATION AND CENTERING PRAYER

So, we reap in action what we plant in the soil of contemplation. Meditation is one of the most helpful tools we can use to begin to clear the ground for the death of the old and the birth of the new.

As I have said, one of the greatest sources of stress is the belief that we must defend an identity. Because of our attachments to the identities we have developed, we tend to see ourselves through the eyes of those for whom those identities are important. In our jobs, we might think about how others perceive we are doing there—not so much how we are doing, but how others perceive us. If we are a pastor or church officer, we might attend to the image we are projecting as we fulfill those roles. If we are husbands, we might be concerned about how well our wives, or even others outside our families, think we are doing the job. As Bonhoeffer put it, many of us are attempting "to make something of ourselves"—whether it be a successful this or that or a saint or a sinner. Seeing ourselves from others' perspectives can become a reflexive habit; we don't have to think about doing it, we just do it. In fact, we do it so "naturally" that we often are unaware that we are doing it. It is a kind of self-objectification; we make ourselves the objects of our own self-evaluation, based on the expectations of our various "publics." We measure ourselves by the yardsticks of others and compare ourselves to other men: how do they think I am doing; how am I doing relative to him; am I going to be okay?

This self-objectification has disastrous effects on us and on others. By handing our self-esteem over to the keeping of others, we lose our peace and joy. Because the expectations are often in conflict and we can hardly ever fulfill all of them or any of them completely, we usually find ourselves in a deficit situation—there is always more to do. To feel good about ourselves, then, we must keep working. We cannot rest and be; we must get up and do. The shame, guilt, and fear we experience when we don't think we measure up result in performance anxiety and overwork. As Thomas Merton says:

As long as you have to defend the imaginary self that you think is important, you lose your peace of heart. As soon as you compare that shadow with the shadows of other people, you lose all joy, because you have begun to trade in unrealities, and there is no joy in things that do not exist.[27]

This self-objectification also has dire effects on our relationships to others. Again, Merton observes:

As soon as you begin to take yourself seriously and imagine that your virtues are important because they are yours, you become the prisoner of your own vanity and even your best works will blind and deceive you. Then, in order to defend yourself, you will begin to see sins and faults everywhere in the actions of other men. . . . Sometimes virtuous men are also bitter and unhappy, because they have unconsciously come to believe that all their happiness depends on their being more virtuous than others.[28]

Judging ourselves—even when we judge ourselves to be right or good—has the effect of increasing our inclination to treat others disrespectfully and thus increases our alienation from them. The alienation fuels our anxiety, which serves to kick us into another round of image management and the defense of our reputation. It is a vicious and downward cycle.

What we need to do is detach ourselves and our self-esteem from these roles and from those expectations. We need to lose our reputation. This is what Merton calls humility—a detachment from our own works and reputations. Only in that detachment do we find joy—the joy of being. In the freedom from captivity to our reputations, we find delight in simply being—being with ourselves, with others, and in and with God. It is to this joy of being that God calls us.

One of the spiritual disciplines that helps us respond to that call is meditation. Among other things, meditation is a practice by which we can learn to break the habit of self-objectification. The various practices of meditation often aim at focusing our attention on something other than the identities we carry and their attendant burdens.

One practice that is helpful is a focus on the breath—its intake and outgo. As we do that, we will become aware fairly quickly that our minds have wandered to some thought, some feeling, or some bodily sensation we are having. When that happens, we can just notice it, name it as a thought, a feeling, a sensation, or whatever it is, and gently bring our attention back to the breath. This is what Jack Kornfield calls "training the puppy."[29] When you put a puppy down and tell it to stay, it often runs off. When you pick it up, bring it back, and put it down again, it runs off again. Our minds are like that. In meditation, when they run off, as they invariably do—into the past or the future—we just pick them up and carry them back to the breath. We do this without negative self-judgment, or without judgment at all; it is just what happens, and when we realize it, we return our attention to the present—to the here and now.

In this process, there are several things that one might notice. First, it becomes clear that many of our thoughts, feelings, and sensations have a kind of life of their own. If we just notice that, without trying to stop them or keep them going, we find that they come and go. They are not permanent; that is comforting—especially when we are dealing with fear, anxiety, or other unpleasant emotions. "Well, there it is again, and there it goes again." In other words, we begin to realize that we are not any particular thought, feeling, or sensation.

We might also notice what led to the thought, feeling, or sensation. Behind it, we often find a set of eyes through which we are accustomed to looking at ourselves. Originally, they might have been the eyes of someone important to us—a parent, a sibling, a boss, a mentor, a bully. They might be the eyes of those in our families, churches, communities, or jobs. We see that we have internalized those eyes and look at ourselves through them. We can notice what feelings—pleasant or unpleasant—come as a result of our looking at ourselves that way. When we realize we are doing that, we pick up the puppy and bring it back to the center; that is, we bring our attention back to the breath. In doing this, we see that those feelings come and go and that we are not the roles or expectations that produce them. We can begin to recognize the image or images we project of ourselves in those contexts, why we might feel the need to project them, and how much energy, time, and attention it takes to maintain them.

We might also begin to see how much it costs us—physically and spiritually—to maintain our image, or reputation, and learn to let it go. The refocusing on the breath is a gentle letting go of that which we often hold on to so tightly. It is to refocus on our being and intrinsic value and away from our doing and striving. Meditation, then, is an expression of compassion for ourselves, that is, for our "inmost" selves. By doing it, we commit ourselves to stop objectifying ourselves—to stop judging ourselves against standards, no matter whose they are. I think this is at least one way of understanding Paul's affirmation that "Christ is the end of the law" (Romans 10:4). In other words, Christ puts an end to all measures by which we judge ourselves and others. It is precisely that process of judging that renders us narcissistically unavailable for the joyful cocreation to which Christ calls us.

In meditation we can also become aware of an awareness of our awareness. That is, we have the sense that someone else is giving us attention even as we give our inmost selves attention. It is one way we experience God. It is similar to the experience Saint Augustine describes in his *Confessions*. As he thought about the fact that he preferred the changeable to the unchangeable, he wondered how it was that he came to conceive of something unchangeable unless he somehow knew the unchangeable itself. Then, in "an instant of awe, my mind attained to the sight of the God who IS."[30] He had this sense that his mind functioned in the horizon of a greater reality, which suffused his consciousness. That is part of what happens in meditation. One has the sense of Another who delights in us and in our delight in ourselves, in others, and in God. That is, God delights in us apart from any role we might play, anything we might do, or any identity we might try to defend. And we delight in God and in God's delight in us and in others.

Basil Pennington has outlined a process called "centering prayer" that he believes is historically continuous with the great spiritual traditions of the Eastern and Western Christian churches, as well as with the spiritual traditions of other religious traditions.[31] Essentially, this method couples the name Jesus with the breathing or heartbeat, while adopting certain postures in order to "bring the mind down into the heart." It is composed of four moments, or stages—*lectio, meditatio, oratio,* and *contemplatio.* In the *lectio,* one receives revelation in whatever ways it might come—sacred Scripture, liturgy, the ministry of others, art, or in the creation. With *meditatio,* notional assent changes into real assent. For example, one might through reading, listening, or seeing come to know of God's delight in oneself or in the reconciling work of Christ and Christ's body. In meditation, one goes beyond intellectual understanding to a more profound awareness: "This is true of me, really true; I can count on it and live accordingly." The *oratio* is the heartfelt response of gratitude and love—for oneself, for others, and for God. In *contemplatio,* one comes to assent with one's whole being and is, thus, freed from one's attachment to roles. One becomes present to oneself, others, and God and capable of decisive service in the world.[32]

CONCLUSION

Remember the diagram of the "lonely warrior":

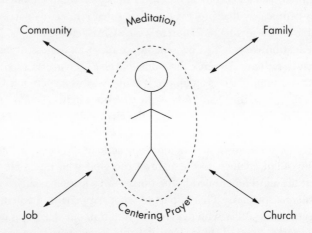

Faith makes possible a movement back toward a centered self. In conversion, the false self dies. Through spiritual disciplines like meditation and centering prayer, we become a midwife to the new self, or new creation, that God is birthing within us. That is, faith and centering prayer reverse the pulls (see the arrows pointing back toward the self) that fragment and enervate us and leave us unavailable to ourselves, others, and God. In other words, God is calling us deeply into our "inmost selves," in order that we might be present to ourselves, others, and God in more just, powerful, wise, and compassionate ways.

By being drawn deeply into our inmost selves, we begin to be healed of our "brokenheartedness" and freed for the ministry of reconciliation to which Christ calls us. The response of faith includes a willingness to walk out of old habits of seeing and acting in the world and into new ones. Most often, we walk not by sight but by a "conviction of things not seen" (Hebrews 11:1). That is, we cannot see exactly where we are going or what it or we will look like when we get there. We realize that some to whom we are connected will choose not to come with us; they may have too much investment in the identities from which we are being called, or they may have their own journey. But we keep walking.

SOMETIMES A MAN STANDS UP DURING SUPPER

Sometimes a man stands up during supper
and walks outdoors, and keeps on walking,
because of a church that stands somewhere in the East.

And his children say blessings on him as if he were dead.

And another man, who remains inside his own house,
dies there, inside the dishes and in the glasses,
so that his children have to go far out into the world
toward that same church, which he forgot.

RAINER MARIA RILKE *(translated by Robert Bly)*

PART THREE

Our Longing for Connection and a Ministry of Reconciliation

Chapter Six

Love Casts Out Fear

All this is from God, who has reconciled us to [God self] and has given us the ministry of reconciliation. (2 Corinthians 5:17)

SAINT PAUL

There is no fear in love, but perfect love casts out fear.

1 JOHN 4:18

When a flame is young, it must be carefully guarded and fed with things which will help it to grow. But when the flame has reached a certain height, and attained a certain vigor, then . . . everything which comes its way is its food—everything helps it to grow. The soul is like that.

JOSEPH CAMPBELL

IN DEALING with our false selves, we need what have been called the theological virtues of faith, hope, and love.[1] These are virtues shaped and empowered by grace. As I have said, faith empowers us to move deeply toward our "inmost self." But that movement out of alienated roles brings with it fear and anxiety, because it is through those roles that we have felt connected to others. The fear is that, by moving out of them, we will live in isolation and endure unbearable loneliness.

In order to continue on this path of faith, we need hope. And there is a promise:

And everyone who has left houses or brothers or sisters or father or mother or children or fields, for my name's sake, will receive a hundred-fold and will inherit eternal life.

(MATTHEW 19:29)

For Jesus, losing one's "life"—what Paul referred to as the life of the "flesh"—meant gaining it and gaining a hundredfold more than one gives up. It is like that for us. As we give up those patterns of thinking, feeling, and behaving (i.e., sexist, heterosexist, racist, classist, and anti-Semitic patterns of thinking) that isolate us and cut us off from others and aspects of ourselves, we find new worlds of deeply intimate, empowering relationships opening up to us.

We need that kind of hope in order to keep walking. Eckhart says that in order for the eternal birth to take place, "the mind must have a prevision of what is to be done."[2] We need a glimpse of where we are going. The rest of this book is a small contribution to the cocreation of a vision of where we might be going.

We are invited to a rich banquet. God's *agape,* or universalizing love, calls us and empowers us to step over the barricades that have isolated and diminished us and others. We are called to communion with all sorts of other human beings—women and men; gay and heterosexual; laboring class and owning class; African-American, Native American, and Euro-American; Jew, African, Asian, European, and South American; young and old; able-bodied and physically challenged. We are called to communion with nonhuman creatures and our earth. In other words, we are called to the fullness of communion for which we were made and for which our lovers yearn. Following God through our deep yearning for communion involves us in a ministry of reconciliation.

In the terms of the diagram I have used of the "desperate lover," God's *agape,* or universalizing love, calls and empowers us to step over those barricades that have isolated and diminished us and others:

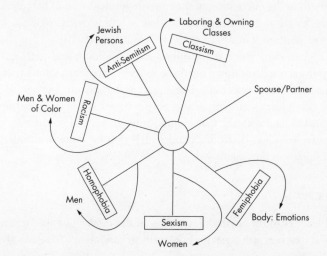

So, we are invited to a rich banquet, but significant parts of us must die for us to gain entrance. There is a great deal within us and in the world that keeps us from communion at the banquet. Emotional, psychological, and even physical violence has been directed at us in order to keep us away from those for whom we yearn; we carry a great deal of fear about getting close to others. In addition, we have acted in ways that have been hurtful and alienating to others; we carry guilt and shame about that. We have been stereotyped and mistreated by others; we carry anger and resentment about that.

The love of God, however, casts out fear and releases us from captivity to sin—that is, the requirement to dominate or be dominated. Our response, our love, then, is not a sentiment; it is not a feeling; it is first a commitment to act on our deepest desire to be connected with others and to act against all those things that get in the way of that connection. It is the act of a mature lover, who refuses either to be addicted to substitutes for this fully human connection or to accept the depression of isolation. Therefore, love brings us into direct confrontation with the external "principalities and powers" and the internal patterns of thought, feeling, and behavior that seem so often to stand between us and others. Love, then, is the act of a mature king who refuses either to dominate others or to stand by passively in the face of structures of domination. Love is also the act of a mature warrior who acts decisively on commitments that are the basis for relationships that aim, not at the obsessive control of others or obsessive self-emptying, but at mutually enhancing, just relationships. Love is also the act of a mature magician who refuses to manipulate others or to be manipulated by them, but who thinks logically, intuitively, inclusively, and justly about what he is being invited by Christ to do in the cocreation of that interdependent web of life intended by God—the kingdom or realm of God. That is, love is the act of those who are "wise as serpents and innocent as doves" (Matthew 10:16).

In order to experience more fully that communion and participate in a ministry of reconciliation, we need the most mature expressions possible of our capacities for connection, justice, strength, and intelligence. We need spiritual disciplines—individual and corporate—that aid us in learning how to love and to deal with the fear, shame, guilt, anger, and resentment that get in our way. We need disciplines and rituals that facilitate both our healing and our initiation into manhood.

INITIATION

Several leaders of the mythopoetic wing of the movement among men have suggested that our industrial and postindustrial societies have not given sufficient attention to the ways we initiate young people into our communities. Michael Meade observes, "In many tribal cultures, it was said that if the boys were not initiated into manhood, if they were not shaped by the skills and love of elders, then they would destroy the culture." He adds, "The way to guarantee that someone will continue to wound others is to keep him ignorant of his own wounds."[3] I think that there is much truth in what he says. Because of our work obsessiveness, we men have little time and attention to listen to and retell our own stories, the stories of our families, the stories of our churches, and the stories of our communities—stories that contain ancient and contemporary life-preserving and life-giving wisdom. We suffer from a historical and, therefore, a relational amnesia. Also, our obliviousness to the ways we have been hurt often leads to our hurting others, no matter how unintentional that might be.

In his workshops and retreats, Meade has found that there is a tremendous yearning in men for

> ritual spaces where there is enough safety to explore [our] neglected emotional and spiritual lives. . . . [B]ehind the boardroom, the locker room, the waiting room, and the barroom, there was a forest of emotional, imaginal life that modern men were just waiting to enter. As men entered that forest, the armor that choked off their emotional, imaginal, and spiritual lives would crack, loosen, and fall clattering to the ground.[4]

It is this kind of exploration of our own wounds that facilitates the healing and integration of our sense of justice, power, intelligence, and compassionate connection; that, in turn, makes it possible for us to stop passing on the violence that has hurt us. We can learn to say and mean, "It stops here."

There are at least three such elements that seem particularly promising for us. According to Joseph Campbell, initiation rites were developed to teach young men and women the skills necessary for the survival and flourishing of the community.[5] For example, in hunter-gatherer communities, young boys needed to learn the skills of the hunt and the courage necessary to use them. For this to happen, there needed to be a ritual space provided in which the old ways of being were cleared out, making room for new, more mature ways of being and acting. Finally, there was a need for elders, who knew the skills, could teach them, and could provide the ritual space in which the transformation might occur.

So, we need opportunities to learn the skills that we and our communities need for our survival and flourishing. We need elders, or mentors, who know those skills and love themselves, our communities, and us enough to teach them to us. We need spaces in which we can move toward mature expressions of our sense of justice, strength, intelligence, and compassionate connection. We are in dire need of such maturity for the survival of our planet and the flourishing of our lives and communities.

At a recent retreat, led by James Hillman and Michael Meade, a man, convinced of their arguments about the need for initiation for young men, asked, "How can we initiate our sons?" Meade said, "We can't, because most of us have not been initiated. Maybe the best we can do is to help each other initiate ourselves and then turn to the younger generations." A sobering thought. The group then began to explore things we could do to help each other.

For those of us who have been shaped by Christian traditions, it might be helpful to explore these initiatory experiences with reference to the initiation rituals of the Christian church. These, of course, are not the only possibilities for life-giving rituals for men, but they do hold promise for us.

Historically, baptism was the means by which persons were initiated into Christian communities. In the pre-Constantinian era, when most converts were baptized as adults, baptism was performed on Easter Sunday. The forty days preceding Easter—what we now call Lent—were a time of instruction and preparation for the initiation ceremony. Candidates for baptism were taught the "first principles" of the faith and engaged in a period of purgation, or purging. That is, they undertook certain spiritual disciplines whereby they distanced themselves from preoccupations that got in the way of their preparation for the initiation rite. This purgation has survived in liturgical traditions in the form of "giving up something for Lent." The purpose of this "giving up" is to take away from oneself something that has become habitual, in order to discern one's spiritual state. Has this become too important to me? Is it causing me to ignore other aspects of my life that need attention? Has it become a kind of idol that is standing in the way of my spiritual growth? In other words, giving up something for Lent is a way of taking stock of one's spiritual life.

If we apply this understanding of Lent and baptism to the needs of men, we might say that, in preparation for initiatory experiences, we give up something in order to assess our spiritual state. In Eckhart's words, we might "cut our selves off" from certain habitual ways of thinking, feeling, and acting in preparation for new birth. In the final three chapters, I will suggest three things we might give up: (1) our deafness to and neglect of our bodies; (2) our competitive feelings and behaviors toward other men; and (3) our neurotic, psychological, and emotional overdependence on women and our attempts to control them.

In the baptismal rite, persons "renounced Satan and all the spiritual forces of wickedness that rebel against God" and symbolically died with Christ and were raised in newness of life.[6] That is, they experienced a painful rebirth in the supportive, celebratory reality of a new community. For us men, we are reborn in a community of resistance to the "flesh," or "world," that served to alienate us from ourselves, others, and God.[7]

Baptism, though a beginning, was not seen as having washed the baptized one completely free of sin. Traditionally, it was thought that baptism freed one of the guilt of original sin, while the effects, or penalties, of original and actual sin remained. Other sacraments and means of grace were available to the Christian to deal in an ongoing way with healing from the effects of both original and actual (before and after baptism) sin. One of the primary means has been the sacrament of penance, or the "rite of reconciliation."[8] This sacrament has traditionally had four elements: (1) contrition, by which one grieves because of the effects of one's sin on oneself, others, and God; (2) confession, whereby one publicly or privately acknowledges the sin and takes responsibility for it; (3) absolution, in which the priest, or representative of the body of Christ, declares one's forgiveness; and (4) penance, by which one is told to "go and sin no more" and is given a task that makes restitution for the sin or contributes to healing and reconciliation.

As men, we might understand baptism, or a similar initiation rite, as an experience in which we acknowledge "the structures of consciousness that bode to our ill-being," receive forgiveness for our guilt for them, and renounce them. We are told that "the powers" were greater than we, that we resisted them as long as we could, and that we are not held accountable for their existence, or for their many effects. This, then, breaks some of the shame that either leads us to deny their existence and effects or paralyzes us into guilty silence.

At the same time, we are held accountable for our collusion with "the powers" and are required to die to them, or have them die in us. In other words, we renounce, for example, the pervasive, insidious, distorting power of sexism in our lives and commit ourselves to rooting it out—in ourselves, in others, and in our institutions. We renounce the powers that oppress us as men and commit ourselves to oppose that which requires men's joyless overwork, the senseless and unfair sacrifice of our bodies and lives, and the low self-esteem produced by the internalization of stereotypes that justify our mistreatment. We renounce the power of racism, classism, anti-Semitism, and other structures of alienation as we are led into further illumination.[9]

But, having acknowledged and renounced these alienating structures of consciousness, we also realize that they and their effects are still with us, that baptism, or the initiatory rite, is just the beginning of a life of "*metanoia*," or repentance and healing. So, how do we deal with lingering effects—both personal and interpersonal? We need rites of reconciliation. The four steps included in the traditional rite are crucial for our renewal, for putting off the old and putting on the new, as Paul would say. The first element of the rite, contrition, corresponds to the fourth stage of grief—depression—that I described in chapter 5. That is, after a man's denial that there is a problem has been punctured and he has worked through his anger and attempts at bargaining, he sees that he must be rid, not only of the effects of sin, but also of sin itself. So he comes to a rite of reconciliation—grieving for what he has done to himself, to others, and to God.

It is important that he confess or talk to at least one other person about what he has realized. He must name what is in us. At first, it is probably best to talk with someone who is like him with respect to whatever pattern of thinking, feeling, and behaving he is dealing with. For example, if it is concerning sexist patterns, he might talk to a man who is committed to ending his own sexism; if it is concerning racist patterns, he might talk to another Euro-American woman or man who is committed to ending her or his own racism. The reason for this "homogeneous" context for confession is twofold. First, if the listener is a member of the class of persons mistreated because of the patterns the man is dealing with, it is possible that her or his hurt and anger will be restimulated. In other words, the listener does not need to hear any more of what has hurt her or him and be expected to forgive and forget. In addition, such a person might end up blaming or shaming the man, with the effect of triggering a paralysis in him that would keep the pattern in place. Second, the man might try to assuage his guilt by presenting a sanitized face to the listener in an attempt to win her or his approval. If the listener is a member of the same oppressor class, she or he will see through that and encourage the penitent to be honest about all the stereotypes, feelings, and actions about which, otherwise, he might be too ashamed to speak. Also, if the man is dealing with his own internalized oppression—ways he has internalized negative stereotypes about himself that justify self-destructive behaviors—it is best for him to talk to someone who understands men's oppression and who does not see his complaints as "whining" and his self-destructive attitudes and behaviors as easily surmountable.

A person of the same class, whether it be an oppressor class or an oppressed class, is also better able to pronounce absolution. That is, because people of the same class know something of the shape and character of the penitent's structure of consciousness, they can honestly say to him that what he has been up against is powerful and that, if he could have chosen differently, he would have. In other words, he did the best he could and should give himself a break. The listener can also assure the penitent that there are divine resources made available within himself (i.e., his inmost self) and within the community that have empowered him thus far and will lead him toward wholeness. By having the paralysis broken in this way, the penitent is freer to use his intelligence to begin to analyze more critically why he has come to think, feel, and act in ways that are hurtful to himself, others, and God; to assess his current situation and see that he doesn't have to continue to live in these patterns; and to develop commitments to think, feel, and act differently.

Finally, the listener helps the penitent to do penance, that is, to develop those commitments to think, feel, and act differently—in ways that contradict the ways we are accustomed to. In addition, he becomes part of a community in which he develops relationships with persons, like and unlike himself, who both challenge him to make those commitments and empower him to keep them. In other words, penance is the active pursuit of reconciliation with others, aspects of oneself, and God; it changes us and the world around us. As we commit ourselves to moving out of our isolation, we will begin to build connections with members of groups from whom we have been alienated.

The rest of this book is a part of that exploration. What skills do our communities need from us for their survival and flourishing? What ritual spaces can we construct in order to learn those skills? Who can help us construct that space and learn those skills?

In the remainder of the book, I want to suggest and explore three skills that men might learn on the way to a fuller and more integrated expression of our first natures—our sense of justice, strength, intelligence, and compassionate connection. Those skills are (1) developing responsiveness to and responsibility for our bodies (chapter 7), (2) developing close relationships with other men (chapter 8), and (3) developing close relationships with women (chapter 9). Said more simply, we need to learn how to take responsibility for and care for our bodies and our relationships. In terms of the diagram of the "desperate lover," we need to work at taking down the barriers of alienation and isolation between us and our bodies and others. In each chapter I will suggest ways in which we might structure spaces to learn these skills and will identify some mentors from whom I have learned something about each skill.

Again, this list is not exhaustive, but a contribution to a growing discussion about what we men can do to "take hold of our own souls," as the fourth-century desert ascetics would say.[10] Many of us feel as though we are in the midst of a deep, dark forest and we, like Ralph, are not sure how we got in here or how to get out. Chapters 7–9 are some signposts that mark at least part of the path out. The path is not for saints; we will make mistakes; we will make wrong turns. But we cannot be afraid of mistakes or even of risking heresy. We cannot be afraid of our shadow sides, as frightening as they might be for us. We simply cannot go on splitting off these frightening parts of ourselves and repressing them or projecting them onto others. That is killing us, others, and the earth. Repression is not sanctification. We must move out of our denial and deal honestly and forthrightly with that which is in us. We must learn to take chances, learn from our mistakes, and keep moving toward wholeness. We must, in the words of Luther, be willing to "sin boldly" if we are to experience more fully reconciliation and participate more significantly in the ministry of reconciliation we have received from Christ.

UNTIL ONE IS COMMITTED

Until one is committed, there is hesitancy, the chance to draw back, always ineffectiveness. Concerning all acts of initiative (and creation) there is one elementary truth, the ignorance of which kills countless ideas and splendid plans: that the moment one definitely commits oneself, then Providence moves too. All sorts of things occur to help one that would never otherwise have occurred. A whole stream of events issues from the decision, raising in one's favor all manner of unforeseen incidents and meetings and material assistance, which no man could have dreamed would come his way.

Whatever you can do,
or dream you can, begin it.
Boldness has genius,
power and magic in it.

GOETHE

Chapter Seven

On Being Body-selves: Body Wisdom and Body Care

> When I sense the holiness of my own body, I begin to sense the holiness of every other body.
>
> JAMES NELSON, *Intimate Connection*

> For you were bought with a price; therefore glorify God in your body.
> (1 Corinthians 6:20)
>
> SAINT PAUL

BECAUSE OF SOME of the demands of the kind of masculinity I described in part 1, many men's bodies are systematically cut off from meaningful, life-giving, empowering contact with other people, earth creatures, and the earth. We experience not only touch but also sensory deprivation. In turn, we tend to think of our bodies, to the extent that we think about them at all, as separate from our essential selves.

The consequences of this alienation from our bodies are a forgetfulness, or ignorance, of the body's wisdom and neglect for the care of our embodied selves. The effects of this forgetfulness and neglect are devastating for us and, as I have said, for others. According to a position paper on men's health problems (1985) by the American Public Health Administration, health education is more effective in reaching young girls than boys. Therefore, boys "miss information on contraception, venereal disease, sexual abuse, obesity, sexuality and nutrition."[1] Men tend not to participate in health promotion and prevention activities. For example, men are less likely to seek medical assistance and less likely to follow the prescribed medical routine when we do. We die in large numbers from cancers of the respiratory system, genitals, bladder, and oral cavity, which are considered to be preventable and/or accessible to early diagnosis. In addition to our having higher mortality rates than women, we also have higher prevalence rates for chronic diseases. Therefore, older men have higher and longer rates of hospitalization.

The reasons for this body forgetfulness and neglect are legion. I will summarize just a few of them here, before I begin talking about what we can do to overcome them. It is important that we see clearly what we are up against.

First, this sort of disassociation from the body is almost required by the oppressive roles we are expected to play as protector and provider. In order to sacrifice our lives for others, militarily or economically, many of us are trained to repress not only fear but also compassion, affection, and empathy—for others and for ourselves.

Our work lives often reinforce this objectification of our bodies, that is, the transformation of our bodies from sensual, vulnerable, sensitive, intimately connected organisms into machines. For men in the middle sector, work is actively disassociated from the body; we aspire to avoid working with our hands. As I said in chapter 2, we are to "work smart, not hard." Success in these lines of work requires what James Dittes has called a monastic seclusion and emotional austerity.[2] We narrow the focus of our lives; we eat, drink, and sleep our work and limit contact with people and things that might distract us. According to Sam Keen, among the unwritten rules of success for men in this class are "The less contact you have with real stuff . . . the more money you make" and "Those who stay indoors and move the least make the most money."[3]

In addition, a physical and psychic conditioning often takes place in the workplace—a conditioning that for some of us leads to a physical dependency on overwork. Many middle-sector men have the experience that whatever they do, it is never enough; they could have always done more. As I have said, superiors hardly ever say, "Well done, good and faithful servant." Rather, the message is more likely to be something like, "Yes, you did that, but what about this?" This is intended to motivate us; the assumption is that we are lazy and need this kind of negative response so that we do not become complacent. The effect of this kind of conditioning is similar to that of a greyhound on a dog track. The dogs chase a mechanical rabbit that always stays just out of reach; they never quite catch it. No matter how hard they run, they never quite reach the goal.

It seems to me that compulsive work habits are inscribed in the bodies of many men in a similar way. We never quite reach the goal; it is always moved a little farther out of reach; the production goals always increase, they never decrease. We are rewarded only if we continue the pursuit at breakneck speed. A man I know told me that when he is working, his pulse rate decreases and when he is not, his pulse rate increases. That sounds like an addiction to me.

For many of us, work has become, not just a way of earning money and providing for our families or a way of expressing our creative, generative capacities, but a physical necessity that masks our underlying fears of inadequacy and failure. The consequence is that overwork is a means of deadening our bodies to these unpleasant feelings.

Another reason for men's body forgetfulness and neglect is the shape of our sexuality. One of the stereotypes believed by others and ourselves is that we men are sexually compulsive. We are not—at least not inherently—sexually compulsive. That does not mean that we don't act out in sexually compulsive ways. We often do, but we don't have to continue to do that. The compulsiveness is not biologically rooted; much of it is the result of a violent conditioning process. As I said in chapters 1 and 2, our sexual expressions are channeled into the very narrow confines of heterosexual, genital sex with one woman. The consequences of this kind of sexuality are genitalization and touch deprivation. Our desire to touch and be touched is funneled into our genitals, and other parts of our bodies and psyches are ignored and neglected. Often, what we pursue is sensation, not feeling.[4]

Finally, our body alienation derives also from the role of violence in our lives. Another of the stereotypes believed about us, by others and by ourselves, is that we are violent. We are not—at least not inherently so. The violence we feel and sometimes act out is the result of the heavy doses of violence—physical and emotional—that we have internalized in our lives and in our bodies. As a result, a great deal of pain, fear, and shame is stored in our bodies. Said another way, dammed up in many of us is a tremendous reservoir of violent feelings. Without constructive and healing ways of releasing this reservoir, many of us act out the fear with violence or find ways of numbing our bodies to the pain, fear, and shame.

To counteract our body forgetfulness and neglect, we need, then, to learn how to listen to our bodies and to care for them. In the rest of this chapter, I will identify some commitments we might make as we move toward that attention and care. In addition, I will identify some skills we will need, spaces we might create, and mentors who might help us in each area.

BODY WISDOM: LISTENING TO OUR BODIES

Commitment 1: "Instead of ignoring the messages my body is sending me, I will listen attentively to learn what this part of my self is trying to teach me."

This is an important commitment. Part of what happens, when we treat our bodies as machines that are supposed to perform no matter what, is that we see our physical and emotional pains as negative obstacles that threaten to thwart our purposes and goals. Consequently, we tend to seek medications or behaviors that will either alleviate or mask the pain in order to function more efficiently. The problem is that the pain is often a symptom of a deeper disorder that needs our attention. We should see the pain, then, not as an enemy but as a friend that is trying to tell us that something is not right—that something needs to be corrected.

A man at a workshop told of having a headache every day for three months. He would take four aspirins and two sinus tablets every afternoon to get rid of it. Finally, because of lower-back pain, he went to a chiropractor. After a month of treatments, he stopped having the headaches. He then started paying attention to when his back tightened up and why. He found that some of the episodes were related to stress at work and others were related to anger he had in several of his relationships. As he realized these things, he began to change some of his work patterns and to deal with the relationships more honestly. The episodes became less frequent and less severe. Had he kept taking the medication that masked the pain, he might never have begun to look at the stress levels at work and learned to say no to responsibilities that were adversely affecting his health. It might have taken him much longer to deal forthrightly with the persons with whom he was in relation. Listening to and acting on this particular message of his body improved the quality of his emotional, spiritual, and physical life in significant ways. It also improved his ability to relate more healthily to the people close to him.

Phil Porter and Cynthia Winton-Henry have developed a technique and philosophy called Interplay to help people listen to the messages of their bodies.[5] They encourage and help people to attend to three levels of awareness of physical experience. The first level consists of body data, which are the "bits of information we are constantly receiving about the present: my feet are cold; I am hungry; my back hurts; I am worried about tomorrow's meeting; I remember sitting in the auditorium the day I graduated; I am excited about seeing a friend. . . ." Since we are constantly receiving this information, we ignore most of the messages unless we have a particular reason to attend to one of them. So, one part of Interplay is the spiritual discipline of attending to specific body data.

The second level is body knowledge, which results from paying attention to accumulated body data and discerning patterns of experience. And the third level is body wisdom, which is body knowledge integrated and used in service to self, others, and God. They point out that wisdom is somewhat different from intelligence. While body wisdom can be profound, it "might be as simple . . . as knowing that a good start to having good friends is to be a good friend, or that violence begets violence."

Based on these insights, Winton-Henry and Porter have developed a notion of "the physicality of grace." They point out that when people are asked to talk about stress, they easily describe its physical manifestations—"tense, constricted, harried, nervous, closed, pressured, tired, confused, etc." Is there, they ask, a positive state that serves as a counterpoint to stress and heals it? Again, when asked, people usually describe a state that is "open, relaxed, breathing, calm, peaceful, generous, energized, etc." When seen as a physical experience, grace can be noticed more easily as body data, and its patterns can be assimilated by body knowledge. In other words, grace can be seen "to occur in some places more than others, with certain people more than others, in the midst of one activity rather than another." When we know this, we can then act to increase the amount of grace in our lives; we see that we receive grace from the action of others and that we are agents of grace to others. This, they say, is body wisdom. And wisdom it is.

Let me give one example of body data that we might listen to, assimilate as body knowledge, and act on through body wisdom. Anger is an emotion that many of us men have trouble with. Often, it is the emotion through which we express many others. It can be bound to other emotions, such as fear and embarrassment, so that we might feel angry when what has happened might more properly cause us to be frightened or hurt. The anger, because it is more acceptable to those around us, masks the other emotions, which we feel are less acceptable. So, our anger is confusing for us. Unfortunately, some interpretations of Christianity encourage us not to be angry and, if we are, not to act on it.

Beverly Harrison argues that "a major source of moral insensitivity derives from being out-of-touch with our bodies." For her, anger is a bodily feeling that can fuel our moral sensitivity and action. She says that "anger is not the opposite of love"; rather, it is "a feeling-signal that all is not well in our relation to other persons or groups or to the world around us" and "a sign of some resistance in ourselves to the moral quality of the social relations in which we are immersed."[6] Further, she says that "anger does not go away or disappear" but "in interpersonal life it masks itself as boredom, ennui, low energy, or it expresses itself in passive-aggressive activity or in moralistic self-righteousness and blaming." In other words, anger denied "subverts community." She believes, then, that we need not only to pay attention to our anger, but also to ask the moral question, "What do I do with what I feel?"

I think her insights are very useful for men. We need to attend to the anger that is in us; and I think there is a lot of it there. I imagine that some of what I have said in this book has evoked anger, even outrage. Writing it and thinking about these dynamics certainly has for me. It seems to me that some of the questions we need to ask are: What has caused this anger? What part of it is legitimate, and what part is not? And what do I do with it? Dealing with those questions in the company of just, powerful, clear-thinking, and compassionate friends, like and unlike us, can go a long way toward our understanding the ways in which we and others have been mistreated, what is fracturing our communities, and what we might do about it. In other words, this kind of connection to our body-selves (lover) increases our moral sensitivity (king) and energizes us for decisive action to resist that which is hurting us and others (warrior).

Another area in which we need to make a commitment to attend to our feelings is in our sexuality. We need to commit ourselves to experience, in their fullness, our sexual feelings—not just the physical sensations connected to genital sex. In other words, we might attend to times and situations in which we feel safe and others in which we do not feel safe. We might ask ourselves whether this expression of physical intimacy is drawing us closer to another human being and ourselves or getting in the way of the closeness we and they seek. As just one example, Herb Goldberg speaks of the inability to maintain an erection, not as impotence, but as the "wisdom of the penis."[7] That is, our inability to sustain an erection can point us to body data or body knowledge to which we need to attend. We might feel unsafe being that intimate with the person we are with; we might sense that engaging in genital sex would damage our relationship with that person; or we might feel that we simply cannot be present to that person in a way that is consistent with the physical act of lovemaking.

It seems to me that the process Porter and Winton-Henry have developed helps men rehabilitate our capacity for compassionate connection and also an aspect of our intelligence. In developing body wisdom, there is a turn toward our right-brain, intuitive, unitive reason. This kind of relearning to be aware in the present moment holds profound promise for the restoration of our health, or salvation. In the church, this relearning would better equip male clergy to help infuse even more of the physicality of grace into worship and other ministries—something we all, women and men, desperately need.

Listening to what is taking place in our bodies is crucial for our life and health and contradicts the internalized messages that our bodies are bad; that they are distractions; that they deserve to be mistreated. If we can't sleep, we need to ask ourselves why. If we are in pain, we need to ask ourselves why. We and others have a lot to gain from the answers.

Commitment 2: "I will embrace my limitations, including my mortality."

This is in some ways an extension of the first commitment. One of the things that the masculine expectations I have described encourages us to do is to ignore our physical and emotional limits. This is part of why we often overwork and do not schedule time for recreation. In talking with men, my sense is that many of us have become too good at delayed gratification. We find ourselves in a cycle of overwork and sensory deprivation followed by "downtime," which consists not of "re-creation" but of "instant gratification," by which we compensate our bodies and psyches for the deprivation they have experienced in our overwork. I say this is not "re-creation" because the pursuit of instant gratification (e.g., alcohol, nicotine, strenuous or competitive exercise, objectified sex, overeating) does not replenish us; it further abuses the body and psyche, so that many of us find the cycle to be a downward spiral.

My sense is that the anxious striving, or works righteousness, that certain masculine expectations condition in us contributes greatly to the high levels of stress and those feelings of being "tense, constricted, harried, nervous, closed, pressured, tired, and confused." By attending to such body data, we can begin to recognize the limits of our physical, emotional, and psychic capacities. That is, we can develop body knowledge about our finitude. Rather than making deals with our psyches and our bodies in order to engage in overwork, we need to make realistic and sober assessments of what we can do and what we cannot. We need to learn to say no to demands and expectations that routinely stretch us beyond the capacities of our bodies. In other words, we need to set firm boundaries (warrior energy) in service of our sense of justice (king energy) to ourselves and to others. From this body wisdom comes a certain release, or freedom, and the grace of deep rest and profound re-creation.

Embracing our bodies and their limitations leads us into an awareness of the ultimate limits of our bodies—death. Ernest Becker and Otto Rank have said that anxiety about death leads us to flee our bodies.[8] So, in embracing our finiteness we also learn to embrace our mortality. Embracing our mortality is crucial for us to overcome what James Nelson has called an "ethics of death." For those who live in denial of death, human existence becomes an attempt "to grasp, to possess, and to control." It is a survivalist ethic based on an ethic of fear; the nuclear arms race has been one of our most graphic testimonies to such ethics of fear and death.[9] How can we men begin to turn and embrace that from which we have been conditioned to run? How can we embrace our own finitude and mortality and stop projecting, as Dinnerstein says we do, our fears onto women and our need for differentiation and transcendence onto our fathers and God?

Coming close to death ourselves or being touched by it in someone we love can be a grace-filled opportunity for us. One of the things researchers have found in persons who have had "near death experiences" is that after they experience the beginning stages of death and then come back to life, many of them lose their fear of death. For many, it is a very "pro-life" experience. Life is sweeter and the present more poignant. Many such people experience a transvaluation of priorities. Some things that were important before become less important, and other things that were less important become more important. They become less concerned for material things and more spiritual, though not necessarily more religious in an institutional sense.[10]

This is the kind of transvaluation that happened to early Christian martyrs and confessors who faced persecution and death. As Ignatius of Antioch was being escorted to his death in the Roman Coliseum, he said that "there burned within him no more concern for material things."[11] In addition, he believed that his only way to life was through death to life "in the world." Using the terms that I introduced in chapter 4, we can understand Ignatius to mean that the way to life is through dying to the "principalities and powers" that rule the "world." That is, if we are to experience life in the next world or in this one, we must die to the power of things like sexism, racism, heterosexism, classism, and anti-Semitism in our lives. We must not be afraid of and avoid that death. For those of us who are Christians, we can, in the power of Christ's resurrection among us, embrace it.

Being confronted with our own physical mortality can serve to focus our attention on the present in ways that help us in that process. One of my mentors in embracing mortality has been Bill Brantley, a wonderfully wise, alive gay man who was diagnosed as HIV positive in 1987 and has more recently exhibited several of the many manifestations of AIDS-related complex. In response to the foreshortening of his life, he has turned deeply into himself. As he has explored his psyche, Bill has confronted his own internalized homophobia as a gay man in our society—the feelings of abnormality, immorality, inferiority, and shame. Saying that "I live my life on fast-forward," he has decided that he does not have time for those negative messages and has committed himself to rooting them out of his life. That has led him, in turn, to analyze the external institutional, social, and cultural structures that have treated him and others like him disrespectfully and inculcated those negative messages about himself. His reflection and reevaluation have moved him to work actively in the church and society against the mistreatment that our world, and, unfortunately, too often the church, directs at gay, lesbian, and bisexual people. The disease in his body has led him to die to "the world" and live in Christ. In the process, he is experiencing profound healing of his sense of justice, power, intelligence, and compassionate connection. He is what Bonhoeffer referred to as a "man and a Christian" who serves for me, as the martyrs and confessors served the early church, as a beacon toward spiritual maturity. He and others like him can help us men toward the freedom to stop anxiously reaching toward the future and to live in the present.

Commitment 3: "I am going to feel, and I am going to find places to express those feelings!"

As Bly has said, many of us men, when asked how or what we feel, look down into our chest cavities and simply don't see anything. Many of us are frozen emotionally. In Dante's *Inferno,* the lowest pit of hell is a sea of ice in which human beings are stuck. This, not fire and heat, describes the most inhuman way for human beings to live. Many of us men live in a hell of emotional isolation and stasis. We need an emotional thaw, so we must contradict the messages we have internalized that we should be numb to our feelings or that we should not express the ones we have. When we make such a commitment and begin to act on it, the tremendous reservoir of repressed emotion stored in our bodies will begin to be expressed. That is, the fear, anxiety, hurt, and embarrassment that caused us to develop our old coping mechanisms in the first place will resurface when we act against, or outside of, these old patterns of thinking, feeling, and acting.

In order for that to happen most effectively, we will need safe places to attend to those feelings and to express them. In other words, we need to develop "sanctuaries" for men where we can, as Ralph did, reimagine our biographies and cry "for the first time in twenty-two years," or shake, or rage, or laugh in the company of compassionate, intelligent, just, and empowering listeners.

These sanctuaries are sacred space; that is, they are particular spaces and times set off by intentional covenants and rituals that provide a safe container for our healing. I will say more about same-sex and cross-gender sanctuaries (group settings) in chapters 8 and 9. Here, I want to discuss some ritual spaces and practices—drumming and storytelling—that many men are finding helpful as they reconnect with their feeling lives. A lot of media attention, much of it critical, has been directed to this aspect of the mythopoetic work among men. There are, however, powerfully transforming things going on in these retreats and workshops. From my perspective, what seems helpful in some of these events is that men are enabled to reimagine our own stories as they relate to the stories (myths and folktales) of our peoples or communities.

In these retreats, men are experiencing sufficient safety and social permission to begin to descend into and go through emotional cycles required to heal from trauma that has produced self- and other-destructive behaviors and ways of being. That is, they can, for a day, a weekend, or a week, put down the burdens, responsibilities, and pleasures of their offices and, because of the safety provided by the ritual space and the social permission of other men, begin to heal.

Many leaders of the mythopoetic movement hold their retreats in the woods or other isolated locations. Why is that? Mythologically, the woods are outside of or on the boundaries of society's institutions and offices. There men can take a moratorium on the often onerous duties of our offices and see and experience ourselves not first as officers or functionaries, but as human beings; not in terms of what we do, but in terms of who we are. Here we might focus not on works, but on God's grace in creation and in redemption.

This does not, of course, have to happen in the woods. What we need is the creation of sacred space by ritual practices by which we suspend the "normal" patterns of thinking, feeling, and behaving. For example, on a retreat, wherever that might be, a group might light candles at the beginning of a session and blow them out at the end. They might agree to certain "rules of engagement," such as not interrupting each other and speaking as much as possible from their own experience. That is, we can establish a context in which we take a moratorium on the violent ways we have been conditioned to treat each other. In other words, ritual space is created by certain acts and agreements that mark off a special space and time as different from what we usually experience.

In addition, time spent on the underside of the oppressive aspects of society's "order" can become transforming sacred space. For example, a Euro-American man can experience sacred space by sitting in an African-

American church listening to what it is like for a black person in the public schools or local loan offices; by sitting in a space where women feel safe enough to talk about what it is like to walk our streets, sit in our classrooms, or try to make it in corporate settings; and by sitting in a space where gay men, lesbians, and bisexual persons can share what it is like to come out to their families, friends, and churches.

Drumming can, for some, add a vital dimension. The drum speaks to the body; the percussive sound and rhythm take us out of our cortices and into our bodies. Neurologically, drumming activates the midbrain—the seat of most human emotions.[12] In other words, drumming can stimulate and dislodge our emotional lives; it can help unfreeze us. Many of us desperately need this.

Storytelling, accompanied by drumming, in the context of safe space can be a powerfully transforming experience. The stories might be personal stories recounting pivotal experiences of transition in a man's life that have shaped his character for good and for ill. A story might recount a family event or series of family events that have shaped him and those he loves. The story might come from the collective unconscious of one's own people or from other peoples in the form of fairy tales, folktales, and myths. Another powerful source for stories is the scriptural traditions contained in the Bible.

Much important work in recent years has focused on the ways in which stories that emerge from a people's life shape the characters of its members.[13] The stories contained in the Bible are what narrative theologians call "master stories," because they have been influential in shaping people's consciousness and values for millennia. These stories belong to us and we belong to them. They express the many and varied ways in which we have struggled to understand God and ourselves. Using Bible stories with men is, however, not uncomplicated. Some men are turned off by Bible stories and shut down emotionally when they are read or told. On a recent retreat, every time I drummed and told a segment of the Jacob and Esau story, one man would disconnect. During the discussion time, he said simply that the story did not speak to him. I asked him what experiences he had had with the Bible in the past. As we continued the discussion with other men joining in, something began to emerge. What many of us had experienced was that someone, usually a male pastor or Sunday school teacher, using left-brain or linear reason, had tried to convince us of some "truth" of the Bible that we were then to internalize and obediently live out. In other words, the richness of the biblical narrative was flattened out into moral or intellectual maxims that we were then to swallow. It is what Freire would call the "banking method" of education in the church. The pastor or Sunday school teacher made deposits of his interpretations of the stories into the heads of students and parishioners. The Sunday school class or "sanctuary" became the scene of "cultural invasion"; no wonder sanctuaries haven't felt very safe for many men.

When other ways of understanding the story are added to the left-brain ways, however, the stories can come alive for men. The drumming, by switching the mind from the left brain to the right brain, aids in the enlivening of the stories.

Let me give a brief example of how this works. At one retreat, after drumming and telling a segment of the Jacob and Esau story, I asked the men present to tell the group what detail of the story caught their attention. When a man responded, I then asked him what feeling came up for him.[14] The responses were varied and powerful. Here are some examples.

One man said that he always felt Jacob was a jerk, because he tricked his brother, but when he heard the story again in the retreat context, he identified with Jacob and felt that it was unfair that Esau was going to inherit everything and Jacob was going to get nothing. He was angry that Isaac loved Esau more than he loved Jacob. He went on to say that it was like that in his family and that he felt it had taken him a long time to stop trying to get his father to love him. He added that he felt terrible because he realized that he had done a lot of things, not because he enjoyed them or wanted to do them, but because he thought that doing them would win his father's approval.

Another man mentioned that the reason Esau was to receive everything and Jacob nothing was the ancient Near Eastern practice of primogeniture. Another man asked what that was and why the Israelites practiced it. Still another man responded that giving the whole estate to the eldest son was a way, in an agrarian economy, to keep the family's holdings intact and thus maintain economic power. This economic power was, consequently, concentrated in the hands of one man—the family patriarch. We began to explore the implications of that economic arrangement.[15] One son is treated unfairly; his mother, Rebekah, is reduced to manipulating her husband through her son, in order to assure the latter's security. Jacob must flee the violent wrath of Esau and becomes an artful dodger. He is cheated by his uncle, Laban, after working seven years to marry Rachel. In other words, Jacob is struggling for his life and his survival.

One man wondered whether that struggle for survival in Jacob, in Rebekah, and in others was the struggle in which we all are engaged. He further wondered whether, in that struggle, we are indeed wrestling with God. He was moved when he recalled that, after the wrestling match with the strange figure in the night, Jacob was called "Israel"—one who wrestles with God. My thought now is that Bonhoeffer might say, yes, God is right here in the struggle, not beyond it or behind it; God is at the center of our strength, not where our strength gives out. The struggle is messy and we get messy, but that is where God is.

Another man resented the way women were treated in the story. The story was about men. When women were mentioned at all, it was always because of their attachments to the men. Women were portrayed as simply instruments of reproduction or as manipulative. I asked him how he felt when he saw women treated as if they were invisible. We talked awhile about what it must feel like for women in a sexist society and what kinds of thoughts, feelings, and behaviors that might evoke in them.

Another man identified with Isaac; he felt that in some ways Isaac was blind and could not see his sons very clearly. We then talked about how it is when our fathers have not seen us very clearly and the ways in which we pass that on to our sons and other younger men and women.

When a biblical story is told in this kind of ritual context accompanied by drumming, our imaginations may be fueled in ways that make listening to the stories like a trip into a kind of "virtual reality." Rather than being one- or two-dimensional, the stories take on a depth and personal quality that allow us to walk into them and identify with characters, dynamics, and feelings contained in these ancient repositories of wisdom. We are reminded of similar experiences or dynamics in our own lives, and those memories bring up the emotions that are associated with those experiences.

These moments can become the occasion for a number of important things to happen. We might use the safety and attention of the group to go through an emotional catharsis. One might realize that he focused on this part of the story because he has experienced a similar kind of thing in his life. He might then ask himself or the group, "What does the story tell me about the reasons I might have experienced that, and what I can do about it now?" In other words, through the medium of the mythological, we can move to the psychological level and see that the concrete level of experience is not just the way things are and have to be, but that there are some very specific, historical reasons for the feelings we have and for the behavior patterns in which we and others engage. We can then use our intelligence (magicians) to begin analyzing why certain things have happened to us the way they did. That often will lead us to think more carefully and empathically about the lives of members of our families or others close to us. By thinking about them in this way, we can be moved to think about the systemic ways in which we and other people are mistreated in our society, what forms that mistreatment takes, and how we internalize that mistreatment. We will also be led to think about the ways in which we have been empowered by our families, churches, and communities and made whole.

We might also realize that we don't have to agree on *one* meaning of the story, and therefore don't have to convince the other guy that he is wrong and that we are right. That is like trying to convince him that what happened to him didn't happen to him or that it is not important. No, he was there; he has experienced what he has experienced, and I have experienced what I have experienced. The issue rather is, What can we learn from one another? What can we help each other learn from the story and from our own lives? This is not about one person having the answers and giving them to everyone else. It is about engaging in a dialogue with mutual respect and in anticipation that something new will come out of the process.[16]

So, to summarize, it seems to me that drumming and storytelling, by moving us out of our left brains and into our right brains, make our memories and feelings more accessible. These, in turn, contain the seeds of our healing and moving toward more just, empowering, intelligent, and compassionate relations with aspects of ourselves, others, and God.

BODY CARE: NURTURING OUR BODIES

To give our body-selves the kind of nurturing attention they deserve and to care more intentionally for them, we might consider several commitments that involve stopping certain kinds of behavior and fostering others kinds.

Commitment 1: "I will stop numbing my body with _____."

One of the ways many of us deal with the pain induced in our body-selves by the violent socialization and conditioning processes I described in part I is to numb the pain with a variety of substances, processes, and relationships. These include alcohol, nicotine, caffeine, and food; work, compulsive exercise, and objectified sex; and "romantic" (read: addictively dependent) relationships with women. Here, I do not think it is helpful to moralize; we do many of those things for good reasons. They dull the pain that we feel from the many things that distort our lives; they have helped us survive. The question, though, is whether we want to continue simply to survive or whether we want to flourish. To flourish, we will need all of our feelings, the unpleasant ones as well as the pleasant ones. And to have them, we will need to wean ourselves from those things that have helped us mask them. My sense is that addictions are a symptom of an unhealthy lover; that is, they result from not being compassionately connected in all the ways our psyches and bodies need and desire. Because of a lack of connection or inadequate connection in various areas of our lives, we overattach to certain other things, processes, or relationships. Without stepping over the barriers that cause our isolation, recovery programs tend simply to substitute one addiction for another. What we need is to move out of the addictive cycle. To do that, we must engage in reconciliation on as many levels and in as many areas as possible. In other words, sexism, heterosexism/homophobia, racism, classism, anti-Semitism, and our own oppression as men feed our addictions. To move out of our compulsions and addictions, we must take concrete steps to connect with others and parts of ourselves.

This means also that many of us will need to change the way we work. In order to spend the number of hours and expend the enormous amounts of energy we do on the job, many of us, for most of the day, ignore the needs of our bodies for rest, stillness, and pleasure. We make deals with our psyches and our bodies that reward this physical and emotional austerity with delayed and often instant gratification. To heal our addictions and begin to care for our bodies, we will need to change this way of being in the world.

Commitment 2: "I will nurture and care for myself as a body-self."

In dealing with the nurture and care of our body-selves, we might think about the treatment of "dis-ease" and the promotion of "ease," or health. The ultimate authority in the care of our bodies is the body and its wisdom. Consequently, it is important for us to take responsibility to know as much as we can about our own bodies and to call on those who have learned the various traditions of wisdom concerning the care of the body.[17] Those include both physicians trained in allopathic medicine (i.e., in traditional medical schools) and healers, therapists, and practitioners using other models for the promotion of health. The relationship between a physician, or other healer, and a patient must be a dialogical one.

It is important to choose a primary care-giving physician, whether that be a family practitioner or a specialist in internal medicine, who knows your complete medical history and appreciates the necessarily dialogical relation within which he or she stands with you—that is, someone willing to take the time to listen to you and talk with you about what he or she is doing and why. Regular physical examinations can help detect and prevent such chronic and acute diseases as high blood pressure, arteriosclerosis, testicular cancer, and respiratory diseases. Especially important diagnostic tests for younger and middle-aged men are blood tests for cholesterol, triglycerides, and blood pressure levels. Be sure to ask not only whether the counts are satisfactory but also for the numbers themselves.[18] High levels of triglycerides, a blood fat, indicate poor cardiovascular health and are often associated with high sugar intake, smoking, and high stress levels. High blood pressure levels often contribute, in younger and middle-aged men, to heart attacks and strokes. Of the factors one can control that increase blood pressure, emotional stress levels are the most important. These numbers represent important body data that can help us understand what is going on with our body-selves and what changes we may need to make in what we eat and what we do—at work and at home.

In addition to medical doctors, there are other health-care professionals who can help us with both the prevention of "dis-ease" and the promotion of health. Among these I would mention three—nutritionists, herbalists, and chiropractors.

The old dictum, "You are what you eat," probably means for many of us that we need to pay more attention to what goes into our mouths. The National Research Council implicates nutritional factors in six of the ten leading causes of death—heart disease, cerebrovascular disease (strokes), cancer, adult diabetes, arteriosclerosis, and alcohol-induced cirrhosis of the liver.[19]

For many men, decisions about what we eat have been made by either our mothers or our wives or female partners. They often have adopted their culinary repertoire from their family traditions—traditions that may or may not be informed by sound nutritional information about carbohydrates, fiber, fats, amino acids, vitamins, and minerals.[20] I say these things not to criticize women, who with the best of intentions often do what we have asked them to do and what they have been expected to do. It is simply to make the point that we need to take responsibility for finding out about sound nutritional principles and applying them to our own lives.

For example, with respect to cholesterol levels, diet (relatively less saturated fat and more polyunsaturated and monosaturated fats and fish oils) can reduce LDLs, while exercise is the only thing that can increase HDLs. For cardiovascular health, we need both; one without the other will not promote our health.[21] A good place to start learning about nutrition is *Jane Brody's Nutrition Book;*[22] it is easy to read and has sound, basic nutrition information. *In How to Be Your Own Nutritionist,* Stuart M. Berger surveys recent controversies about recommended daily allowances, discusses the relation of food allergies to disease, and develops what he calls preventive nutrition, which is aimed at helping people develop individualized prescriptions for nutritional health rather than relying on statistical averages of the general population. For developing a diet and exercise plan, Jack N. Wilmore's *Sensible Fitness* and Donald B. Ardell's *High Level Wellness: An Alternative to Doctors, Drugs, and Disease* are helpful.[23]

To supplement what James Green calls Western "allopathic, technological, crisis medicine," some people are turning to herbalism as a healing art.[24] Pharmaceutical drugs save lives in the face of serious infection, catastrophic injury, and life-threatening conditions such as heart failure. However, Green and others suspect that a host of unpredictable side effects appear when "active chemicals are administered in a concentrated, isolated form." In addition, pharmaceutical drugs, being of a completely nonnutritive nature, are not well suited for most preventive care. Consequently, herbalists believe that whole plants, with all their constituents organized in a "synergistic matrix," are safer and more effective than many concentrated forms. Because of the natural biochemical compatibility with the body's metabolic chemistry, the inert constituents in herbs and vegetables balance and buffer effects of the active constituents. Based on centuries of empirical observation and knowledge, herbalism uses medicines that work more slowly and systemically; that incorporate time as an ally for healing; that nourish and rebuild body tissue; and that attempt to support and enhance the body's natural immune system rather than suppress and replace it with the actions of serums and chemicals. Green believes that the scientific work of isolating, naming, and categorizing individual plant constituents provides important information for the safe and effective use of plants in the promotion of health and the healing of disease.

Another supplementary healing art is chiropractic. This involves spinal manipulation for symptoms such as chronic back pain and headaches. There are a number of different techniques and theories about why and how spinal manipulation works. Some orthopedists are referring patients who do not yet need surgical crisis intervention to chiropractors for preventive treatment. In selecting a chiropractor, it is important to look for one who uses a relatively noninvasive technique (e.g., Gonstead) and who takes a holistic approach, giving attention to diet and exercise.

A primary health-care model in which practitioners of allopathic and alternative medicine communicate directly with each other would benefit us all.

Commitment 3: "I will replenish my senses."

As I have said before, one of the conditions that certain aspects of masculine conditioning and socialization produce in us men is touch deprivation; I would expand that to sensory deprivation. Because of the lack of sensory input, we find ourselves at times depressed, enervated, and compulsive about genital sexuality. We need to take steps to reconnect our body-selves with

other body-selves and with other aspects of the earth. Here are some suggestions about things we might do with respect to replenishing each of our
senses:

1. *Touch:* Our largest sense organ is our skin; with it, we are constantly
taking in body data. The primary thing Jesus did to heal people was to touch
them. When Mother Teresa goes to an outlying village, the first thing people
want to do is touch her. Without compassionate, safe, nurturing touch, we
cannot maintain psychological, emotional, and physical health.

Here are some examples of things you might do to attend to your need for
life-giving physical contact. Pay attention to the furniture you regularly sleep
on and sit on; make sure it is both supportive and comfortable. Care facilities
for senior adults have found that stroking small animals has a calming and
healing effect. The same is true for all of us; so, you might adopt a pet. Treat
yourself to a regular massage by a licensed massage therapist. Learn the techniques of "stroke massage" (the least intrusive of the many massage techniques) and use it on yourself; encourage your spouse or partner and your
friends (male and female) to learn it, so that you can give and receive regular
physical attention. Degenitalize your sexuality by giving and receiving physical attention other than genital stimulation with your sexual partner. Exercise
for twenty minutes at least three times a week—it is good for your heart and
soul. Try a discipline like yoga, with its slow, gentle stretching and focus on
breathing, which is very helpful in arresting our attention in present-time
body awareness.

2. *Taste:* Lionel Tiger in *The Pursuit of Pleasure* has argued that our
sense of taste has played an invaluable role in our survival as a species.[25] We
are able to distinguish at least four tastes—salty, bitter, sweet, and sour.
Sodium, which is always salty, is important for water retention and is vital for
human life. Sugars taste sweet and supply calories. Alkaloids, found in poiso-
nous substances, are often bitter. Acids, when taken together with sugar content, help us determine the ripeness of fruit. In other words, the pleasures of
our palates have helped us survive as a species and therefore are, according
to Tiger, evolutionary entitlements.

We can enhance the enjoyment provided by taste in a number of ways. We
can plan meals with attention not only to nutritional balance, but also to the
various tastes associated with the foods we prepare and the ways we prepare
them. We can take time to prepare meals and eat them in peace. Try avoiding
other media of sensory stimulation. For example, try turning off the TV, par-

ticularly the evening news, when eating. Pay attention to which flavors you like and which ones you do not. Experiment with new recipes and spices.

3. *Smell:* Smells are significantly associated with memories. With one whiff, memories of crisp autumn days, warm summer nights, fresh spring mornings, or cold winter afternoons can come flooding back with all sorts of sights, sounds, and feelings attached. It is important, then, to pay attention to the ways in which smells affect you. What smells trigger good, safe feelings and memories? What smells trigger bad, threatening feelings and memories? What are the characteristic smells of your house or apartment; do they evoke anxiety or calm? How do your favorite foods and drinks smell? What are the smells associated with the people you feel closest to? What are your favorite smells in the outdoors? With this kind of body knowledge, we can find ways of nourishing our olfactory pleasure and sense of well-being.

4. *Sound:* This is a very powerful sense. Martin Luther believed that faith came primarily *ex auditu,* from hearing. Protestant theologian Karl Barth once said that he could more easily make it through the day without reading the Bible than he could without hearing Mozart. As I said with reference to drumming, our feeling lives become more accessible by the stimulation of sound. There is nothing more effective in soothing the savage breast or stirring the passion of the masses than the right song.

So, pay attention to what you feel when you listen to particular sounds, voices, or music. Do they evoke fear, comfort, joy, sadness, delight, anger, anxiety, or peacefulness? Why? Based on that body knowledge, be more intentional about what you listen to and when. You might find it helpful to expand the range of sounds you hear. Explore, perhaps with the help of a music-appreciation textbook, different kinds of music and the various sounds of instruments. Take a walk in the woods and listen to what is there.

5. *Sight:* When asked why he quit writing his great *Summa Theologiae* without finishing it, Saint Thomas Aquinas said, "Compared to what I have now seen, all that I have written seems like straw to me."[26] Vision, both physical and metaphorical, is a powerful medium of grace. Through it, we feel God's delight in us and can express our delight in God. As Alice Walker's character Shug said, God "is always trying to please us back" so "I think it pisses God off if you walk by the color purple in a field somewhere and don't notice it."[27] For our sakes and for God's, let's pay attention to what we see and sometimes don't see. One of the difficulties we have here is that many of us are no longer trained to be discriminating, critical viewers. Sight has become a very passive sense for us. We need to realize that what we focus on,

both physically and metaphorically, enlarges and becomes more important.[28] So, we need to be more intentional about what we look at and how we look at it.[29]

When you look at someone, what do you notice? Why? Who does that person remind you of? What feelings are associated with that memory? What colors and figures do you like? What colors and figures do you dislike? Why? Look around your home and workplace. What do you see? How does it make you feel? When in a crowded room or on the street, move your eyes to places you usually do not look. Whom or what do you notice? What is the effect? Based on this body knowledge, you might then make decisions about what is best for you to focus on.

Commitment 4: "I will attend to and care for the earth and its creatures."

Reconciliation with our body-selves calls forth reconciliation with the earth and other earth creatures. This becomes clear as we replenish our senses and care for our body-selves. Our pursuit of pleasure and health leads us to care for the earth. As Tiger points out, pleasure has enabled us as a species to survive; if we, other earth creatures, and our earth are all going to continue to survive, we must pay more attention to it.[30] In addition, we need to think more clearly about our interdependence with the earth. For example, Sallie McFague points out that

> we literally live from breath to breath and can survive only a few minutes without breathing. Our lives are enclosed by two breaths—our first when we emerge from our mother's womb and our last when we "give up the ghost" (spirit). Breath also knits together the life of animals [including human ones] and plants, for they are linked by the exchange of oxygen and carbon dioxide in each breath inhaled and exhaled.[31]

In many ways, plants are more important than we are for the survival of the planet; their quantity and health are certainly crucial for our survival as a species. The quality of our lives is directly dependent on the quality of the air we breathe, the water we drink, and the food we grow. And the quality of that air, water, and food is directly dependent upon the quality of our characters as human beings. And our characters are being questioned by the messages our earth is sending us.

According to biologist Norman Myer, our "assault on the Earth constitutes the worst trauma life has suffered in all its 4 billion years of existence."[32] A provocative image we might use to think about our current relationship to the earth is that of cancer. In many ways, human beings constitute a cancer in the body of the earth. We are growing randomly and rapidly and are producing toxins that threaten the life of the body. The traditional therapies used for checking or killing cancer employ chemicals, radiation, and radical surgery. In many ways, we, as human beings, are subject to forms of each of these therapies. Environmental pollutants are choking us, ultraviolet rays are irradiating us through holes in the ozone, and we are killing each other in large numbers by means of starvation and increasingly sophisticated and effective weaponry. To personify the earth for a moment, we might say that it is trying to get rid of us before we destroy it.[33] This is a sobering thought, but one we should entertain.[34]

There are many signs calling us to mature, responsible renewal. Do we have ears to hear and eyes to see? We must.

To facilitate that hearing and seeing, McFague advocates an "attention epistemology," which produces a knowledge that comes from paying careful attention to things other than ourselves and taking them seriously in and of themselves.[35] She names three ecological sins, or lies, to which we need to give attention. First, we must see that we live in unjust relations with others of our own kind; there is an inequitable distribution of space and land. When we think about the physical living conditions of billionaires and the homeless, the industrialized world and the two-thirds world, chronically obese and starving people, sin takes on a more concrete, physical shape. We cannot effectively address our relationship to nonhuman beings unless we are doing our homework in our own species.

The second sin involves our refusal to appreciate other species and the ways they are different from us and from each other. We need to see that those differences require "special and particular habitats, food, privacy, and whatever else each species needs to flourish." This is not to say that we are just "one species among species"; there are differences between human and nonhuman beings and we may have to make ethical decisions based on those differences, particularly in the current ecological context of overpopulation and scarcity in some areas of the world. But neither are we "the crown of creation" who can lump all other animals into an inferior category, treat them as alien creatures, and numb "ourselves to their real needs, preferences, and ability to feel pain so that we can continue to use them for our own benefit."[36]

Finally, the third sin is our obliviousness to the fact that we are not only "connected to nature but that all its parts, including ourselves, intermingle and interpenetrate." In addition, as the only self-conscious part of the ecosystem, we too often ignore our responsibility for nature. We need both to see our complex and intimate unity with nature and to appreciate "the intrinsic and particular differences of various species, biotic regions, oceanic eco-systems," and other things. We then need to act decisively on their behalf, understanding that we are also acting on our own. We can survive and flourish only to the degree that our earth and other earth creatures survive and flourish.

God is calling us to understand ourselves as body-selves and as part of a wonderful creation in and through which we encounter God. To love God and our neighbors as ourselves, we must love our bodies and the earth.

THE WIND, ONE BRILLIANT DAY

The wind, one brilliant day, called
to my soul with an odor of jasmine.
"In return for the odor of my jasmine,
I'd like all the odor of your roses."
"I have no roses; all the flowers
in my garden are dead."
"Well then, I'll take the withered petals
and the yellow leaves and the waters of the fountain."
The wind left. And I wept. And I said to myself:
"What have you done with the garden that was entrusted to you?"

ANTONIO MACHADO *(translated by Robert Bly)*

Chapter Eight

On Loving Our Brothers

In general, most men do not have an intimate male friend of the kind that they recall fondly from boyhood or youth.

DANIEL LEVINSON, *The Seasons of a Man's Life*

People should walk down the street as if they belonged to each other.

ETIENNE DECROUX

BRINGING SOME MEN together is like bringing the same pole of two magnets together—the closer they come, the more repulsion there is. I think that the primary emotional dynamic that causes the repulsion between men is fear—fear of being ridiculed by other men; fear of being shamed for being close to other men; and fear of being physically assaulted by other men.

The result is, as Daniel Levinson has observed, that too many of us do not, in adulthood, have the kind of intimate friendships that we might have had when we were boys. Because we are inherently relational creatures, this absence damages us. As Robert Moore has stated, "If you are not being admired by an older man, you are being hurt; if you are an older man and you are not being admired by a younger man, you are being hurt."[1]

John Landgraf, at the time a marriage and family therapist, recounts a time just after his estranged wife, son, and the family dog moved away. With his divorce drawing near, he sought therapy. In the midst of a session, his therapist asked him, "When are you going to go after the friends you want in your life, instead of just processing whoever happens to show up?" The question, says Landgraf, hit him hard. During a long, sleepless night he realized that he had never "intentionally, assertively made a friend—a friend *I* chose, one *I* wanted, not as a business associate, teacher, or romantic partner, but as a friend."[2] He had had friends, but for him friendships either happened with people who might be in proximity or they didn't. He had wooed and won teachers, training opportunities, employers, and lovers but had never intentionally pursued a friendship. It had never occurred to him until that day to do so.

Aelred of Rievaulx, the twelfth-century monk and abbot, referred to some of these relationships as "worldly friendships," because they are most often prompted by the desire to have temporal and material advantages.[3] These advantages may include such things as alliances in office politics, recommendations for advancement, derision of mutually shared "enemies," and favoritism with respect to financial remuneration and other perks. But, when the relationship becomes a liability, more than likely one or both of the "partners" will abandon the other.

I am reminded of the pattern of Ralph's relationships. Outside his family, the only people he spoke of and probably had time to relate to were his colleagues at work. When he started dealing with the shape of his life and the pain it caused him, he realized, by their ridicule and "excommunication," that although he had spent sixty hours a week with them for seventeen years, they hardly knew him, nor did they want to. That is pretty sad, but those are worldly friendships; they cannot foster the kind of human trust that empowers us to be centered body-selves capable of strong, decisive action on our own and others' behalf. Though he was "paid more than any two of [the men in the group] put together, supposedly one of the top decision-makers in the country," when it came to his own home and his own life, he didn't even know where to begin. And he lost the only people (Ginny, Randy, and Ralph, Jr.) he ever loved in the process.

From a similar place, John Landgraf concluded that he needed to learn how to be single, or to put it in his terms, how to "single." For him, "singling" must be a conscious process of taking responsibility for oneself in the context of one's relationships. Singlehood involves learning how to be increasingly "self-aware, self-preserving, self-affirming, self-fulfilling, and autonomous (self-governing)." Singlehood, redefined in this way, can be "a high level of wellness"; one can be single and sexually whole; one can be well married to oneself; and one is free to have a life mate or not to have one. Far from leading to an isolated self-centeredness, such singleness leads to the ability, from the strength of a centered body-self, to live "*inter*dependently" in life-giving relationships with others, rather than in the mutually deadening dynamics of "addictive dependencies." The opposite of being single, then, is not being married, but rather being nonsingle. That is, nonsingle is the state of not having a centered self.[4] Often, such a person is so focused on his or her own dependency needs that he or she is not very free to be present to another—even a life partner—in friendship.

Because of our conditioning toward relational isolation and an overdependence on the primary woman in our lives, many men have never successfully singled. We need to. We need to take responsibility, not only for our bodily well-being, but also for our relational well-being.

What Ralph needed and what we all need, says Aelred, are "spiritual friendships," in which we can develop deep levels of trust that others love us, not for what we can do for them, but for who we are, and that they will be there for us through thick and thin. Said another way, we need people in our lives who are committed to seeing and mirroring back to us our first natures, or inherent capacities for justness, strength, intelligence, and connection, as well as those patterns of thinking, feeling, and behaving that are mature expressions of those capacities. We need them also to be honest with us about our modes of being that are distortions of those capacities and hurtful to ourselves and others.

These kinds of spiritual friendships, says Aelred, are the "medicine of life." It seems to me that Jesus recognized the importance of spiritual friendships. John McNeill recently pointed out at a conference I attended that Jesus' family of choice apparently was three single people—Mary, Martha, and Lazarus.[5] In addition, he apparently had an especially close relationship with John, the "disciple whom Jesus loved."[6]

As I have said, there is much that gets in the way of our developing spiritual friendships with men—primarily fear. And there are very good reasons for our fears. I have mentioned a few. Also, in our churches, dominative masculine men ridicule kenotic masculine men for being weak, naive, unfair, and pandering to "special-interest groups," while kenotic masculine men ridicule dominative masculine men for being tyrannical, authoritarian, violent, and "out-of-touch." Many of us have been hurt in these ways by other men and have felt abandoned by older men, including our fathers. We are hurt and strike back; they are hurt and lash out again; we retaliate. And on and on it goes.

For this reason, if we are ever to get close to other men, we need to deal with the fear that we have of them in our psyches and our bodies. Landgraf points out that we need to learn "to love other men without the fear of homosexuality."[7] He is right. Homophobia is usually defined as "an irrational fear or hatred of homosexual people."[8] Many of us men are deathly afraid of homosexual people and of homoerotic sexual expression. We have good reason to be; we have seen gay men, lesbians, and bisexual persons targeted for verbal and physical violence in our society and in our churches.[9] When they have been honest about who they are, they have lost jobs or been denied employment or advancement; they have been asked to leave our churches or denied places of leadership. We, ourselves, may have been targeted if we have expressed emotional or physical closeness to another heterosexual man or to a gay man or lesbian. For some of us, that fear has risen to the surface when another man, whether gay or heterosexual, has expressed a desire to be emotionally or physically close to us.

In light of all these experiences that put distance between us and other men, we need to expand the definition of homophobia. As I said in chapter 2, homophobia literally means "fear of the same," so perhaps it might be helpful for us to say that homophobia is the fear, not just of gay men, but of men in general.[10] Understood in this way, homophobia is that which leads men to mistreat not just gay men, lesbians, and bisexual persons, but also other men much like us, as well as men who are different from us in various ways. Since "there is no fear in love," we must confront and deal with our homophobia if we are going to be able to love other men. We must put a stop to this violence against one another; we must interrupt the cycle of violence. We must find ways of creating "demilitarized zones" in which we call a moratorium and begin to address the fear that motivates much of it.

We need spaces in which we call a moratorium on the emotional and physical violence we habitually inflict on one another, so that we might experience sufficient safety to begin to trust one another. To develop spiritual friendships with men, we must establish new patterns of relating to them.

Spiritual Friendships and Sacred Space

To facilitate spiritual friendships, we need to clear safe spaces—sanctuaries—in which we can learn and practice the kinds of spiritual friendship–making wherein deep, human trust can germinate and flourish. Sam Keen has said:

> Friendship exists as a sanctuary that is situated between the private world of family, the ambiguities of sexual love, and the public world. . . . Friendship is a sanctuary precisely because within it we may be more than, and different from, the destiny we must wrestle with in the family, or the roles we must assume to enter the contractual order of civility.[11]

In other words, the healing space of friendship exists between those private and public worlds that sometimes rend our psyches. It is a space within which profound healing can take place for all of us, but particularly for men. The trouble is that, because of the demands of those two spheres, many of us have never put a premium on or given much explicit attention to what it takes to develop intentional, or spiritual, friendships.

Aelred of Rievaulx provides a helpful framework for thinking more intentionally about some of what we may already be doing, as well as pointing us toward things we might do to facilitate more meaningful friendships. He speaks of four stages of friendship—selection, probation, admission, and harmony.[12]

In choosing our friends, we should see the other as clearly as we can and make judgments about the other's character. He advises us to avoid angry, fickle, suspicious, and talkative people, as well as those who slander, reveal confidences, and persist in hurting people we love. We should pay attention to our attractions—emotional, intellectual, and physical. He says in addition to seek out persons whose temperaments and habits suit our own. I would add that, while it is important to pay attention to such attractions, sometimes some of our best spiritual friends may not have been initially attractive to us, though there must be something to which we are attracted if we actively pursue friendship. Also, his advice may lead us to persons most like us and thereby keep us in the small, homogeneous circles encouraged by the "principalities and powers." My sense is that that is a good place to start, and on the basis of those spiritual friendships we can move out across the barriers that separate us from persons who are not like us in significant ways.

Next, Aelred says, there must be a period of probation; to begin to build trust, we must explore various aspects of the relationship. He suggests that we look for four things in individuals to whom we are relating. First, do they demonstrate loyalty? Can we count on them; do they make time for us and for our relationship; do they continue to do hurtful things to us and to the ones we care about, after we have named those things to them and asked them to stop? Second, do they have good intentions? Do they want to know us and care about us for who we are with our strengths and weaknesses, or do they want to be friends with us as a means to another end for them? Third, are they discreet? Can they keep confidences; can we trust them not to use what we tell them—as heretical, antisocial, childish, or grandiose as some of it might be—in ways that might hurt us? Fourth, do they show patience to us? Can they allow us to make mistakes in the relationship; can they accept our weaknesses as well as our strengths; do they see our best intentions and remain loyal to us?

The key here is to learn when and how to open ourselves to others—how to be vulnerable to others. One of the reasons we men don't seem to be vulnerable is that we haven't learned how to be appropriately vulnerable.[13] We have been encouraged and conditioned to bare everything to our wife or significant other and almost nothing of emotional significance to anyone else. Consequently, for many of us, vulnerability is an all-or-nothing kind of enterprise; we haven't been taught to make judgments about the levels of vulnerability—emotional, intellectual, psychological, and spiritual—appropriate to our various relationships. As Aelred says, we can't love everyone, "but we can embrace them differently, without having all of them as intimate friends."[14]

I believe this difficulty in making discriminating judgments about the trustworthiness of others is one of the psychosocial roots of our objectification of others—that is, our unwillingness to be vulnerable to others. We are reluctant to allow ourselves to be known by others because we don't know how to do so without being hurt. Consequently, we withhold important information from them and, thus, inhibit their ability to act as fully informed agents, or subjects, in their own right. We know them, but they do not know us very well. This gives us an unequal balance of power and undermines the intimacy we so need and want.

After we make sober and deliberate decisions about the trustworthiness of another, Aelred says we can admit her or him into friendship. Said another way, we make a commitment to that person and she or he to us. In doing so, we freely offer to acknowledge and accept a claim that the person has on our attention and care, and we ask her or him to do the same. As Margaret Farley points out, there are various levels of commitment we can make, but the key to fulfilling them is "the way of fidelity." By that she means, in part, a commitment to be present to another; that is, we promise to give our attention, as best we can in the context of the commitment, to the other person and to the relationship.[15]

Before moving to the last stage of friendship, it is important to note that, as Aelred says, it may become necessary to end a friendship or, at least, renegotiate the level of intimacy in a relationship. There are a number of reasons for this, including unrepentant betrayal.[16] When this becomes necessary, he says that it must be done slowly and with compassionate deliberateness, in order to avoid bitterness, quarrels, and enmity. It is, he says, "shameful to wage war against someone who has been your intimate."[17]

The fourth stage of a spiritual friendship is harmony, says Aelred:

> It is in fact a great consolation in this life to have someone to whom you can be united in the intimate embrace of the most sacred love; in

whom your spirit can rest; to whom you can pour out your soul; in whose delightful company . . . you can take comfort in the midst of sadness; in whose most welcome friendly bosom you can find peace in so many worldly setbacks; to whose loving heart you can open as freely as you would to yourself your innermost thoughts; through whose spiritual kisses—as by some medicine—you are cured of the sickness of care and worry; who weeps with you in sorrow, rejoices with you in joy, and wonders with you in doubt.[18]

It is in this sort of sacred space that our capacity for compassionate connection is healed.

SPIRITUAL FRIENDSHIPS AND MATURE MANHOOD

Developing these kinds of spiritual friendships with men and women demands of us and draws forth mature expressions of our capacities for justness, strength, intelligence, and compassionate connection. Aelred says that spiritual friendships are ruled by justice, guarded by fortitude, moderated by temperance, and directed by prudence. These friendships must be just relationships; that is, we recognize the sovereignty of our friend and insist that she or he recognize our own. In other words, *philia,* or friendship love, involves a mutuality that demands equality. To preserve that equality and mutuality, we also commit ourselves to act with fortitude, or strength, against those persons or institutions that would treat our friends and ourselves disrespectfully and establish and maintain inequality. Sexism, heterosexism, the oppression of men, racism, classism, and anti-Semitism, among other oppressive structures, are the enemies of friendship and make us all poorer. Finally, love, or our desire for compassionate connection, is, according to Aelred, the source of friendship. And love requires reason to keep it pure and affection to keep it sweet.[19]

To facilitate developing spiritual friendships with other men, we could undertake two commitments or, as I said before, two penances by which we commit ourselves to ways of feeling, thinking, and acting that contradict the ways we usually interact with other men and that lead us toward reconciliation.

Commitment 1: "I will stop competing with, shaming, ridiculing, and otherwise hurting other men."

This is a difficult one. A commitment to stop doing violence to other men does not mean that we are naive about the fact that other men can and will do violence to us. We only have responsibility for what we do, not for what others do. Consequently, there are times when we will need to protect ourselves by exercising "appropriate vulnerability," that is, by determining how much we want to open ourselves to other men who may unwittingly or maliciously hurt us. We will also need to decide when and how we will name and call attention to those unconscious and conscious violent patterns of other men. In other words, we need to learn how to be "wise as serpents and innocent as doves" (Matthew 10:16).

Commitment 2: "I will actively identify with, care for, and think about what it is like for men similar to and different from me."

This is not something that comes easily or naturally to us. The violence we experience at the hands of other men and the fear it evokes in us often produce a kind of paranoia around other men. We are often so busy protecting ourselves that we don't have much time or attention to see them very clearly. As we feel safer around other men and experience their care for us, we will be able to see them more clearly for who they are and to distinguish this particular man from other men who might have hurt us. We will be better able to admire their justness, strength, intelligence, and compassion, receive it, and be empowered by it. We will also see more clearly what has and is hurting them and what decisions—for good and for ill—they have made as a result. We might then learn from their wisdom and respectfully and persistently challenge their self- and other-destructive ways of thinking, feeling, and acting. So, to care for another man is to contradict his internalized messages that justify the ways he has been mistreated—to point out that he is not simply emotionally constipated, relationally incompetent, inherently violent, and sexually compulsive. Caring means helping another man recover the parts of himself that have atrophied or have been repressed.

To care for another man also means challenging the ways he may be mistreating others and the stereotypes he has internalized about others that justify their mistreatment. For example, if a man speaks about or treats women disrespectfully, we can point that out and then invite him to think about why he is doing that and to make a commitment to stop it. The same is true of heterosexist/homophobic, racist, classist, and anti-Semitic patterns of thinking, feeling, and acting. Just as the violence between men must stop, our violence and disrespectful treatment of others not like us must stop. We must hold each other accountable on both scores.

SPACES FOR ENACTING THE COMMITMENTS

In this section, I want to discuss three contexts, or spaces, where we might live out these commitments to developing closer relationships with other men. Those contexts are personal friendships, mentor relationships, and men's groups. We might see them as ritual space, in that they are, as Keen has said, often found on the boundary between private and public space and intentionally constructed by rules or guidelines that provide sufficient safety for trust to grow and intimacy to flourish. In other words, each of these contexts can be containers in which spiritual friendships with men can develop.

Personal Friendships

In developing personal, spiritual friendships with other men, we can look to Aelred's advice about choosing a potential friend, testing him, and admitting him to friendship as a guide. I want to note here some of the barriers we might face in developing friendships, even with men who are most like us.

First, and perhaps foremost, many men don't have or make much space and time in their lives for such friendships. Many don't see the need to. This is something we need to understand and think about. For those of us who are divorced or single, we may feel that this is particularly true of married men, or men in partnership relationships, whose loyalty may be solely to the partner or the family. None of us needs more rejection from men. Consequently, we need to clear out time in our own lives before we can expect other men to do so. Also, we may need to be direct with a person we see as a potential friend about whether he has or will make time to foster a friendship with us.

Second, we need to remember that other men have the same fears of emotional and physical intimacy with men that we do. Therefore, it is helpful, as the relationship develops, to be direct about what we want and are comfortable with in the areas of emotional intimacy and physical contact and ask him to do the same.

Finally, many men have not given much thought to intentional friendships with other men and may be perplexed by the whole idea. Here you might suggest that you both read something about men's lives.[20] In doing so, you may develop a common vocabulary that enables you to name with each other important issues and dynamics that will foster mutual understanding and care.

John Landgraf tells of his decision to "woo and win the most desirable friend" he could find. It was a man Landgraf respected for his wisdom, thoughtfulness, and leadership, but who was married and had many professional commitments. He found the courage to ask him to lunch and reports:

> As the small talk played out and lunch was served, we both fell into silence. It was my move. Looking more at my plate than at him (not good technique at all, but I was embarrassed and afraid of rejection), I

said softly, "I've been watching you from afar for some time. I like what I see. I am seeking a friend, and the reason for this lunch is to ask you to consider becoming my friend. I don't know how close we'd want to get or what form our friendship would take, but we could start now and see where it wants to go. If you can make time for an occasional meeting like this and are willing to try . . . " As my voice trailed off I looked up—to see him crying! He was lonely too. No one had ever approached him this way. He was touched. We became fast friends. What a great feeling!

The first time I read this passage I cried and have every time since then. I don't quite know why. Part of it is the way what Landgraf did contradicts so much of my experience in life. Here is a man much like me risking vulnerability with another man. He did it in a clear, respectful way that gave the other man a choice. He admired another man and told him so; he also told him he wanted to be closer to him and was clear about what that might mean, at least in the beginning. The other man responded with his own vulnerability; he was moved and he showed it. It was a sacred moment between two maturing men.

Of course, it might not have turned out this way. The other man might have reacted with consternation, embarrassed silence, defensiveness, or dismissiveness. The man might have been grateful for the invitation but might not have had time in his life at that moment for what was being requested. Or he might, for other reasons, not have wanted to enter the level of friendship that was offered. Those and other responses are all possibilities. But the possibility of friendship, which in this case was reciprocated, made the risk Landgraf took worth it. By acting in spite of his fear and insecurity, Landgraf dropped part of his armor and made possible a sacred space where healing could take place. I am sure these two men had many more such sacred moments. For me, this account contributes to a vision of what is possible among men and provides a partial model of how to move toward it.

Mentor Relationships

As I said in the beginning, Robert Moore believes that we need to both admire and be admired by older men and younger men. In light of that, we might make commitments to develop friendships with older men and younger men we admire and respect.

As men, we need the affirmation and respect of older men. It has a way of securing us in the world and giving us a sense of pride in our maleness. Some of us got this admiration and respect from our fathers, and some of us did not.

I always had the sense that my father respected me, and as I moved into adulthood he has told me directly and indirectly that he admires who I am, the decisions I have made, and what I am now doing. We haven't always agreed about the direction of my life, but I have always known his respect. I think that baseline of respect and admiration has enabled me to move with confidence into my adult life and to do many of the things I have done. I am very grateful for that.

As I have done that, I have been gifted with other older men who have respected me, encouraged me, and admired me. One of these was my academic mentor, George H. Williams. Holding a distinguished chair and having been at Harvard for almost forty years when I met him, Professor Williams was an imposing figure for this recent graduate of a state university from a small town in east Tennessee. He had white hair, wore three-piece suits, knew and routinely used more ancient and modern languages than anyone else I've ever known, lectured brilliantly on every period of the history of the church, and had the respect, and sometimes fear, of many of the graduate students I admired. In fact, overwhelmed, I dropped the first course I ever took from him.

In the last year of my three-year master's program and as I was applying to doctoral programs, I did a presentation in his class on theories of salvation in early Christianity. As I filled the blackboard with the typology I had worked out, I turned around to find him taking notes. I had never seen him do that before. I assumed he was writing down his criticisms and saving them until I had finished. When I ended with a comment about which of the theories I found most compelling, he asked why that was and we engaged in a lively discussion.

Several weeks later I went to his book- and paper-cluttered office in Widener Library to ask him to write a recommendation for me to doctoral programs. He said that he would be happy to and would mention how much he had learned from me. I remember walking away from his office in disbelief. He had learned something from me? I had never known him to be disingenuous, so he must have been telling me the truth. That was a turning point for me. I began to see myself in a different light. I began to appreciate and have confidence in my own intellectual ability in ways that I never had before. An older man, whose magician I admire as much or more than anyone else I have ever known, blessed mine.

Another of my mentors has been a colleague and friend, John Collins. During my divorce and its aftermath, I would often go to him either sunk in

confusion, guilt, and pain or exhilarated with some new insight or realization. If he could, he would make time to listen to me as I sorted through the
difficult dynamics of love, sex, romance, friendship with women, and friendship with myself. He would also share thoughts with me from his considerable wisdom on matters of the heart and soul. In the sacred space he offered,
I learned something about what Dietrich Bonhoeffer called the "grace of in-
terruptibility"—the willingness to make time in the midst of a busy schedule
for a fellow traveler. I learned also that a man can love and care for another
man in ways that, until that time, I had mostly experienced with women. In
doing so, he helped wean me from my addictive dependence on the women
in my life for emotional support and freed me to see them more clearly and
treat them more respectfully. I also learned that I could seek this kind of emotional intimacy from other men. A man whose compassionate connection I
admired, admired my lover and provided space and skills for its rehabili-
tation.

Good relationships with older men can aid us in reconciliation with our
fathers. They no longer have to be those independent, autonomous, completely powerful persons we have often needed and expected them to be. We
can let them be who they are. We can appreciate what we received from them
while acknowledging some of the things we did not. We learn that we can get
some of what we have needed from other men and from ourselves. That frees
us to see our fathers more clearly and more compassionately. We see that
they have their own histories, their own father wounds, and their own ways
of dealing with all of that.

Healthy mentor relationships, as well as reconciliation with our fathers,
also go a long way toward rehabilitating the image of God as a father. For
many men, God as a father has meant domination, not justice; intimidation,
not strength; manipulation, not wisdom; and absence, not presence. However, as we experience the justness, strength, intelligence, and compassionate
connection of men in our lives, the image of God as a just, powerful, wise,
and loving father becomes both believable and meaningful.

These mentor relationships also enable us to give attention to the younger
men, particularly our sons, in our lives. It is attention that they desperately
need and attention we need to give.[21] Our sons need more from us than the
thirty-seven seconds per day we average with them in their first three
months, or the hour per day later. If we are fathers, fathering is a part of our
vocation. It is not something we help our wives with; it is part of who we are
and what we are called to do in the world. Consequently, we need to make a

commitment to be there for them; to spend structured and unstructured time with them.

They need our physical, psychological, and emotional presence. They need to follow us around learning what we do and why; learning what we feel and why; learning what we know and why; and learning how we love and why. They need to know that we respect and admire them as they begin to make their own decisions about what they will do, how they will feel, what they will learn, and whom they will love. They need us close enough that they feel safe to explore, but not so close that that exploration is obstructed. They also need to know our friends and have the opportunity to relate intimately with other adults in mentor relationships.

For those of us without sons, we can offer similar gifts to younger men—nephews, students, advisees, protégés, or strangers. There are plenty of young men in the world who need our attention. So, choose one and develop a relationship with him. Spend time with him, think well and clearly about him, and offer him your admiration. It is a balm for the soul—yours and his.

Men's Groups

In addition to personal friendships and mentor relationships, men's groups can serve as sanctuaries where men call a halt to mutually destructive violence and develop skills in caring for themselves, other men, women, children, and the earth.

Recently, a center for men "seeking refuge from fierce competition at work and from their families" opened near Kyoto, Japan.[22] Yoko Hirooka, who operates eight homes for unmarried mothers and abused wives, says that she is surprised at the growing number of men seeking counseling who are exhausted from work and life in general. She adds, "There are few places in society that will accept hurt people as they are. This is meant to be a movement to liberate homes." Father Richard Certik, the head of the center and a Roman Catholic priest, observed, "I am neither a counselor nor a psychiatrist, but I can listen to people with problems."

Many men need a place where we can be accepted as we are, not for what we can accomplish, and where we can be listened to as we put together the pieces of our lives and point them in more self- and other-nurturing directions. We need many centers of the kind Ms. Hirooka and Fr. Certik are operating in Kyoto. In addition, for men who cannot take the time away from work and family that such an experience requires, we need regular times and spaces that serve the same purposes. Increasing numbers of men are finding that space in men's groups that help them disengage, for an hour or two each week—some less, some more—from those dynamics that pull and tug us in ways that distort us.

There are several reasons why some of this work is best done in all-male groups. First, part of the task is to wean men from emotional overdependence on women. It is important that a man come to know and feel that significant emotional needs can be met by other men. Second, because the mutually disabling, complementary gender dance between men and women often sets up a power struggle between them, men and women end up blaming and shaming each other in some of our most vulnerable areas. The shaming often shuts men down emotionally, and we get used to being silent in the presence of women about issues involving our emotions and relationships. For this reason, too, a man will probably feel more understood by other men and more likely to begin to break his silence, as Ralph did, about some of the most important things in his life. Finally, in the context of being understood and appreciated, a man is more open to being challenged about the ways some of his patterns of thinking, feeling, and behaving might be destructive to himself and others. When a brother, who has spent time with us, listened to us, and understood what life is like for us, names ways in which we have internalized, for example, sexist or racist stereotypes and patterns of behavior, we are in a better position to hear that in a nondefensive way.

Because of the considerable forces that produce fear of other men in us, we need to structure men's groups with rules, or guidelines, that create space in which we can learn to treat each other with respect, to begin to trust men, and to count on them to be there for us. Here I want to share some examples of guidelines that I and others have found helpful in structuring such space and then discuss some of the things men might do in such groups to foster spiritual friendships.[23]

GUIDELINES

1. *Composition and Selection:* Somewhere between six and ten members is a good number. The group is too big if each member does not have sufficient time to share his concerns on a regular basis. The desirable size also depends on how frequently the group meets. The group is too small if the absence of one, two, or three members means that the group does not function well. With respect to whom you invite to be in your group or what kind of group you join, several factors are important. First, if this is your first or only group, you might want a group of men who are similar to you in terms

of socioeconomic class, sexual orientation, and race. The reason for that is that many of us need to learn to deal effectively with lesser differences before we can move on to greater differences with any degree of confidence and hope for success. Age and marital status are also factors. In my own primary men's group, half of the men are married and half are not. The balance has been helpful. We have also found that a spread of ages (two in their fifties, two in their thirties, and two in their twenties) is useful. The inclusion of these differences has been enriching; it has caused us to work through conflicts that the differences cause.

Another matter to think about is preexisting relationships. A good way to get a group off the ground is for each man who is organizing the group to ask one or two friends to join. Sometimes, however, men who move in the same professional or social circle do not feel safe in the group because of the possible ramifications of things said in the group for their lives and relationships outside the group. This can be dealt with by talking about specific fears or concerns and requiring a strict confidentiality. For this reason, a men's group composed completely of men from the same church congregation might have some barriers to overcome. Many men (particularly pastors) sometimes have professional and social investments in their relationships at church, which makes honest self-disclosure to other men in their church too risky and difficult. If that is the case, groups composed of some members of a congregation mixed with men from outside the congregation would be helpful.

It is also helpful to include men whose concerns about men's issues are similar to yours—that is, men who are open to looking at and discussing some of the dynamics I have been dealing with in this book. Said another way, a man doesn't have to be in stage five (acceptance) of the process I described in chapter 5, but if he is in deep denial, having him in the group will be more frustrating than helpful. It is also important that a man be willing to take responsibility for his own feelings and thoughts and have enough attention to listen respectfully to others. If a man is in crisis, chronically depressed, or has a heavy addiction, he might need therapy before he is ready to be a contributing member of a men's group. Almost every man I know needs a men's group; the question is, Do you want him in yours?

Having said that, let me enter a caveat. I don't know too many men who aren't in crisis at some time, who are not depressed at least some of the time, and who are completely free of addictions. When we think of any particular man whose neediness we fear might sink our group, we realize that "there but for the grace of God go I." The only thing I can say is, Be open to your brothers, but also take care of your group—it is a precious and rare space.

2. *Time:* Set a regular meeting time, and stick to it. It might be from ninety minutes to three hours each week or every other week. You can adjust it depending on the needs and desires of the group. You might start by meeting at the same place for the first several months (e.g., someone's home, a room at a church, a private dining room, an office conference room), or you might rotate the meeting place among the members' own living spaces, if privacy and comfort can be accommodated. It is helpful in the beginning to set an initial termination point of the commitment (e.g., six months to a year), followed by a reevaluation and renewal or ending, in order for men to feel comfortable making an initial commitment.

3. *Leadership:* Usually, one or more men will need to take responsibility for establishing the contacts, arranging for the meeting times and places, and circulating mutual agreements, or even a set of guidelines such as these, to get a group going. As I have said, it is not easy to get men together, and it is not easy for us to stay together once we come together. As time goes on, the leadership can be shared as other men take ownership in the group and grow in their ability to assume responsibility for its process.

4. *Process:* Within the group, certain things are required to create the safety necessary for trust to develop. As an example of a set of specific guidelines a group might want to develop, I reproduce here a set compiled by a group of men that began meeting in my city.

MEN'S GROUP

It is the intention of this group to establish a safe place to explore the areas of our lives which we have traditionally ignored or denied. In order to achieve the needed security for each individual, it is appropriate to establish certain guidelines. This list is not intended to be restrictive or all inclusive.

1. Certain basic values are necessary for our effective sharing and safety. Among these are honesty, respect, and confidentiality.

2. We are each responsible for establishing our own boundaries and protecting ourselves emotionally and spiritually, as well as physically. Each of us is encouraged to say as much as we want to say but ONLY what we want to say. While we may encourage each other to speak what is on our mind, we must respect the boundaries of each individual.

3. Group size will initially be limited to no more than eight people, with six being considered the ideal size for our group at this time.

4. If a man wishes to become a member of this group, he should be "presented" to the group PRIOR to an invitation being offered. The intention is not to restrict inclusion, but rather to assure a continuation of the safety on which this group is founded. Any discussion of the individual should not be considered criticism, but rather assurance of a "good fit" with the other individuals.

5. If a current member of the group wishes or finds it necessary to leave the group for any reason, he is requested to inform the group in one of our regular meetings. This is not intended to put anyone on the spot, but rather to assure understanding among the group and to allow "closure" for the relationship which has developed and to say "good-bye."

6. The regular meeting time for this group will be every second and fourth Tuesday from 9:00 P.M. to 10:30 P.M. This time frame is open to change at the pleasure of the group.

7. The intention of this group is to deal with men and their feelings. This is not really a forum for discussion of theoretical issues as our primary topic, although material can be shared among us. The focus should remain on men's feelings and how to deal with them effectively in today's society.

8. While our relationships with women will from time to time be a topic of discussion, this group is not established to demean or malign women. It is recognized that women are facing many problems of their own in today's society. However, this group is established to help men deal with feelings from a man's perspective.

I will make just a few comments. Guideline 2, with its concern for appropriate vulnerability, is very important. In fact, a men's group is a very good place for a man to develop and test his capacity for self-revelation and to determine appropriate levels of intimacy. Also, the way one enters and leaves relationships is important (guidelines 4 and 5); learning to be intentional here can help us be more intentional and respectful in other relationships.

The commitments to acknowledge one's feelings and to deal with them, rather than with abstract, theoretical issues (guidelines 2 and 7), are crucial to the success of a group. This, of course, does not come easy for us. As I said before, our masculine conditioning encourages the development of our left brains, so that we are much more comfortable debating the relative merits of abstract ideas than we are articulating our feelings and questioning why we might believe what we believe to be true. Because of what Keen calls our "warrior psyche," it is also difficult for us to allow different opinions about things we believe strongly. We tend to get competitive about our ideas and find it easy to ignore the emotional investment we and others have in them. Consequently, our ostensibly nonpersonal polemics can be very personal and very hurtful. Staying on the feeling level, rather than on the level of the ideas, helps us to stay out of an attack mode and allows us to be more present to the person speaking.

Finally, because of the overdependence of many men on the women in our lives, we might be tempted to focus our attention on them and share our complaints with each other, rather than take responsibility for our part in whatever dynamic it is that we don't like. It is important to keep our own thoughts, feelings, and behaviors in front of us and get help on those (guideline 8). It is also important to keep in front of us the ways in which sexism distorts our lives and the lives of women. This means that we will experience and express, in our groups, our anger, hurt, shame, and guilt, as well as the delight, joy, empowerment, and exhilaration that come as a result of our relationships with women. We need to focus, however, on taking the locus of control of our lives back into ourselves.

ACTIVITIES

A men's group is a wonderful context in which to do a number of things that are healing for us. I will mention a few here.

1. *Drumming and storytelling:* A men's group is an excellent context for doing the kind of drumming and storytelling I described in chapter 7. In listening and responding to stories, we unearth the wisdom of our historical communities, gain insight into our own personal stories, and uncover body data that become available for body wisdom.

2. *"Reimagining our own biographies":* Michael Meade has said that the traumas, shocks, mistakes, and losses in our lives are portals through which we might pass into deeper levels of spiritual maturity.[24] Men's groups can provide the attention necessary for a man to "reimagine his own biography" and with the "eye of initiation" see where initiatory breaks have taken place. Saint Augustine's *Confessions* is an excellent example of the way the reimagining of his own life story served as a means of recognizing grace in his life.

In *Your Mythic Journey,* Sam Keen and Anne Valley-Fox outline an intentional means of attending to and writing our own "personal mythology." By personal mythology, they mean autobiographical stories that contain our personal answers to questions like "Where did I come from; why is there evil in the world; with whom do I belong; what are my duties, my obligations; how close should I be to this person or that person; what is the purpose of my life, my vision; who are my enemies; and who are my allies?"[25]

In the context of good attention by others, they encourage people to tell the stories of their lives. In order to prime the pump, they suggest exercises that trigger memories of important aspects of our lives and help us attend to them. For example, to unearth the past, one might draw a map of one's home, make a list of the family's ten commandments, or make a list of the people or institutions that have made you the angriest or most resentful. To get underneath the present, one might make a list of ten words that describe you best and make a list of the secrets you have never told anyone. To get a sense of one's aspirations for the future, one might make a list of what one would do if one had a month to live. These are just a few of the suggestions they make to structure our thinking about our lives. A man could do these exercises in a private journal and then share what he thought might be appropriate in the men's group. He could, of course, begin to share some of his story with other friends as he felt comfortable doing so.

3. *Learning to listen:* A men's group is not only a good place to learn how to make friends; it is a good place to learn how to be a friend to others. Perhaps the most important skill we need to develop is the ability to listen to others. One of the things masculine conditioning breeds into us is what Warren Farrell calls "self-listening." In our competitive mode, we listen just long enough to switch off and begin to develop our rebuttal or to clarify our own unique contribution. Therefore, we don't remain very present to the person we are, ostensibly, listening to. We need to reeducate ourselves around listening. We need to "be quick to listen, [and] slow to speak" (James 1:19).

Part of what frees us to listen to others is having been listened to. The more good attention we get from others, the more we will have to give to others. Keen and Valley-Fox say that telling stories "will hollow you out so you can listen to the stories of others. . . . And that remains the best way we storytelling animals have found to overcome our loneliness, develop compassion, and create community."[26] Listening enlarges our compassion by correcting misinformation we have about others or by simply supplying information we have not had. As we see others and the world more clearly, we will begin to see those things that are hurtful to others. In other words, listening with empathy stimulates our sense of justice, which, in turn, can stimulate our analysis of those unjust "structures of consciousness" and lead us to oppose them decisively. Only this sort of process can create real community in the face of the barriers standing between us.

Robert Brizee, in a wonderful little book called *The Gift of Listening,* identifies some of the dynamics of good listening. He says that a listener's role is twofold—reflecting and waiting with caring.[27] Reflecting is sharing back what has been said. This is mirroring activity by which we say back to people what we have understood them to say. We might say something like, "It sounds like you . . . " This lets people know that they are really being listened to and helps them get even clearer about what they are trying to articulate. Waiting entails allowing people to find their own words to put with their experiences. Caring involves empathy or "a feeling along with the other person." In waiting with caring, we "rejoice with those who rejoice, [and] weep with those who weep" (Romans 12:15).

Good listening is a spiritual discipline. Brizee says that it may feel stilted and unnatural at first, and so it should. This sort of listening is very different than "the 'put-downs' and 'zingers' we hear so often" in the media and in our own lives. It is very different than the "self-listening" that has been encouraged in us men. He says that to "help another person blossom is to enter a strange new world"—the world of grace:

To listen to another person is to offer a gift.

To listen with caring to another person is to offer a gift of awareness.

To listen with acceptance to all facets of another person is to offer a gift of healing.

To listen with patience for new ways to see the past events of another person is to offer a gift of freedom.

To listen with reverence for new becomings emerging within another person is to offer a gift of grace.[28]

To listen to another is to serve as a kind of "midwife" to that which is being born in another person. That for which we wait is sacred; it may well be what Eckhart called the "eternal birth" of another human being.

4. *Learning to touch:* As I have said before, many men experience touch deprivation. We often attempt to get our needs for touch met by genital, sexual contact with women. This cannot meet those needs and puts a terrific burden on women. A men's group is a good place to begin to develop other ways of getting our need for touch met. This is not easy. Because touch has been associated with genital, sexual activity and because of our fear of homosexuality, touching men and being touched by them is a scary area for many

of us. I think that is one of the reasons we ritualize our touching; that is, we recognize places and times where physical contact with other men is acceptable. For example, we shake hands in social situations, and we hug or slap each other on the backside on athletic fields and courts. In other words, we have places and times in which we feel safe enough to touch men. Nothing else is going to happen. In a sense we have guidelines and rules that protect them and us from our fear that it might lead to something more involved and more intimate. The rituals ensure that our own homoerotic desires and those of other men don't get out of hand, so to speak.

I am grateful for these ways of touching other men; they are good and meet some of my needs for the empowering experience of touch. But they are not enough. We need to explore other ways of touching men and begin to be more honest about our desires for that.

In that exploration, it is important to remember that just as words can mean different things in different contexts and to different persons, so too can nonverbal acts. We cannot know for sure how someone else is going to interpret or experience a particular physical act. So, it is important to check out whatever we want to do with the other person.

We might begin with hugging. For some men, this is no big deal; for others, it is a very big deal. So, before you do it, you might ask the other man's permission by saying something like, "I'd like to hug you as we leave. Is that okay with you?" In a conversation with a friend or in a men's group, we might see that a man is feeling pain, sorrow, grief, or fear. Sometimes, reaching out to touch his shoulder, take his hand, or put our arm around him will empower him both to stay with the feeling and to express it. That is, physical closeness can help with the discharge of that reservoir of stored feeling many of us have. On the other hand, touching in this way may stimulate other fears and distract the man from what he is feeling. So, again, one might ask, "Would you like for me to put my hand on your shoulder?" or "Would it help if I sat a little closer to you?" or without touching him at all, "It's all right, stay right there with what you are feeling; I am right here."

Another avenue for touching might be massage. There are relatively noninvasive techniques of stroke massage that we can learn and practice with each other. For example, we might ask another man if he would like to exchange a ten-minute back rub. There is a beginning, a clear idea of what kind of touch is involved, and a clear ending. Experiences like this can help us learn that touching does not necessarily have to lead to erogenous stimulation. At some point we may want to be open to that, but we can always decide whether we want to act on that desire or not. These more intentional and formalized ways of touching help us learn to take responsibility for determining how we want to touch another man and be touched by him. They provide a safe "container" wherein we learn appropriate vulnerability, and they free us to be increasingly spontaneous about our desires and needs to touch and be touched.

I think learning how to exercise appropriate vulnerability in this area will go a long way toward helping men deal with our fear of gay men and facilitate our reconciliation with them.

RECONCILIATION WITH GAY MEN

An important means of overcoming our homophobia is developing spiritual friendships with our gay brothers. This is not easy. On their side of the oppression barricade, there is a great deal of anger, hurt, and suspicion directed at us—and for good reason. On our side, there is a great deal of fear, misinformation, and ignorance of what life is like for them. What is needed, then, is an intentional, deliberate commitment on our part to step across that barricade in respectful and honest ways. My own commitment came as a result of my relationships with an upstairs neighbor and a fellow church member. My upstairs neighbor was a gay man who was HIV positive and who developed AIDS. Though we would talk occasionally and had a cordial relationship, he never told me that he was gay or that he had AIDS. Over a period of months, I could hear him getting increasingly sick. His mother would come and stay all week with him, and his father (they were divorced) would come on the weekends.

One morning an ambulance driver knocked on my door by mistake. I told them they probably wanted the apartment upstairs. I stood in the backyard with his mother as they put my neighbor in the ambulance. His body was emaciated, and he was delirious. As I talked with his mother, she said several poignant things. First, she said, "Steve, it took nine months to bring him into this world, and it has taken nine months for me to help him go out." Words are not adequate to express my admiration for that mother.

But then she said something very disturbing: "You know the one thing I regret is that he is angry with God." I asked why. She said that he believed that God did not love him, because he was gay and he had contracted the virus. My mind flashed to the gay men I knew from my work in the American Academy of Religion who were writing wonderfully insightful books about homosexuality and Christianity.[29] They were working hard on their own internalized homophobia, recovering from the low self-esteem it caused them, and doing constructive theological work from their perspective. I thought,

Why couldn't my neighbor tell me he was gay? Why didn't I ask? Why did I not offer him some of the resources I knew about that might have helped him with his spiritual struggle?

I asked his mother if she wanted me to come to the emergency room with her. She said no, he would be all right. I returned to my apartment, thinking that I would not want my mother dealing with this alone. So I got dressed and drove to the hospital. When I got there, my neighbor had already died. Holding his hand, she looked at me and said her sweet son was gone. I walked over, hugged her, and we cried together.

Something changed for me that day. I saw how ridiculous it was that I could not talk to gay men—that there seemed to be something between us. Then I thought about a gay friend I knew at church. I liked him and admired him, and we shared many perspectives on spiritual things. But I realized I didn't call him for dinner or to spend time together, as I did with straight men friends. The reason, I guessed, was my homophobia, which, in this case, was my fear of gay men. A week later, I made a commitment to myself, in the presence of a group of close friends, that I wanted to take steps to work on my homophobia.

The first step toward this kind of commitment is to recognize and name the barriers between us and others. That is, we need to look at the ways in which gay men and, for that matter, lesbians and bisexual persons have been mistreated and discriminated against in society and our churches because of the ways they love others and themselves. We can, then, examine how our ways of thinking, feeling, and acting have contributed to their mistreatment. Theologically, these social, institutional, and personal forms of mistreatment can be identified as sinful, calling for penance, or a commitment to change.

The commitment might be something like, "I will not let homophobia get in my way of making friends with gay men, lesbians, and bisexual persons, and I will actively oppose the violence and hatred directed at them." Although this chapter focuses on male–male relationships, I include lesbians and bisexual persons of both sexes in the commitment because our homophobia serves as a barrier to friendships with all of these people. I will say more about women in chapter 9 and focus here on our relationships with gay men.

There are several steps we can take on the personal and social or institutional levels to act on this commitment. First, the point is not to go out and make a token gay friend. Rather, it is to not allow our fears and stereotypes to keep us from being friends with men with whom we would probably be friends if they weren't gay. Many of us, whether we are aware of it or not, know gay men already. If you don't know an open, or "out," gay man, join an organization like Parents and Friends of Lesbians and Gays (PFLAG) or a denominational organization that is working on gay and lesbian issues. Go to meetings and start talking to gay persons there. If you express an openness to gay persons, you will probably soon "find" more than a few in the circles in which you usually move. If you know an open, or "out," gay man that you would like to get to know better, treat him as you would treat any other potential friend: move closer to him, talk, ask him to get together, share mutual interests, and explore trust levels. In the process, you will see more and more about what the world is like for him.

Some of what you learn will be painful and enraging. Often, gay men, or lesbians or bisexual persons, have spent a significant part of their lives hiding their sexual orientation and relationships from others. If they decide to come out, the result can be and often is isolation from those most important to them—their families, churches, and friends. They have been labeled immoral sinners by religious institutions, sick or sad by too many psychologists, criminals by the legal system, and in some cases, they have been disowned by their parents. Until recently, there has been a virtual silence in the media, schools, and professional organizations about gay persons and almost no positive images about the ways they love others and themselves.

This will make you angry. Whereas before, you may not have been able to tolerate the thought of a gay person and the sexual acts you might imagine him to engage in, now you will begin to be indignant about the disrespect and mistreatment your friend has to face daily in almost every area of his life.

Some of what you learn will be inspiring. I have found that many gay men, in coming out of the closet and "ruining their reputation" as masculine men, have made more progress than most straight men in the tasks I have identified with mature masculinity. In other words, by rejecting what Robert Moore has called immature masculinity, many gay men have done much to reconcile themselves with their bodies, with other men, and with women. That is not to say that there is no body hatred, homophobia, and sexism in gay men; there is, and they must continue to work on those distortions of their humanity. It is to say that we straight men can learn much about being mature men from our gay brothers.

The second part of the commitment is to actively oppose the hatred and violence directed at gay persons. Here it will be important to work collectively on what is affecting the lives of gay men, lesbians, and bisexual persons—under their leadership. You might start on the local congregational or community level by joining an organization that is working to educate people about homophobia and heterosexism and to end discrimination against gay persons. This will not be easy. There are very good reasons why we have ignored, been suspicious of, or even hated gay persons in the past. A lot of social censure and violence has been directed at us if we haven't acted in those ways. When we start acting against those patterns of behavior and make friends with gay persons, we will experience a lot of old fear and will probably be targeted for social censure and maybe even violence. We will need all the spiritual friends we can get—men, women, gay and heterosexual—in order to carry on and see the difficulties as blessings rather than curses.

CONCLUSION

We need a repatterning of our relationships with men; we need to experience our relationships with them as not disempowering, but as empowering. To do that, we need to create spaces where we can take a moratorium on the competition and shaming that too often characterize our relationships with men. In doing so, we will begin to experience a lot less fear in our lives and bodies and a lot more grace.

In addition, we need to know that the quality of our relationship with women is directly proportional to the quality of our relationship with men.[30] A sobering thought, but true.

As we turn to look at our relationships with women, I recount the observations of a man on a recent retreat. He is going through his third divorce and has made a commitment to himself. He has decided that before he gets involved with another woman in a significant-other relationship, he is going to make one good, male friend. Therefore, he has decided not to return to the local Parents Without Partners or Single Again groups, because he finds that many of the men there are looking for romantic partners rather than male or female friends. It is just not a good place to find a potential male spiritual friend. A wise man.

And I know that the spirit of God is the brother of my own,
And that all the men ever born are also my brothers. . . .

WALT WHITMAN

Chapter Nine

On Loving Our Sisters

Men and women are infinitely ingenious in their ability to find ways of being unhappy together.

LAWRENCE KUBIE

Today we begin again; I look at you and see someone who is trying—as best they can to live, to love and be loved. . . . Today I see you . . . maybe for the first time. I know that when you hurt me it's because you're hurting. Today I will try to love you. This love will not be easy to give or receive.[1]

LISA ALLRED

DEVELOPING close relationships with women means that we have to begin to move across the barriers between us caused by sexism. It means also that we invite our sisters over the barriers caused by the mistreatment of us as men.

We have been socialized and conditioned to devalue and mistreat women, as well as to repress important parts of ourselves that are labeled feminine. This repression leads us to feel and believe that we must join to a woman in order to be whole and complete. So, we have been conditioned both to be radically dependent on women and to devalue and resent them. Women to whom we try to relate, particularly in primary relationships, have been socialized and conditioned to devalue parts of themselves labeled masculine and look to us for their completion. We end up underfunctioning in the private, relational parts of our lives, while they often overfunction. In the public sphere, we often overfunction, and they tend to underfunction. Too often, we end up resenting our partner's "private" overfunctioning and "public" underfunctioning, and she resents our "private" underfunctioning and "public" overfunctioning. While this "complementarity" is supposed to lead to harmony and fulfillment, it often leads to unhappiness. As Lawrence Kubie has said, "Men and women are infinitely ingenious in their ability to find ways of being unhappy together."[2]

We often find ourselves either in a resigned, silent détente or in aggressive attempts to overcome the incompatibility produced by the "complementarity"—a complementarity that promised compatibility but often fails to deliver it.[3]

As for friendships with women who are not our primary partners, well, as Harry (Billy Crystal) said in *When Harry Met Sally:* "Men and women cannot be friends; the sex thing always gets in the way." It is not just the sex thing that gets in the way of our developing friendships with women; there is a lot standing in the way. But because we tend to funnel our desire for intimacy through genital sexuality, the sex thing is usually somewhere in the middle of the difficulty. When the passion wanes in our primary relationships, as it is wont to do with the advent of mutual resentment, it is tempting to look for that promising other half in someone else.[4] That search is often sexualized and hooks the fears of abandonment in our primary partner, if she knows about it. Her fear hooks our own fear of abandonment, and we either jump ship into another incompatible, complementary relationship or stay in the one we are in and begin to view other women, particularly if we are attracted to them, as dangerous. We feel like we can't afford to get too close to them, because the closeness might become sexual and wreck our primary relationship. If a woman is married or partnered, we also fear what her partner would feel, think, or do if we got close to perhaps his only supply of emotional, physical, and sexual intimacy.

Needless to say, these dynamics are not very conducive to our developing spiritual friendships with women. My point here is not that dependence on women, as with other men, is bad or unhealthy; no, we need our sisters in order to be most fully whom God intends us to be. Rather, we need to find our way toward healthy interdependence with them—an interdependence that empowers both us and them.

We need deep, mutual friendships with women. We have been significantly cut off from the justice, strength, intelligence, and compassionate connection of half the human race; no wonder many of us have a sense of personal powerlessness. And women need deep, mutual friendships with us. They need us as allies in the struggle to stop what is hurting them, and we need them as allies to stop what is hurting us. We both need reconciliation.

We need and they need for us not to move away from them, but from our distorted views of them. We need to stop projecting our anxieties about our own finitude, mortality, and sexuality onto them. We need to recover from the fear produced by our perception of their smothering power. We need to deal with our anger at the ways in which we have been objectified as "success" or relational objects by women. We must stop abdicating responsibility for our emotional and relational lives to them and begin to be honest with them about what we want.

Remember Maggie Scarf's image of women chasing men emotionally, with men running just fast enough not to be caught, but not fast enough to get away. What we need to do is stop, turn around, and begin to deal with real women, not those images of women informed by our old wounds and fears. We need to begin to understand and say to them how we feel, what we want, and what we don't want. We need to define ourselves clearly and stay in contact with them. This will make us anxious, and it will, at times, make the women we relate to anxious, but it is the only way to find our way out of the tangles so many of us have wandered into. To do that will take all the mature justice, strength, intelligence, and compassion we can muster.

But how? What can we do? How can we develop spiritual friendships with women? We need some clear ideas and practices that will contribute to our emergence from unhealthy enmeshment in primary relationships and lead to an increased capacity for intimacy with all women, rather than the attraction–avoidance patterns produced by these symbiotic dynamics.

I suggest at least three commitments we can make to help us toward the goal of reconciliation and friendship with women:

1. "I will stop underfunctioning in certain physical, emotional, and relational areas of my life and stop asking women to do more than their share."
2. "I will stop overfunctioning in the physical, economic, and sexual areas of my life and resist those sexist dynamics that exclude women from doing their share."
3. "I will develop one spiritual friendship with a woman in the next year."

As in chapter 8, I am talking primarily about friendships with women most like us. As I have said before, it is difficult to learn to love even people most like us, and we may need to start there before we can effectively move out to persons unlike us in significant ways. So, most of what I say will apply principally to our relationships with those women, though I will suggest ways of connecting with women less like us.

STOP UNDERFUNCTIONING:
MUTUALITY IN THE PRIVATE SPHERE

By a commitment to stop underfunctioning in certain physical, emotional, and relational areas of our lives, I mean that we need to stop asking women to carry the responsibility for those areas and learn to do them for ourselves.

As I said in chapter 2, many of us, because of our sense of disability in these areas, look for the woman or women in our lives to plan and cook meals for us, clean our homes, pick out our clothes, and raise our children. We ask her also to be our emotional filter; she is to help us interpret to ourselves and to other people what we are feeling. Often, then, she becomes the relational switchboard; she mediates many of our relationships both inside and outside the family.

As long as we are asking women to do these things for us, we will not be able to love them for who they are; we will need them too much to be and to do what we are convinced we need them to be and do. If we are to be present to them and to see them more clearly, we will need to learn to take responsibility for these aspects of our lives.

In chapters 7 and 8, I discussed a number of things we can do to reclaim that responsibility for our own bodies and for our relationships. My point there was that we need to be doing these things for ourselves; my point here is that those things will also greatly improve our relationships with women. I said at the end of chapter 8 that the quality of our relationships with women is directly proportional to the quality of our relationships with men. It is. I would add that the quality of our relationships with women is also directly proportional to the quality of our relationships with our own bodies and with our children. Let me add a few comments to what I have said about these areas already.

Growing up at my house meant that the children helped with things around the house. There were two different kinds of things to do—outside things and inside things. My father supervised the outside things, and my mother supervised the inside things. Outside, I cut grass, pruned bushes, carried wood, raked leaves, and shoveled snow. Inside, I helped in the kitchen, made beds, dusted, vacuumed, and folded clothes.

I am grateful that my mother expected me to do these inside things. I never saw it as particularly women's work or something that I should not do. It was just part of the things that needed to be done around the house. During my marriage and after my divorce, I realized how different it is to help with the inside things and to shoulder responsibility for them. When I began not only to cook food, but to plan meals and do the shopping, I realized how much energy and time it takes to eat well. My respect for what I saw my mother do, while she worked a full-time outside job, grew significantly.

It also began to dawn on me that one needs a plan to deal with dust, dirt, and clutter. My first semester in college, my roommate and I went for three months without washing the sink in our dorm room. It wasn't a conscious decision; it was just that neither of us thought to do it. Around Christmas, one day I decided to take some bathroom cleanser and a brush to it, as I had done every other week at home. I was amazed at the transformation! It was beautiful; it also made me feel a lot better about living in the room and about myself. I had learned in school to focus on and take pride in my academic accomplishments, but I had not learned to focus on and take pride in my home. I am still learning about that.

Many of us men, in fact, feel like aliens in our homes, whether we are married (or have partners) or not. It is just not a place where we have focused a lot of our attention. If we are married or partnered, we often see the house or apartment as the sphere of our female partner. As it was with my home growing up, that is the area of a woman's responsibility and expertise. Consequently, we often feel that we have very little or no private space of our own. Unfortunately, we too often seek that private space at work. If we are unmarried or without a partner, we, as I did in college, still have a hard time focusing on our living space as an important area for our attention and care. Whether we are living with someone or not, we need to give attention to our homes—cleaning them, decorating them, and taking pride in them. If we are married or have a partner, we may need to begin by claiming some place in our homes for which we will take primary responsibility.

As we take more responsibility for both feeling and expressing our own emotions, there are several things we can do. As we pay attention to body data and develop body knowledge and body wisdom, we can begin to share what we learn with others. In order to wean ourselves from an overdependence on women in the emotional area of our lives, we might begin to share that with at least one other man. It is important that we have other places and relationships in which we are developing emotional intimacy. The man I mentioned at the end of chapter 8 is an example of someone who, through much pain and conflict, learned that to be healthy and to have any hope for a healthy relationship with a woman, he needed to have at least one good, male friend. He was right.

We might also keep a journal in which we reflect on our lives—our joys, our pain, our successes and failures, our hopes and our regrets. This kind of exercise can go a long way toward helping us better put words with our feelings. Once we gain facility in doing that, we can decide whether and with whom we want to share those feelings. It might be in a men's group; it might be with a male friend; it might be with a female friend; it might be with our wife or partner; it might be with God; or it might be with no one. We can decide. We have access to information that may have been unavailable to us before. We can also be more present to our friends as they sort out their feelings and as they communicate to us what they need to know from us. This is a liberating ability to develop—one that contributes to the building and maintenance of human communities that empower everyone who is a part of them.

Becoming responsible for our own emotional life is also very scary. For those who grew up with religious fundamentalism, intellectual ambiguity and freedom can be frightening. People accustomed to someone else telling them what they should believe and that no doubts or questions should be entertained develop a level of certitude that provides security and reduces anxiety. A great price is paid for this kind of intellectual captivity, but there are these gains.

I think many men are in the same boat emotionally. Many of us have become accustomed to having someone else tell us how we are supposed to feel. When we begin to feel for ourselves, some scary things start to happen. There is often a great deal of ambiguity, because many of our feelings have at least one other feeling attached to them. As I said earlier, shame at feeling at all is attached to most of our feelings. So, when we begin feeling, we will need to learn how to deal with the feelings of shame that come up. Anger, too, has been attached to some of our feelings—including anger at not being allowed to feel them and to express them. Also, fear emerges: is this feeling right; is it dangerous; will it isolate me if I express it; will people still care about me?

For our own sake and for the sake of the women in our lives, we must develop, to paraphrase Paul Tillich, "the courage to feel." That courage and the courage to express those feelings will come, in part, through spiritual friendships, which draw us into deeper levels of trust and self-disclosure. As God's love draws us into mutual relations, our fear will be dispelled by love.

As that happens, we will want to maintain those relationships ourselves. We will begin to pay more attention to answering personal correspondence, keeping up with birthdays, sending notes of appreciation or celebration, buying gifts, and planning time to see those we care about. These are not things that many of us men have thought a whole lot about. Since the woman or women in our lives have usually done these things for us, we may have to take slow, deliberate steps to begin assuming responsibility for this part of our lives. We might buy various kinds of cards and have them on hand when an occasion arises for which we want to express our care for a friend or family member. We might write the birthdays of friends and family on whatever calendar occupies our attention. We might think about each of our relationships and what kind of time we want to spend with that person. We could then talk to that person about our desires and develop a plan to make the kind of time to see each other that seems appropriate.

As we do these kinds of things, we will feel a lot less isolated, will take more pride in ourselves, and will be more present to the women in our lives.

STOP OVERFUNCTIONING: MUTUALITY IN THE PUBLIC SPHERE

We cannot have mutual (*philia*) relationships with women as long as women are systematically mistreated in our society and in our churches. Mutuality requires that the two persons relating do so on an equal or nearly equal basis. That is, a mutual relationship requires two persons who are fully subjects:

Men	Women
Subject ⟶	Object
*Object ⟵	Subject

By being fully a subject, I mean that a person is able to make her or his own decisions and act on the basis of them. Because women are mistreated as women (sexism), their self-determination is undermined. When their self-determination is undermined, their humanity is distorted. Since we are relational creatures, our own human integrity and well-being are inextricably linked to those of women. So, when their humanity is distorted, our humanity is distorted. In terms I have used before, one of the primary desires of human beings is to know others and be known by others. If women's self-determination, or subjectivity (see the last line of the diagram), is systematically undermined by sexist attitudes and institutional dynamics, they cannot know themselves, others, or us in the ways we want and need to be known.

Two forms of the mistreatment that women have historically experienced are economic disadvantage and a lack of public voice in our institutions—political, religious, and educational. This sexist mistreatment distorts their first natures, or their capacities for justice, strength, intelligence, and compassionate connection. It also, therefore, adversely affects their ability to relate to each other and to us in healthy ways. Because of their relative lack of economic power and public voice, women have often resorted to indirect means of getting what they want and need (e.g., passive aggression and manipulation). That does not feel very good to us, and we need to confront it in our women friends and challenge them to look at and change these compensatory patterns of behavior.

But we also need to realize that what often leads to these infuriating patterns in women are the sexist patterns in us and in our institutions that block their direct access to public power and influence. I have agreed with Luther that men's exclusive responsibility to care for the public political and economic order is onerous and distorts our humanity as men. It is a manifestation, or consequence, of sin. We need to name that, examine it carefully, and resist it. But our anger and resistance should not be directed at women; to participate in the maintenance of unjust institutional structures and then to complain about the effects those structures have on us is a manifestation of our own mystification, or intellectual naïveté. Rather, we must direct the power of our righteous indignation at those personal and institutional attitudes and practices that give us too much public responsibility and women too little.[5]

What most of our sisters are asking from us is not to grant them some unfair privilege, but to stand with them against those "principalities and powers" that are unjust to them and wounding of us. We cannot be friends with women unless we work with them, under their leadership, to resist that which distorts their humanity.

Part of what it means, then, to stop overfunctioning in the public sphere is to renounce the privilege that we as men have been granted by sexist feelings, thoughts, and behaviors. We have and continue to benefit in significant ways from the mistreatment of women. Because we are like most of the people in positions of power, we get hired more readily, are better prepared to understand the systems in which we work, and are more confident that they can work for us. All other things being equal, we still make more money than a woman for equivalent work. We can walk the streets with less fear. We see images of ourselves exercising public power and influence reflected in what we read in school, hear in church, and view in the media.

Renouncing privileges we have as a result of sexism does not mean that we, out of a masochistic sense of guilt, beat up on ourselves and other men and abdicate our responsibilities in public institutions. Rather, it means that we use whatever expertise and power we have in those institutions to oppose the unfair discrimination against women in hiring and promotion practices, wage and salary distribution, and decision making. What we need is to help make the power dynamics of our institutions more fair, open, and inclusive of the concerns of others—in this case women. A place to start is to listen to women talk about what life is like for them in spaces where they feel safe enough to be honest. That might be done by asking your mother, sister, spouse, daughter, or female friends what they have wanted in their lives and what stood in their way. It might be done by reading women's literature (poetry, fiction, and nonfiction), as well as feminist analyses of the situation of women. Another possibility is to join a local, regional, or national organization led by women and working on issues affecting them.

By way of illustration, let me take two issues—men's violence against women and discrimination in the workplace—and discuss some of the things we men can do as women's allies.

Ellen Goodman, in a recent article, observed, "But today, it seems the most deeply felt constriction on [the] daily life [of women] may be fear. Where women go, what we do, and how comfortable we feel doing it are often limited more by a sense of danger than by legal discrimination."[6] The women in a coed class recently confirmed Goodman's suspicion; they talked for several meetings about what it feels like to have to be constantly aware and on guard when they are alone, or even in groups. It causes them to spend time planning strategies to assure their safety. Mostly middle-sector white women, they acknowledged that they experience emotional and verbal violence from other women but that the threat of physical violence from men places the greatest restriction on their lives and movements.

Most of the men in the class had no idea how great the fear of violence was for women and how it affected their lives. They were also surprised that some of the women saw men as irreformably violent. Many of the men had never thought of themselves as violent or that women had anything to fear from them. One of the men said that he had never noticed that men were violent toward women, and we talked about why that was. As we talked, we began to uncover signs of potential violence in men toward women—derogatory language for women, repressed anger and resentment about the dating game, disrespectful jokes, and violent language for sexual acts (e.g., banging, screwing, nailing). We then talked about how being physically abusive to a woman in public was not "cool" in many of their peer groups; however, what happened behind closed doors might be another story.

Some of the men got angry when they realized that they were implicated in other men's violence toward women. I asked if they felt, then, that they had any responsibility in helping to stop it. Since some of the stereotypes about women and disrespectful treatment of them are conditioned in us by other men, they agreed that they did. We then explored what they might do to contribute to changing that conditioning. Among the suggestions were getting involved in the campus rape-prevention program, talking with men about their attitudes and behavior toward women, recognizing and working through our own anger and resentment toward women, dealing with the violence we have experienced at the hands of other men, giving time and money to shelters for battered women, and working with male offenders. There are a host of things that need to be done and that we, as men, can do.[7]

With respect to discrimination against women in the workplace, I will focus on the church. In chapter 3, I surveyed some typical reactions—defensive denial and guilty silence—by men to protests about the mistreatment of women in Christian churches. I do not want to suggest with that analysis that no progress is being made or that no men have been effective allies of women in the struggle against their exclusion from institutional influence. There has been, and there are.[8] The fact remains, though, that we, as well as many women, have been reluctant to welcome women into positions of leadership in our churches. Though we are graduating increasing numbers of women from our seminaries, it is still difficult in many places for them to find positions as senior ministers or at the top levels of our denominational organizations.

I see several reasons for men's reluctance to welcome women into leadership positions in the church. In many of our churches, even churches with congregational polity, there is a tendency to buy into notions of leadership and authority as they are understood in an objectified paradigm. That is, there is often an invisible pyramid of authority with the senior minister at the top and other staff members and laypeople arrayed below. No matter how much we talk about and prepare people for lay ministry, many of us don't feel "ministered to" without a visit by the senior minister. We allow that person to affect us; that is, we open ourselves and are vulnerable to that person and, for too many of us, to that person alone. But being vulnerable is a frightening prospect for most of us, so we often want to have some control over that person. Many of us would rather open ourselves to a senior minister whose salary and job description we have some control over than to the brother or sister next to us in the pew.

Given these dynamics and fears, why have many churches had difficulty welcoming and embracing female ministers? If Dinnerstein is right about our fear of the perceived omnipotence and omniscience of the mother and our need for a male counterbalance to the perceived power of women, we need a figure other than a woman at the top of the ecclesiastical-power pyramid. Since emotional self-disclosure and intimacy are often associated for us with genital sexuality, it would also be helpful if that person did not hook our sex-ual feelings and thereby constitute a threat to our relationships with our wives or partners. Finally, it would be preferable if that figure did not need to disclose too much about herself or himself and have us attend to it. In other words, it seems to make our lives a lot more comfortable, less anxious, and less complicated if the minister is male.

I don't think it is surprising or accidental that, even in denominations that have recognized the inclusion of women in leadership as a justice issue, we do not observe a great deal of movement. What would it take, then, for us to overcome those dynamics in ourselves and in our institutions that block women from direct access to public power and influence in our churches? First, by taking back responsibility for our physical, emotional, and relational lives, we dismantle our perception of women's power over us and dissipate our fear of them. Second, by expanding our circle of intimate relationships and spreading out our desires and needs for emotional and physical close-ness, we degenitalize intimacy and will be less likely to sexualize a relation-ship with a female pastor. Third, this widening circle of spiritual friendships will also reduce our need for a nonmutual relationship with our ministers. We will get our pastoral needs met by any number of our brothers and sisters in the "unglorified body of Christ" and will even have some attention to allow our ministers to be self-disclosing and vulnerable to us.

All these things will enable us joyously to welcome our sisters as cher-ished leaders and partners in the ministry of reconciliation. As we do that, we will encounter the resistance of some, or even many, of our brothers and sis-ters.[9] With them, we will need to "speak the truth in love."

We will not be able to develop spiritual friendships with women until, when we see them at work, we do not dread them but delight in their justice, power, intelligence, and compassionate connection.

Spiritual Friendships with Women

By taking responsibility for underdeveloped aspects of our own lives and by re-sisting those things that threaten to disable women in aspects of theirs, we are in a much better position to develop mutual, spiritual friendships with women. As we pursue those friendships, we might, again, follow Aelred's advice con-cerning the selection, testing, and commitment to a potential female friend.

As we choose a female friend, we need to pay attention to the same quali-ties we look for in a male friend—someone who is not perpetually angry, sus-picious, and overly talkative, someone who does not slander others, reveal confidences, and persist in hurting people we love. In addition, someone who is looking for a significant-other relationship with a man is not a good candidate—at least not if she is aiming that search at us.

Another thing to look for is the quality of her relationships with other women. Does she value other women; does she enjoy being in their company; do other women trust her; does she care deeply for them and exhibit loyalty to them? These are all indicators of how she feels about herself and how grounded she is in mutual relationships outside of a significant-other relationship. The potential for the quality of her relationship with you is proportional to the quality of her relationships with other women.

You might also look at whether she has intimate relationships with other men. Does she like men; has she developed friendships with other men; can she see men's first natures; does she appreciate the positive aspects of men's second natures; does she see clearly and name the negative aspects? It is important that your potential friend not be in denial about men's sexist patterns, but also be able to see and appreciate our goodness. A woman who cannot see or doesn't want to see how she has been mistreated as a woman will be less able to be honest with you about your patterns of thinking, feeling, and behaving that are hurtful to her. And we need that honesty and that challenge, if they are to trust us and be vulnerable to us. Without it, intimacy, at deep levels, will be impossible. A woman who cannot or does not want to see men's goodness—both potential and actual—will be tempted to pedestalize you as the one or one of the very few good men in the world. This, too, kills the possibility of deep intimacy. She may be using you to avoid dealing honestly and vulnerably with other men. And you might be tempted to be less than honest with her about the parts of you that you know she will not like. You might also distance yourself from other men in order to maintain her approval. This is death to a spiritual friendship.

During the period in which you are getting to know your female friend, it is important to establish levels of appropriate vulnerability. Since many of us have a tendency with women to be compulsively self-disclosing or not disclosing enough, we need to find our way to a middle ground. As we do that, we will need to look for several things. Does she keep confidential those things you ask her to? Does she challenge you when you have done or said hurtful things? Is she willing to forgive you when you change? Is she relating to you or to a projection of what she thinks she needs in a relationship with a man? As our trust level grows, we will be better able to determine what we want to share with our friend, what we do not, and why.

It might be helpful here to say something about sexuality. With James Nelson, I think it is important for us to think of our sexuality as our fully embodied way of being in the world as men and women.[10] Therefore, sexuality is a part of every relationship we have—with men and women. As I said in the last chapter, it is important to talk about what level of physical contact is appropriate for you and for your friend. In what ways does it feel right, good, and empowering to touch and be touched by your friend? What do particular expressions of touch mean to you? What do they mean to your friend? Physical acts, like words, are context-specific and can mean somewhat different things to different people, depending on our histories and the context within which the acts take place. In order to say what we mean to our friend and mean what we say, we need to talk about it.[11] Whatever you decide to do, it should contribute to your level of trust and draw you closer to your friend.

When we are dealing with a female friend, we need to pay careful attention to this. As I have said, many of us men have been conditioned to associate intimacy with genital sexuality. As we develop intimacy with a female friend, our tendency, then, might be to move toward genital sexual expression, before that level of vulnerability is appropriate for us or for her, if ever. The difficulty is that genital sexual expression tends to elicit many deeply seated yearnings for touch and communion, as well as fears of abandonment—ours and those of our female friends. Consequently, genital sexual expression requires clear, mutual understanding of its meaning for both people and a strong commitment on the part of both to care for the relationship and the things that come up as a result of that level of intimacy.

Genital sexual expression can also enmesh us both in the mutually alienating, complementary gender dance I described in chapter 2. We men might be tempted to substitute physical intimacy for emotional and intellectual intimacy and neglect certain aspects of our own lives and our relationships with others. As we do that, we will find it difficult to see our female friend very clearly, apart from what we might need from her. Our female friends might find themselves making us the object of their compulsive relational fantasies about a future mate. They might, then, neglect certain aspects of their own lives, such as the public part of their vocation and their relationships with others. They would then find it difficult to see us very clearly apart from what they might need from us.

Considering these dynamics, it might be best to consider a moratorium on genital sexual expression with a female friend, at least in the probationary stage of the relationship and perhaps permanently.[12] Whatever you decide, it is important to acknowledge these concerns and discuss them with your female friends. Denial of sexual attraction and desire is also not conducive to a spiritual friendship.

As our trust level grows, we might make a conscious decision to commit ourselves to an ongoing friendship with her. It is a commitment to care for the relationship in whatever ways are mutually agreed upon. Among other things, the commitment to friendship means that we commit ourselves to focus on the first nature of our female friend, as well as to be aware of aspects of her second nature that might be a distortion of her first nature.

For example, we will have occasion to admire, learn from, and comment to her on such things as her refusal to accept her own mistreatment, that of her sisters, and of others; her decisive action on her own and others' behalf; her flexible and incisive thinking about the world; the quality of her relationships with aspects of herself, others, God, and the earth; and the deep compassion that draws her into those relationships and issues from them.

We will also have the occasion to challenge her, with kindness and gentleness, when she mistreats herself or others, including us; accepts what she need not accept and can and should do something about; undervalues her own intelligence and neglects its full development; and becomes enmeshed in a relationship in such a way that she can no longer see the other person or herself clearly.

In other words, with a spiritual female friend, we commit ourselves to "speak the truth in love" and to listen to her as she does the same for us. I have found that, because they do not share masculine socialization and conditioning, at least to the degree that we do, female friends can be of great help to us in pointing out where certain patterns of thinking, feeling, and behaving are distorting our characters. For example, they might raise questions about the ways in which our unconscious fear of failure feeds our work compulsiveness or why we engage in such violent and competitive dynamics with other men.

MENTOR RELATIONSHIPS

In chapter 8, I echoed Robert Moore's observation that we men need both to be admired by and to admire older and younger men. I believe that we also need to admire and be admired by older and younger women.

Because the admiration of our mothers is sometimes fraught with conditions and expectations, it is helpful to receive admiration from other older women. We need to be seen clearly by older women who value our strengths and can teach us things others cannot.

During a time when my own relationship with my mother was strained, I was a teaching fellow for a divinity school course. One of the students in the class was a woman who had returned to school later in life and had children just a few years younger than I. Though full of brilliant right-brain insights, she was struggling to read and write in the critical (left-brain) ways demanded by the academic study of theology; she appreciated my help with that. After the course ended, she invited me to lunch, and we talked about her life and mine. When I mentioned that my mother was having difficulty with some of the choices I was making, she looked me straight in the eye and said, "Steve, I wish your mother was able to appreciate what a fine young man you are." I'll never forget that lunch or that moment. She blessed me in ways that, at the time, my mother could not. I had the sense that she saw at least parts of my life clearly and that she liked what she saw. I am still not entirely certain why this brief exchange was so important to me. What is clear is that I needed the admiration she offered and that, perhaps, she was one of the few people who could have given it to me.

There have been other older women who have admired me and shaped me in important ways. One of those is an academic adviser, Margaret Miles. Watching her work, I learned that academic work does not have to be alienated work; we can and do take our own concerns and passions to our reading, writing, and teaching. I learned, too, that students can and should be treated with respect and that we are most positively and significantly formed by "attraction." That is, our lives are shaped by those things and people that delight us. Coercion and intimidation in the educational process not only violate the dignity of the student and teacher, but also do not ultimately teach us very much of what we want to know. She learned some of these things from Saint Augustine, one of her mentors; I am grateful that she passed them on to me. These kinds of mentor relationships with older women can aid us in our reconciliation with our mothers—a reconciliation that we and our mothers need. It is also a reconciliation the world and the earth need.

Insofar as we have unconsciously projected onto our mothers a sense of their omnipotence and moral superiority, and our finitude, sexuality, and mortality, we need to stop. We also need to refuse to internalize her projections onto us. Many of us have had certain expectations or conditions attached to our mother's affirmation of us. We have felt that unless we fulfilled those expectations, or at least appeared to, we would be excommunicated from her and, since our mothers were usually the emotional hub, from our families. For a man who is otherwise pretty isolated, that is a terrifying prospect. In addition, our mother might have communicated to us that her happiness and perhaps even her life depended on our fulfilling whatever role she needed us to play for her. There comes a time when, for our sake and hers, we must detach from those expectations and, empowered by our relationships with others, deal with the guilt, shame, and fear of abandonment that will inevitably come up. Both of these movements—ceasing to project unreal expectations onto her and ceasing to accept them from her—are part of what it means to grow into manhood and into a mutually empowering relationship with our mothers.

As with our fathers, we cannot redo our childhood relationship with our mothers. Many of us were loved and valued deeply by our mothers; for that we remain forever grateful. Many of us have also been hurt by some of the things she did or did not do, because of her coping mechanisms and the decisions she made. The wounds are real and must be dealt with. But they are ours to deal with, and we must take responsibility to focus on our own healing. Our mothers are not now the same persons with whom we had a relationship when we were hurt. They are limited in their ability to help us in our present healing; we will need to look to others for this. I think that is why spiritual friendships with older women are important to us.

The healing makes it possible for us to see the human being who is our mother more clearly and to develop an adult relationship—possibly even a spiritual friendship—with her. As we reclaim our own bodies, embrace our mortality, and develop other relationships in which we receive the human attention we need, we can begin to see our mothers more clearly. It is helpful to get to know our mother's history: what kind of family did she grow up in; what kind of expectations shaped her life; in what ways was she cherished and nurtured; what were her strengths; what were her virtues; what were her visions and dreams; how was she touched by sexist disrespect and mistreatment; how did that block the development of the full range of her sense of justice, power, intelligence, and compassionate connection; how did she compensate for that; how did she overcome some of those limitations; what is her legacy to us?

Our differentiation from and reconciliation with our mothers is crucial for healthy relationships with other women. I think that a mutually reinforcing relationship exists between them. As our relationships with our mothers improve, our relationships with other women improve; we can begin to stop projecting our anger, shame, or guilt onto other women and can begin to see them more clearly for who they are here and now. As we gain experience in successfully developing honest relationships with other women, we gain confidence in doing the same with our mothers.

As we come to see our mothers as finite, mortal human beings like the rest of us, we can more deeply appreciate their often considerable gifts to us. And we can experience a new openness to imagining God with female images, supplementing, for example, our images of God as father with the images of God as mother. Thinking of ourselves and all of creation "as bodied forth from the divine being," using imagery such as gestation, giving birth, and lactation, can be powerfully transforming for us. We have a more profound sense of the whole of creation as being "dependent on and cared for by the divine life."[13] Sallie McFague has pointed out that such imagery, which has precedents in the Hebraic-Christian tradition, is the most powerful imagery available for expressing "the interdependence and interrelatedness of all life with its ground"; that is, that "we live and move and have our being in God."[14] That sense of the interdependence of all things, conjured by such images of God as mother, is, she rightly argues, one that we need desperately in a world threatened by nuclear and environmental destruction.

My observation here is that our ability and willingness to embrace that imagery and the interdependence it discloses to us is crucial to the survival and flourishing of the human species and, indeed, of all God's creation. And that ability and willingness requires our reconciliation with our mothers. It is a reconciliation that calls forth our maturity as men.

Our relationships with younger women—particularly our daughters— are also important. They need our interest, attention, care, and admiration. Victoria Secunda has written about the ways in which a daughter's relationship with her father shapes her and her patterns of relationships with men.[15] We can learn much from her analysis of those patterns about what we can do, as fathers, to contribute to our daughters' growth and the maturation of their capacities for justice, powerfulness, intelligence, and compassionate connection.

Secunda says that many daughters are hurt by their fathers' sins of omission rather than commission. In other words, they are most hurt by our absence, or unavailability. Perhaps the most important thing our daughters need from us is our emotional, physical, and intellectual presence. I asked a female friend, whose life was profoundly affected by her reflection on Secunda's insights, how she would have liked to have been treated by her father and what advice she would offer fathers. She wrote:

1. Hug your daughter; don't be afraid to touch her.
2. Do things just with your daughter; teach her to mow the grass, shoot basketball, fish, build birdhouses, plant seeds, use tools, tend a garden.
3. Show interest in and encourage her academic and physical development.
4. Treat her with the same respect as a son; do not protect her in ways you would not protect your son.

My thought about her suggestions is that what she and other daughters have needed from their fathers is their presence, active connection, and respect.

I would add that part of that respect is to share with your daughter some of the places where you might be unsure, confused, weak, or afraid. This goes a long way toward helping daughters see that their fathers, too, are mortal, finite, and vulnerable. They need to see that, and we need for them to see it—particularly in our relationship with them. Secunda urges a father (as well as mothers) to, at some point, have the courage to say to his daughter, "Here is where I failed you. I am not the same person today I was when you were born and were growing up. I am ready to accept my part in your emotional confusion. Can we talk about it?" Starting such a conversation is one of the greatest gifts a father can give to his daughter (or son).[16]

These are just a few things my friend thought of immediately. It is not an exhaustive list, but I hope her suggestions serve to prime the pump for your own thinking about your relationship with your daughter, or with other younger women who need older men who are not their fathers in their lives.[17]

In chapter 8, I suggested the commitment: "I will not let homophobia get in my way of making friends with gay men, lesbians, and bisexual persons, and I will actively oppose the violence and hatred directed at them." There, I discussed some of the things we might learn from gay men. Here, I want to say something about what we might learn from lesbian friends.

I have learned a great deal about relationships from lesbian writers— Christian (Beverly Harrison and Carter Heyward) and non-Christian (Mariana Valverde). One of the most important things I have learned is that mutuality is a necessary precondition for just and, therefore, fulfilling relationships. I don't think it is an accident that these women have seen this and are writing about it the most clearly.

We heterosexuals pursue sexual fulfillment with persons of the other sex. Because of the systemic mistreatment of women (sexism) and the mistreatment of men (men's oppression), there is a great deal of structural inequality between us, as well as anger and resentment. We often end up objectifying one another with the result that desire decreases. When mutuality (*philia*) is absent, it becomes impossible to maintain the erotic tension between our desire to know (*libido*) and our desire to be known (*eros*). Because we do not often look at these dynamics that pit us against one another, we are mystified as to why we don't have more sexually fulfilling relationships. Equality must be the basis for mutually enhancing sexual relationships between human beings. It just doesn't work very well when inequality exists, and there has been and continues to be structural inequality between women and men in a society plagued by sexist discrimination and the mistreatment of men.

Because lesbians are erotically drawn to other women, less structural inequality affects their relationships (though racism, classism, and anti-Semitism still intrude). Consequently, there are lesbians who have thought long and hard about the nature of sexual relations, the erotic, and the mutual relations necessary for a healthy sexuality. Carter Heyward, an Episcopal priest and theologian, has articulated the connections between justice, the erotic, and our yearning for God.[18] Discerning those connections and acting on the basis of them have been spiritual disciplines instrumental in my reconciliation with my body and sexuality, as well as with others and God.

Coed Groups

It is helpful not only to develop personal, individual friendships with women, but also to participate in groups where there is sufficient safety for us to be honest with one another.[19] In fact, this might be a good place for some men to start. We need cross-gender groups where we can explore with each other who we are, what has hurt us, and whom we hope to become.

This is difficult, because we tend to shame each other when we get together to talk about things that really matter to us. You know how that goes. Men say things like women are too emotional, irrational, nagging, naive, manipulative, etc. Women say things like men are too overbearing, condescending, silent, violent, etc. And on and on it goes. We tend, with such accusations being hurled about, to shut down or become defensive and attack. To see each other more clearly, we need to learn to talk with mutual respect and empathy. We need a "demilitarized zone," or sanctuary, that calls a halt to the rhetorical violence we aim at each other so that we can experience enough safety to begin to be honest and even vulnerable with one another. Again, we might construct such a ritual space with certain rules that we can all agree upon.

In what might be called "gender reconciliation groups," it is important to have male and female cofacilitators. You might begin by reading material from women's perspectives and from men's perspectives. When the group meets, divide it into two subgroups—the men and the women. At times you will want to meet together and at other times in the same-sex groups. In the latter, participants can speak more freely about their concerns without fearing that they will offend the other group or be shamed by it. In these same-sex groups, led by the same-sex facilitator, you might make a list of questions for the other sex on whatever topic the group is considering that day. When the two groups come together, sit interspersed and have the female facilitator ask the men the first question. As the men answer, the women keep quiet and listen respectfully, except to clarify something that might be unclear about the question. The men should be as honest as they feel comfortable being. Sometimes a man might say, "Some men I know think this or that or do this or that." That way he can be honest about patterns he might share but doesn't have to be put on the spot about it. When the men are answering, the male facilitator can encourage them to be honest and gently challenge them when he feels that they are putting up false appearances. After every man has had an opportunity to speak, the male facilitator asks the men's first question of the women, and the procedure is repeated, with the same rules.

If the group is an ongoing group, I have found that a couple of other ground rules are important. First, what is said in the group is held in confidence, or at least, the content of any person's contribution is not shared with his or her name attached to it or anything else that might identify that person. Second, it is best, for the duration of the group, for the members not to develop a new sexual or romantic relationship with someone else in the group. This will be tempting to do, because the participants will feel close, perhaps closer than they have ever felt, to members of the other sex. However, sexual/romantic relations and the dynamics they often bring with them can have a chilling effect on the group. What often happens in groups like this is that men get a glimpse into the world of women and women get a glimpse into the world of men. We begin to become less mysterious to one another as we begin to understand what causes some of the feelings, thoughts, and behaviors that have too often been hurtful to us. We see that persons of the other sex often don't want to act in ways that are hurtful to us, themselves, and others. In such groups we can learn to love one another, not for the neurotic needs the other might meet, but for who that person really is and wants to become; we can learn to be allies for each other against the "principalities and powers" that too often pit us against one another. In other words, such groups can be sacramental spaces where we can begin to see each other more clearly and slowly learn to "love our enemies."

PARTNERED RELATIONSHIPS

Finally, I have a few comments about partnered or significant-other relationships with women. Sydney Harris has observed:

> I should guess that for every one case of true incompatibility, there are 20 cases in which the word is used to disguise a deeper fact: that at least one of the marriage partners is not compatible with himself or herself. . . . Getting along with someone else, at close quarters, for long

and steady periods, first implies the ability to get along with oneself. A person who is disjointed is looking for opposite things in the same mate—like the woman who wants a "strong" husband whom she can nevertheless dominate . . . but nobody can be "right" for long if you are "wrong" with yourself. . . . Being the right person is more important than finding the right person. It is not merely that too many couples become divorced prematurely; it is that far too many become married immaturely.[20]

This is another way of saying what John Landgraf has said: "Good marriages can be made and sustained only by singles." Again, what he means by a "single" is someone who, because he or she has developed a centered body-self, has the ability to live interdependently with others and is, therefore, free to have a life mate or not to have one.

If one decides to have a life mate, my sense is that one indicator of the quality of that significant-other relationship is whether it makes other relationships more significant. Said another way, when two people who are well married to themselves come together, a surplus of attention and care is produced. Muriel James and Louis Savary depict such a relationship as

$$1 + 1 = 1 + 1 + 1$$

The extra 1 produced by the relationship of two "single" persons represents the extra attention those persons have because of the mutually empowering quality of their intimacy.[21] Because of the trust and intimacy that are fostered in a relationship where both persons respect and encourage the integrity and centered embodiedness of the other, something new emerges. Each person is more deeply connected, grounded, and centered than he or she would have been without the care and attention of the other. Because they are having some of their inherent, authentic dependency needs met, they are each more powerful and have more attention for themselves, each other, and others— those outside the friendship itself. So, the something new, or *extra,* that is produced is an increased reservoir of care and attention in the world. In a heterosexual couple, their attention for each other may literally produce (when the procreative function is joined with the unitive function of genital sexuality) a third person—a child. It is a child for whom there is sufficient attention from both parents, and from their friends, to grow to her or his full God-given potential. They do not have a child to get their attention needs met but rather because they have surplus attention to give. They may decide not to or be unable to have biological children and may direct that surplus attention to other persons, including children in need of the kind of parental generosity they are able to provide.

Thanks to the insights of the women's movement and to the more recent movement among men, there are exciting new possibilities for friendship between women and men.

ADVICE

Someone dancing inside us
learned only a few steps:
the "Do-Your-Work" in 4/4 time,
the "What-Do-You-Expect" waltz.
He hasn't noticed yet the woman
standing away from the lamp,
the one with black eyes
who knows the rhumba,
and strange steps in jumpy rhythms
from the mountains in Bulgaria.
If they dance together,
something unexpected will happen.
If they don't, the next world
will be a lot like this one.

BILL HOLM

Epilogue

As I come to the end of this book, I am again aware that this and other books like it are only a beginning of the conversations that need to take place. Men more or less like me need to talk with other men like us, with men not like us in significant ways, with women similar to us, and with women not so much like us. There are many things to discuss and do. I have touched on some of those things. I see, however, many threads that could be picked up and taken further. As I close, I want to summarize some of the main points I have tried to make and comment on some of the directions in which they might lead.

I agree with Martin Luther that patriarchy—the public rule of men—is a result, or manifestation, of human sin. Because we can only love God by loving our neighbors and our own inmost selves, that public rule of men and its effects manifest a deep alienation from God. It has led to the systematic violation of the God-given sovereignty of our sisters and caused deep alienations within them and between them and us. In us, it has required the inculcation of a dominating form of masculinity that prepares us for our ruling functions in society's institutions.

That dominating masculinity often produces in us lonely warriors and desperate lovers. If we are expected to rule others, we can't afford to get very close to them. We forfeit much-needed intimacy with them and with aspects of ourselves. And they, rightly, end up resenting us for violating their sovereignty as human beings. This business of ruling is killing us and others—human and nonhuman—around us. In addition, many of the institutions we lead are infected with diseases like sexism, heterosexism, racism, anti-Semitism, and classism. These further cut us off from life-giving human intimacy and lead to no little desperation about the relationship with the significant woman in our lives.

That isolation distorts our capacity for compassionate connection, which in turn distorts our abilities to see and understand some of what is happening in the world, to judge justly, and to act decisively. To return to Saint Augustine, he said that right order (God's reign) consists in our doing no harm and helping whomever we can. If we are acting out of the active pole of the distorted expressions of our capacities (tyranny, sadism, manipulation, and addiction), we will harm others. Defensively denying the harm we and others like us do serves to perpetuate it. If we are acting out of the passive pole (weakness, masochism, naïveté, and depression), we will not be able to help others when they need it. That is, guilty silence usually does not do anything to remedy the systemic attitudinal, behavioral, and institutional harm done to the targets of sexism, heterosexism, racism, anti-Semitism, and classism. Nor does it repair the harm done to us as participants in the perpetuation of these alienating structures. Guilty silence also does nothing about the oppression we experience as men.

Between defensive denial and guilty silence, we must find a third way—a way that enables us not to fight or to flee, but to be "wise as serpents and gentle as doves." This means that we take a hard look at the harm that we, often unwittingly, do to others and the harm that has been done to us. It also means that we need to stay in contact with others—otherwise we will not be able to see clearly very much at all. Both of these are difficult. It is hard to look at the harm we do and the harm that is done to us without getting lost in shame or anger. But look we must. It is scary for many of us to stay in close contact with others; it contradicts the masculine imperative to have an independent, separate identity. But scary as it is, we must not withdraw in hostile indignation, paralyzed shame, or silent self-pity. We must find ways to stay in contact with others and pursue honest, mutually respectful dialogue with them.

To do that, we will need to deal with fear. I think that, because of the violent masculine conditioning we experience, many of these masculine ways of thinking, feeling, and acting are held together by fear. If we are to recover from the distortions that fear produces in us, it must be cast out of our minds, hearts, and bodies.

The whole, or complete, love of God casts out the fear that leads us to try to dominate others and aspects of ourselves. It is important to affirm that God never intended for us to "lord it over" anyone. We need release from this "life in the flesh." And here, I depart from Luther. I believe that we are called out of this captivity by Christ in this life, as well as in the next. Ours is an eschatological hope, but it is not just that. In the strength of God's grace in creation and redemption, more can and should be done right here and right now.

We do need order in the world—an order that upholds the just intentions of God and compassionately guards our human vulnerability from abuse and exploitation. Many of us men, because of our love of God and our neighbors, have served self-sacrificially in the institutions that order our society. However, we have not always been wise enough when it comes to discerning the actual effects of the "order" we are serving. What may look like order to those on the top of a hierarchical pyramid may not look or feel like order to those on the bottom. In other words, we have not always seen the degree to which the "order" we are upholding can contain dynamics whereby whole groups of people (e.g., women, gay people, African-Americans, Jews, working-class persons, and many men of all sorts) are treated disrespectfully. However, God is daily drawing us deeply into our "inmost selves" and out over the barricades that isolate us from others. These two movements are related. A deep connection to our "inmost self," because of its inherently relational nature, leads us to a deep connection to others.

God, through the anguished and powerful, angry and compassionate voices of members of these groups and others, is calling us to an awareness of these dynamics and to a new ordering of things—the reign of God. For those of us who are Christians, we interpret that drawing in the light of Christ.

Throughout history, human beings who have participated in the "prolongation of the incarnation" have been and are women and men; gay and heterosexual; African-American, Native American, South American, African, Asian, and Euro-American; of Jewish descent and of non-Jewish descent; laboring class and owning class; young and old; able-bodied and physically challenged. All kinds of people have been Christ for others and, therefore, for me.

In addition, those who do not call the name of Christ can, by the grace of God, be Christ for us.[1] When people insist that they be treated with the respect due all of God's creatures or offer us compassion and insight into the ways in which we are alienated from them and, therefore, from God, they become the "Word made flesh" for us. Whenever we listen to the "least of these," we are listening to Christ.

Further, in Christian community we experience empowerment to listen and find our way beyond denial and silence to a third way of life. We do not have to respond to the challenges of others or to our own mistreatment by fighting or fleeing. We can justly, assertively, intelligently, and compassionately act in ways that extend God's reign "on earth as it is in heaven."

Christian communities that empower us in this way are full of spiritual friendships between and among men and women, older persons and younger persons, gay, bisexual, and heterosexual people, African-Americans and Euro-Americans, among others.

As I said at the end of chapter 9 with respect to men and women, spiritual friendships produce an *extra* dimension; there is an increased amount of compassionate attention in the world—more than either of the friends has by himself or herself, or even when taken together. In other words, spiritual friendship produces something that is greater than the sum of its parts. Spiritual friendships can be, then, sacramental; through them grace is mediated to us, to our friends, and out toward others. It is a grace that transforms those partners in a spiritual friendship and opens them out to be transforming presences in the world. We all need more of this kind of grace in our personal and collective lives. We need, therefore, to find ways in our lives, communities, and churches to be more intentional about recognizing, honoring, and supporting those grace-mediating friendships.

VOCATION

This brings me to some reflections on men's sense of our vocation. I believe that many of us think about our vocation, or calling to meaningful, creative work in the world, almost exclusively in terms of public, even institutional, roles. Consequently, we devote most of our time and energies to the fulfillment of the tasks and responsibilities required by those roles. We, like Ralph, often do not have much time or quality attention for our partners, children, friends, the earth and its nonhuman creatures, or our own inmost selves. As Sam Keen has observed:

> Within the community of men, I have learned that men's loneliness is a measurement of the degree to which we have ignored the fundamental truth of interdependence. In devoting ourselves to getting, spending, and being entertained, we simply forget that we inevitably feel alienated when we do not live within a circle of friends, within the arms of the family, within the conversation of a community. There is no way we can recover a secure sense of manhood without rediscovering the bonds that unite us to others and reaffirming our fidelity to the "We" that is an essential part of "I."[2]

Because God created a world that is fundamentally interdependent, we need to begin to think of our relationships and their quality as a part of our vocations. We need to understand that there is a significant and irreducibly relational aspect to our vocations. We are being called to spend time and attention on the compassionate care, cultivation, and nourishment of our inmost selves, our relationships to others close to us and still others not yet so close to us. Taking sabbatical time from the demands of our jobs, families, communities, and churches in order to meditate, pray, and listen to the wisdom of our bodies is an essential part of our vocation. For those of us in partnerships with women, taking an equal share of the responsibility for thinking well about and caring for that relationship is part of our vocation. For those of us who are fathers, giving our children some of the best time, attention, and thinking we have is part of our vocation. The initiation, nurture, and maintenance of spiritual friendships are an essential part, also, of our vocation. So, too, is our responsiveness to and care for the earth and its creatures. These are things not incidental to what we are to be about in the world; they are central to it.

STEPPING ACROSS THE BARRICADES

It is, of course, easier to develop spiritual friendships with persons most like us. Part of our vocation, however, is the development of friendships and alliances with persons not like us in both small and significant ways. In this book, I have focused most of my attention on stepping across the barriers of sexism and heterosexism and developing relationships with women and other men, both heterosexual and gay. I have had less to say about stepping across the barriers of racism and classism. The reason for that has been the progression of my own awareness of the need to address these dynamics. I do not know if the order of this awareness is unique to me or is shared by other men like me.

What is clear is that sexism and heterosexism are intimately related. They are, in many ways, the barriers closest to home for most of us and the ones over, under, around, or through which we first need to step. In other words, we need to be reconciled with the women in our lives, aspects of ourselves labeled and suppressed as feminine, and other men closest to us (heterosexual and gay) in order to free up enough attention to move toward persons from whom we have segregated ourselves. We need to make peace with those with whom we live before we can honestly hope to make peace with those with whom most of us do not.

In another context, Paul Tillich made a point that seems germane here. With respect to the relation of Christianity to other world religious traditions, he said that we cannot go up and out over our own tradition to some external, objective place and relate significantly to other traditions. Rather, Christians must go deeply into our own traditions and know them intimately in order to find connections with other traditions.[3] Only by going deeply into ourselves and our own traditions can we find "common ground" with others. As we recover from our historical amnesia and develop a deeper appreciation of our own cultural heritage, others will be less threatening to us. We can more fully appreciate the richness and contributions of their cultural creations. It is on the basis of knowledge and appreciation of ourselves that we can know and appreciate others.

So, by doing the work closest to us, we can move more resolutely, powerfully, intelligently, and compassionately toward others over racial and class barriers. In doing that, I am beginning to see how racism and classism are intimately related.

At a recent workshop, James Forbes, the African-American pastor of Riverside Church in New York, gave a stirring presentation on the ways in which racism distorts the humanity of African-American men. His passionate anger and his compassionate openness to the Euro-American men there was moving for many of us. Afterwards, I told him that this is the kind of dialogue—"speaking the truth in love"—we need to have in all our communities. He responded by saying something like, "Steve, this is nice, but what if we were back in your community. Your people and my people would be competing for the same resources. Then dialogue is not so easy. It can happen only when a black baby and white baby born in the same hospital in your community come into a world in which they have the same opportunities." I am still thinking about what he said.

What I now see is that for African-Americans and Euro-Americans to "speak the truth in love," we must become their allies in creating more just economic conditions. We need the material conditions for honest, mutual dialogue. To do that, we must begin to look at the class structure in our country and the ways in which it, coupled with our own white racism, has historically functioned to keep most African-Americans from being integrated into the mainstream of American economic and political life.[4] While doing that, we need also to reach across the residential, social, and cultural barriers that separate us. You might find a group that is working on issues that affect African-Americans and join the work under the leadership of African-Americans. You might do work on your own to learn about African-American history and culture. In order to survive, many African-Americans have spent a lot of time learning what life is like for us. It is important for us to take responsibility to do the same. These suggestions are just places to start; much needs to be done here.[5] Again, the point is not to make token African-American friends, but rather not to allow our own stereotypes, guilt, and fears to keep us from being friends with persons who are African-American.

As we look at class structure, we see also that our relationships with Jewish people have not only been colored by anti-Semitic Christian preaching and teaching, but have also been linked historically to classism. Distorted and inaccurate images of Jews have been perpetuated in too many Christian traditions. The Jews have been unfairly blamed for the death of Jesus. Though Jesus' teaching reflects his agreement with one group of Pharisees over other groups, scribes and Pharisees as a whole have been portrayed as legalistic, controlling, and insensitive. The Hebrew Scriptures, or the Christian Old Testament, have been inaccurately characterized as containing only law in opposition to the grace of the New Testament.[6] In addition, many of us in the laboring sector have lived with an irrational fear that Jews, serving the owning class, exercise power over us through their participation in economic institutions. For us Christians to step over the barricade of anti-Semitism, we need to work on the theological, historical, and sociological misunderstandings that have alienated us from people of Jewish faith and descent.[7] I might add that anti-Semitism alienates us not only from Jewish people but also from other Semitic peoples, as some of the stereotyped and inflammatory anti-Irab rhetoric during the Iran hostage crisis and the Gulf War demonstrated.

WORK

Through the writing of this book, I have become increasingly convinced that, unless many of us change the way we work, we will not be able to do very much about the dynamics that harm others and us. If we give forty to seventy hours a week of our best time, energy, and attention to a job, we simply will not have much left to give to anything else. If our sense of self-worth is bound primarily to our work, we will not be psychologically, or emotionally, able to pursue the relational aspects of our vocations. To be sure, many of us, like Ralph, work as hard as we do in order to provide for our families. But that work, in a tragic irony, takes us increasingly out of the lives of those for whom we are working. In addition, our work may serve to concentrate the ownership of capital and other means of production in the hands of fewer and fewer people. The result is that we, unwittingly, make ourselves, the members of the laboring sector, and the working poor even less self-determining.[8] We need to begin to look at how the work we do affects us and others.

We can begin by asking ourselves questions like, Where and with whom do I spend my best time and attention? Why? For what am I working? For whom am I working? Who is getting more powerful as a result of my job? Who is getting less powerful? What am I sacrificing to work the way I do? Whom am I sacrificing?

As we answer these questions, we can begin to distinguish and sort out the relationship between our jobs and our vocations. Then, we can begin, in solidarity with others with common interests, to negotiate more humane and just relationships with our employers and, perhaps, between our jobs and those affected by them and us.

A Word to the Church

As I come to the end of the book, I want to say just a couple of things to those participating in and leading Christian communities. I return to the reason I used the rhetorical device of posting theses in the Introduction. Luther wrote his theses because he believed that the church's sacrament of penance was not delivering the transformative experiences for which it was intended. Many of Luther's concerns had been articulated in the centuries preceding him. The Roman church had been able, for the most part, to absorb those reform impulses, change, and maintain a certain unity. In the sixteenth century, however, it proved unable to contain similar impulses. One reason is that the papacy, during the Renaissance period, had become fairly rigid and inflexible and was unable to respond creatively to the demands for reform. The result was a split in Western Christendom.

I think we are in a similar situation today. Many voices are crying for reform. They are naming the diseases of sexism, heterosexism, racism, and classism that afflict the church and pointing out how they lead to further harm and alienation, rather than to healing and reconciliation. Harm and alienation are not the only things those speaking have experienced in the church. They have experienced also grace and healing; otherwise, they would no longer be addressing it and demanding its change. But the voices are insistent and persistent; they are not going to go away.

The question today, as in the sixteenth century, is whether those leading our churches can both listen and speak with justice, strength, intellectual honesty, and compassion. And those leading our churches are still mostly men. So, this is a time when our spiritual maturity and response-ability, as men and as Christians, are being tested. Can we, in our personal lives and in our institutions, contribute to the dismantling of the dividing walls of hostility? Can we work together with others to build more inclusive Christian communities? Can we work in more mutual relationships with those we have been conditioned to dominate? Can we be so "rooted and grounded in love" that we address these questions nonanxiously, creatively, and flexibly? We must. The unity of our churches and denominations hangs in the balance, as the responses to the recent Re-Imagining Conference demonstrate.

But, in order for many of us to do that, we need places safe enough for men, like Ralph, to begin to see what has happened to us, what is going on inside us, and what is going on between and among us and others. We need a "sanctuary movement" for men. We need places where we are protected from the violence and oppression we experience in the "world"—places where we can heal; where our characters are reintegrated; where we find our way to integrity; where we reconnect with other men, women, the earth, and God; where we become truly just and powerful in standing for God's realm; and where we become "wise as serpents and gentle as doves."

Is the church that kind of place? Jesus said, "Come to me, all you that are weary and are carrying heavy burdens, and I will give you rest" (Matthew 11:28). Is the church a place where men, including clergy, can come and put down their burdens; where they can experience rest? Or is it a place where those burdens are increased? That is, do we serve in our offices and committees in ways in which we feel we must hide our "inmost selves"? Is the church a place where we can deeply know and love ourselves as human "beings," or do we feel judged and judge ourselves as more or less adequate human "doings"?

Again, "There is no fear in love, but perfect love casts out fear" (1 John 4:18). Is the church a place where a man like Ralph would feel safe enough to express his fear? Is it a place where he would feel safe enough to cry for the first time in twenty-two years?

The church is not always, perhaps not often, such a place. But it can be, and it must be. We need leaders, male and female, clergy and laity, who have experienced sufficient safety to know what it looks like, to know what it feels like, and to know how to help provide it for others. We need men's spirituality groups in our churches, and we need to sponsor them in our communities; we need such groups and men's studies programs in all our seminaries.

Our churches, seminaries, and wider communities need reconciliation groups working intentionally and persistently with people divided by gender, sexual orientation, race, and class.

These needs may seem daunting, just as are the "powers and principalities" that produce them. But we have a promise: "The one who is in you is greater than the one who is in the world" (1 John 4:4). That is, the power of the One who draws us together is greater than that which would drive us apart. Faith is believing that and, sustained in communities of faith, moving beyond defensive denial and guilty silence toward a new way.

Endnotes

Introduction

1. By "dominative" masculinity, I mean those expectations from our culture that say men are supposed to be in control—to affect others while trying not to be affected by them. See chapter 4 for a more complete discussion.
2. See Jaroslav Pelikan, *Obedient Rebel* (New York: Harper and Row, 1964).
3. Carter Heyward, *Touching Our Strength: The Erotic as Power and the Love of God* (San Francisco: HarperSanFrancisco, 1989), 20ff.
4. Kenneth Clatterbaugh, *Contemporary Perspectives on Masculinity: Men, Women, and Politics in Modern Society* (Boulder, Colo.: Westview Press, 1990).
5. J. Michael Clark, *A Place to Start: Toward an Unapologetic Gay Liberation Theology* (Dallas, Tex.: Monument Press, 1989), speaks of writing gay liberation theology that is both confessional ("This is how it is with me") and invitational ("How is it with you?"). For him, theological writing then "is less a culmination of what we or others have previously done, but rather a prismatic focusing of that work, which in turn radiates outward toward new speech, new dialogue, and ongoing theological process."
6. Alton Pollard has explored Howard Thurman's concept of the "common ground" and its implications for social justice in *Mysticism and Social Change: The Witness of Howard Thurman* (New York: Peter Lang Publishing, 1992).
7. Barbara Ehrenreich, *The Hearts of Men: American Dreams and the Flight from Commitment* (New York: Doubleday, 1983), 55–56.
8. Marc F. Fasteau, *The Male Machine* (New York: McGraw-Hill, 1974), and Warren Farrell, *The Liberated Man: Beyond Masculinity—Freeing Men and Their Relationships with Women* (New York: Bantam, 1974).
9. Robert Bly, *Iron John: A Book about Men* (Reading, Mass.: Addison-Wesley, 1990), and John Lee, *At My Father's Wedding: Reclaiming Our True Masculinity* (New York: Bantam, 1991).
10. See Warren Farrell, *The Myth of Male Power* (New York: Simon & Schuster, 1993), chapter 8, for a discussion of the higher mortality rates of men.
11. See James E. Dittes, *When Work Goes Sour: A Male Perspective* (Philadelphia: Westminster Press, 1987).
12. For a helpful treatment of some of these themes see Margaret R. Miles, *Augustine on the Body* (Missoula, Mont.: Scholars Press, 1979).
13. I will say more about each of these in chapter 2.
14. We must, however, be careful that we do not "confiscate" the cultural traditions and insights of other peoples without developing relationships of reciprocity with them.

That is, we must invite them to participate and share in the fruits of their own labor and stand with them against those cultural dynamics that have displaced and threatened their lives and cultures. See Katie Geneva Cannon, "Appropriation and Reciprocity in the Doing of Womanist Ethics," *Annual of the Society of Christian Ethics* 1993, 1, and Christopher Ronwaniente Jocks, "Defending Their People and Their Earth: Native American Men and the Construction of Masculinity," in *Redeeming Men: Religion and Masculinities*, ed. Stephen B. Boyd, W. Merle Longwood, and Mark W. Muesse (Louisville, Ky.: Westminster John Knox, 1996), 132–44.

PART ONE
THE MEN WE HAVE BECOME

CHAPTER ONE   *Lonely Warriors: The Public, Responsible Self*

1. Warren Farrell, *Why Men Are the Way They Are: The Male-Female Dynamic* (New York: McGraw-Hill, 1986), 3–7.
2. Guy Corneau, *Absent Fathers, Lost Sons: The Search for Masculine Identity* (Boston: Shambhala, 1991), 13ff.
3. Farrell, *Myth of Male Power*, 105.
4. See Corneau, *Absent Fathers, Lost Sons,* chap. 1.
5. F. Rebelsky and C. Hanks, "Father's Verbal Interaction with Infants in the First Three Months of Life," *Child Development* 42 (1971): 63–68, and F. A. Pedersen and K. S. Robson, "Father Participation in Infancy," *American Journal of Orthopsychiatry* 39 (1969): 466–72, as cited in Samuel Osherson, *Finding Our Fathers: How a Man's Life Is Shaped by His Relationship with His Father* (New York: Fawcett Columbine, 1986), 29.
6. Osherson, *Finding Our Fathers,* 7.
7. James Carrol, review of *Good Morning, Merry Sunshine,* by Bob Greene, *New York Times Book Review,* June 10, 1984.
8. As quoted in Myriam Miedzian, *Boys Will Be Boys: Breaking the Link Between Masculinity and Violence* (New York: Anchor Books, 1991), 7.
9. Miedzian, *Boys Will Be Boys,* xxiv and 5. Increasing attention is being given to boys as victims of childhood sexual abuse. This includes instances in which women are the perpetrators. See, for example, Mic Hunter, *Abused Boys: The Neglected Victims of Sexual Abuse* (Lexington, MA: Lexington Books, 1990); and Mike Lew, *Victims No Longer: Men Recovering from Incest and Other Sexual Child Abuse* (New York: Harper & Row, 1990).
10. Miedzian, *Boys Will Be Boys,* xxiii. She also believes there is a biological predisposition in men to violence (xxvi) and, therefore, asserts that even more attention must be paid to countering it. However, biologist Anne Fausto-Sterling, *Myths of Gender: Biological Theories About Women and Men* (New York: Basic Books, 1985), 123–56, asserts that the evidence is not conclusive.
11. Miedzian, *Boys Will Be Boys,* 45.
12. The definitions and discussion of socialization and conditioning in the next two paragraphs are from Judith Webb Kay, "Human Nature and the Natural Law Tradition" (Ph.D. diss., Graduate Theological Union, 1988), 81–82.
13. Much of the material in the next two paragraphs was presented by Kreiner at workshops on "Male Sexuality" and "Dismantling the Oppressor Role," Fifteenth Men and

Masculinity Conference, Atlanta, Georgia, May 31–June 3, 1990, and Sixteenth Men and Masculinity Conference, Tucson, Arizona, June 6–9, 1991. See also "About Men: A Conversation with Charlie Kreiner," *Breitenbush Newsletter,* Winter–Spring 1990, 19–27. He is currently working on a book, and I am grateful to him for allowing me to make use of this material before its publication. He may be contacted at P.O. Box 173, Beaver Meadow Road, Haddam, CT 06438.

14. Augustine, *Confessions,* trans. R. S. Pine-Coffin (New York: Penguin Books, 1961), 30–31.

15. Paulo Freire, *Pedagogy of the Oppressed,* rev. 20th Anniversary ed., trans. Myra Bergman Ramos (New York: Continuum, 1993), 57ff.

16. Alfie Kohn, *No Contest: The Case Against Competition* (Boston: Houghton Mifflin, 1986), 139.

17. Joseph Wax, as quoted in Kohn, *No Contest,* 147.

18. Sam Keen, *Fire in the Belly* (New York: Bantam Books, 1991), 42–43.

19. Michael Kaufman, "The Construction of Masculinity and the Triad of Men's Violence," in *Beyond Patriarchy: Essays by Men on Pleasure, Power, and Change,* ed. Michael Kaufman (Toronto: Oxford Univ. Press, 1987), 1–29.

20. Paul G. King, Kent Maynard, and David O. Woodyard, *Risking Liberation: Middle Class Powerlessness and Social Heroism* (Atlanta: John Knox Press, 1988), 30ff.

21. King, Maynard, and Woodyard, *Risking Liberation,* 27.

22. I am grateful to Andrew Blackmon, an undergraduate student, for several discussions in which some of these thoughts were clarified.

23. Charlie Kreiner helped me see some of what I have written about in this section.

24. Augustine, *Confessions,* 46.

25. For Adrienne Rich's reflections on this, see her "Compulsory Heterosexuality and Lesbian Existence," *Signs* 5 (1980): 631–60.

26. See Eric Mendelson, "An Exploratory Investigation of Male Gender-Role Development During Early Adulthood" (Ph.D. diss., University of North Carolina, 1987).

27. Kohn, *No Contest,* 107–11.

28. Kohn, *No Contest,* 122–23.

29. Kohn, *No Contest,* 125–31.

CHAPTER TWO *Desperate Lovers: The Private, Separative Self*

1. Catherine Keller, *From a Broken Web: Separation, Sexism, and Self* (Boston: Beacon Press, 1986), argues that masculine identity is a separative identity. That is, the ego, in an attempt to protect itself from outside influence, "makes itself the absolute in that it absolves itself from relation" (26). But, she asserts, "however much the ego feels single and apart, this feeling may represent not truth but denial. It is less precise to call this ego separate than separative, implying an activity or an intention rather than any fundamental state of being" (9). Consequently, I have called this aspect of male identity a "private, separative self."

2. For helpful reflections on racism, see Andrew Hacker, *Two Nations: Black and White, Separate, Hostile, and Unequal* (New York: Scribner, 1992); Angela Y. Davis, *Women, Race and Class* (New York: Vintage Books, 1983); and Susan Brooks Thistlethwaite, *Sex, Race, and God: Christian Feminism in Black and White* (New York: Crossroad, 1989). Numerous forms of racism and ethnocentrism with discrimination and mistreatment are aimed at many groups. I will focus on the mistreatment of African-Americans because of its special and pervasive nature in the United States. See Hacker, *Two Nations,* chap. 1.

3. King, Maynard, and Woodyard, *Risking Liberation,* 112–16.

4. King, Maynard, and Woodyard, *Risking Liberation,* 61.

5. This image came to me after Charlie Kreiner observed that, while there are 1,000 ways of being connected, 999 are taken away.

6. Stephen Boyd, "Hanging by a Thread," interview by Michael Arges, *The Canadian Baptist,* October 1991, 10–14.

7. Keen, *Fire in the Belly,* 15.

8. I am grateful to the members of several classes of my Gender and Religion course, as well as to Lisa Allred, members of the Wake Forest University Counseling Center, and Meg Davis, for their help in developing this chart.

9. Simone de Beauvoir, *The Second Sex,* trans. H. M. Parshley (New York: Random House, Vintage Books, 1974; original, 1949); Nancy Chodorow, *The Reproduction of Mothering: Psychoanalysis and the Sociology of Gender* (Berkeley and Los Angeles: Univ. of California Press, 1978); Betty Friedan, *The Feminine Mystique* (New York: Dell, 1974); and Carol Gilligan, Nona P. Lyons, and Trudy J. Hanmer, *Making Connections: The Relational Worlds of Adolescent Girls at Emma Willard School* (Cambridge: Harvard Univ. Press, 1990).

10. Recent authors whose work has informed the development of the part of the chart dealing with femininity are Nancy Friday, Carol Cassel, Barbara Ehrenreich, Lillian Rubin, and Anne Wilson Schaef.

11. Herb Goldberg, *The New Male: From Macho to Sensitive but Still All Male* (New York: Signet, 1979); Goldberg, *The New Male-Female Relationship* (New York: Signet, 1983); and Goldberg, *The Inner Male: Overcoming Roadblocks to Intimacy* (New York: Signet, 1987).

12. Mariana Valverde, *Sex, Power, and Pleasure* (Philadelphia: New Society, 1987), 37ff.

13. See Gilligan, Lyons, and Hanmer, *Making Connections,* 6–27, for their sense of how this happens to adolescent girls.

14. Keller, *From a Broken Web,* 28.

15. Herb Goldberg's reflections have been helpful here; see *The Inner Male,* 41ff.

16. These "compulsive relational fantasies" do a lot to disable women relationally and to make them miserable. Because of their need for a "successful" relationship, shaped by formulas depicted in various cultural media such as fairy tales, romances (Harlequin and Danielle Steele), and soap operas (daytime and prime time), women do not see men very clearly. As Warren Farrell has pointed out, this is women's equivalent of pornography. Through romance novels and soaps, women relate not to real men, but to figments of someone's imagination. This, I think, is an important contributing factor to women's disillusionment about relationships with men and about men in general.

17. Quoted by Bly, *Iron John,* 62.

18. Dorothy Dinnerstein, *The Mermaid and the Minotaur: Sexual Arrangements and Human Malaise* (New York: Harper & Row, 1976), chap. 7.

19. Dinnerstein, *Mermaid,* 161–67.

20. Dinnerstein, *Mermaid,* 38.

21. Dinnerstein, *Mermaid,* chap. 8.

22. Chodorow, *Reproduction of Mothering,* 104.

23. Kenneth Adams, *Silently Seduced: When Parents Make Their Children Partners* (Deerfield Beach, FL: Health Communications, 1991).

24. Dinnerstein, *Mermaid,* 134.

25. See Mendelson, "Male Gender-Role Development."

CHAPTER THREE *A House Divided: The Punishment of Adam*

1. I am indebted to Judith Kay for several important concepts, distinctions, and terms, including this one, which is taken from "We Are Not as We Appear: Thomistic Virtue in the Moral Agency of the Oppressed" (paper presented at the Annual Meeting of the Society for Christian Ethics, Washington, DC, January 20, 1990). She is doing important work constructing a liberation theory that uses Thomas Aquinas as a resource in developing an emancipatory notion of human nature. See also her "Human Nature and the Natural Law Tradition," chaps. 2 and 4. The interpretation and use of her distinctions here are my own.

2. Kay, "Human Nature and the Natural Law Tradition," 173ff.

3. The work of Robert Moore and Douglas Gillette, *King, Warrior, Magician, Lover: Rediscovering the Archetypes of the Mature Masculine* (San Francisco: HarperSanFrancisco, 1990), from a Jungian perspective has been particularly helpful. What they identify as the archetypes of "deep masculinity"—King, Warrior, Magician, Lover—correspond to what I have termed the capacities for justice/fairness, power/strength, intelligence, and connection/compassion. Their contention also is that these are inherent in men ("hard-wiring") and continue to be present in the psyche no matter how distorted their expression might be. That is what I am calling the continuing presence of the image of God. I will refer to the specific historical, Christian traditions in the notes.

4. John Calvin, *Institutes of the Christian Religion,* trans. Ford Lewis Battles, Library of Christian Classics, vol. 21 (Philadelphia: Westminster Press, 1977), 1504, believed that . this sense of justice, or equity as he called it, was, even after the Fall, the foundation of the moral law that was available to every person, Christian and non-Christian, as a result of the continued, though muted, presence of the image of God.

5. Many of the desert ascetics of the fourth century, the Anabaptists of the sixteenth century, the pietists of the seventeenth and eighteenth centuries, and contemporary Christians associated with the base Christian communities in the two-thirds world affirm this God-given power. It is a grace of creation that is shaped by the grace of redemption.

6. The early Christian apologists, the medieval scholastics, the Socinians of the sixteenth century and their progeny—the Unitarians—and the Deists of the eighteenth century affirmed this human capacity.

7. I got this image from Charlie Kreiner.

8. This has been a strong affirmation of the medieval mystics, Reformation Spiritualists, nineteenth-century Romantics, and those currently employing process thought in their theological thinking.

9. See Fausto-Sterling, *Myths of Gender,* for a review of scientific work about the similarities and differences between men and women.

10. Moore and Gillette's use of archetypal language is difficult for some people. One of the difficulties is that Moore and Gillette do not pay sufficient attention to their own social location and how that influences the way they read and understand the archetypes. Consequently, they tend to universalize from their own experience and understanding without taking into account how others, with different experiences, might understand these archetypes and be affected by their interpretations. For example, the images of King and Warrior are particularly problematic for some of us—men and women. "King" conjures up political images of permanent, nonmutual relationships of domination and submission; "Warrior" elicits associations with aggressive, militaristic, violent, and coercive activities that have historically too often kept unjust, nonmutual power relations in place. For some men, and for many women, people of color, gay, lesbian, and bisexual people, such images simply remind them of the very dynamics and power relations that have stunted and

thwarted their own first natures. So, the use of these images may simply increase the separation between us men and others.

Having said that, however, I believe that important things may be gained from their analysis. One of Moore and Gillette's arguments is that "King energy"—what I am calling a sense of justice and fairness—is generative; is concerned about right ordering, integration, and integrity; and mediates vitality and joy. Moore and Gillette assert that this energy is in each man and that it needs to be accessed and developed in the face of the tyrannical institutions that maintain unjust relations or the weak leaders who ignore them. The "Warrior" is that energy—what I call boundary setting and defending—that serves the generativity and just ordering of the "King." Approached in this way, the "King" and "Warrior" images can be seen to be not only congenial to our modern sense of political and social justice, but, Moore and Gillette argue, beneficial for their realization. I tend to agree with them, as I have found these images, thus understood, to be helpful in my own action on behalf of gender and racial justice. It may not be so for everyone, so I suggest that if these images are used, they must be translated so that they are not unnecessarily obstructive. If we find them harmful to our pursuit of justice, then perhaps we can find more suitable images.

11. See Keller, *From a Broken Web,* for an explication of this metaphor.

12. Moore and Gillette, *King, Warrior, Magician, Lover,* 16–17.

13. I got the idea for doing this from Charlie Kreiner at a retreat he did on men's isolation.

14. *The Fragility of Knowledge: Theological Education in the Church and the University* (Philadelphia: Fortress Press, 1988), 3–16.

15. Victor J. Seidler, *Rediscovering Masculinity: Reason, Language, and Sexuality* (New York: Routledge, 1989), 1.

16. Beverly Harrison, "The Power of Anger in the Work of Love," in *Weaving the Visions: New Patterns in Feminist Spirituality,* ed. Judith Plaskow and Carol P. Christ (San Francisco: Harper & Row, 1989), 218–19.

17. James H. Cone, *A Black Theology of Liberation* (Maryknoll, NY: Orbis Books, 1990), 18.

18. Saint Thomas Aquinas, representing what I believe is the most pervasive theological opinion and contrary to Luther's view, believed that men ruled and women and others were ruled because of men's "natural" superiority. Women were subjugated to men primarily because of their derivative nature (using Genesis 2:4b–24), rational and physical inferiority (following Aristotle), and secondary role in procreation. So, one might say that men's responsibilities for economic provision and coercive rule were privileges that came with a superior nature, given in creation. These roles, then, were believed to have been intended by God in creation.

19. Luther, *Lectures on Genesis,* in Luther's Works, vol.1, ed. Varoslav Pekihan (St. Louis: Concordia, 1958), 203–7.

20. Luther, *Lectures on Genesis,* 203.

21. New York: Seabury Press, 1974.

22. Again, I have profited from Kay's definition of oppression as well as her discussion of internalized oppression and internalized domination; see her "Human Nature and the Natural Law Tradition," 57ff. The interpretation of her work I give here is completely my own.

23. See Gail Pheterson, "Alliances Between Women: Overcoming Internalized Oppression and Internalized Domination," *Signs* 12 (1986): 146–60, for a more technical definition of these dynamics and a good description of a process by which they might be overcome in oppressed and oppressor groups.

24. For a formulation of this, see Harvey Jackins, "On the Oppression of Men," *Men* (Seattle), no. 3 (1985): 14–15.

25. Phyllis Trible, "Eve and Adam: Genesis 2–3 Reread," in *Womanspirit Rising: A Feminist Reader in Religion,* ed. Carol Christ and Judith Plaskow (San Francisco: Harper & Row, 1979), 74–83, makes this point in her reading of the story.

26. For a discussion of paradigms and shifts from one paradigm to another, see Hans Küng, "Paradigm Change in Theology: A Proposal for Discussion," in *Paradigm Change in Theology: A Symposium for the Future,* trans. Margaret Kohl, ed. Hans Küng and David Tracy (New York: Crossroad, 1989), 7.

27. Charles Hartshorne, *Omnipotence and Other Theological Mistakes* (Albany: State Univ. of New York Press, 1984).

28. Dinnerstein might give us at least one clue as to why many of us—men and women—have an investment in seeing God as a "he." She argues that the seeming omnipotence of the mother in the "mother-involved" family is balanced by our projection of our split-off need for differentiation, autonomy, and independence onto the father. An absolute, utterly transcendent, self-sufficient Father offers us a cosmic emotional and psychological counterbalance to the perceived omnipotence of the mother.

29. This view is often called the Latin theory of the atonement, or the substitutionary view of Christ's work. Based on the scriptural language of sacrifice, it came to be a predominant view in Western Christianity, particularly in Reformed (Calvinist) circles. Many advocates of this view point to Saint Anselm's *Cur Deus Homo* (Why God became man), in *A Scholastic Miscellany: Anselm to Ockham,* ed. Eugene R. Fairweather (New York: Macmillan, 1970), 100–183, as the clearest articulation of this formulation. This view employs early medieval political metaphors and Latin legal theory (e.g., God as lord, human beings as vassals) to express the relationship between God and humanity. Robert D. Crouse, "The Augustinian Background of St. Anselm's Concept of *Iustitia,*" *Canadian Journal of Theology* 4 (April 1958): 111–19, argues that Anselm's notion of justice is best understood aesthetically—as God's right ordering of the world. This tends toward a less juridical and more medicinal or remedial reading of Anselm's theory.

30. This may explain the investment many traditional, male theologians have had in separating *agape* and *eros.* If God is male, in fact hypermasculine, and we men are supposed to love God (and our neighbors as ourselves), given the strong homophobic aspect of masculinity, men's love for God cannot have an erotic component. Consequently, men assert that God's love doesn't either. Men are thus encouraged, even required, to keep their bodies, emotions, and sexual passion out of their relation to God. See Howard Eilberg-Schwartz, *God's Phallus: And Other Problems for Men and Monotheism* (Boston: Beacon Press, 1994), for a helpful treatment of some of these issues.

31. Portions of this discussion first appeared in print in the *Journal of Men's Studies* (1993): 323–45.

32. *Annual of the Southern Baptist Convention* (Nashville, TN, 1985), 65.

33. *Partners in the Mystery of Redemption: A Pastoral Response to Women's Concerns for Church and Society* (Washington, DC: National Conference of Catholic Bishops, March 23, 1988).

34. E. J. Miller, *Women in the American Baptist Churches: A Perspective on the Past Thirty Years* (n.p.: Women in Ministry Group of the Minister and Missionaries Benefit Board of American Baptist Churches, 1986), 8–9.

35. Miller, *Women in the American Baptist Churches,* 10–12.

36. "Split, Catholic Bishops Defer Proposals on Women's Issues," *New York Times,* September 14, 1990, A1 and B6. This more conservative Second Draft may have been prompted by the criticisms of laity and clergy, including Vatican officials, who believed the First Draft to be too liberal.

37. "Called to Be One in Christ Jesus: Third Draft/Pastoral on Concerns of Women," *Origins, CNS Documentary Service* 21(46) (April 23, 1992): 772, and "One in Christ Jesus," *Origins* 22(29) (December 31, 1992): 502. Between the Second and Third drafts, an International Consultation was held at the Vatican in May 1991. Five Vatican officials and thirteen bishops from other countries attended, along with representatives of the U.S. bishops. The National Conference of Catholic Bishops voted to issue the Fourth Draft as a committee report rather than an authoritative pastoral letter.

38. "Called to Be One," 772, and "One in Christ Jesus," 502.

PART TWO

THE LOVE OF GOD AND THE MEN WE LONG TO BE

CHAPTER FOUR *"A New Creation": The Call to a Center and Over the Barricades*

1. H. Richard Niebuhr, *Radical Monotheism* (New York: Harper & Row, 1960).
2. Heyward, *Touching Our Strength*, 188.
3. Too much of Christianity has displayed an anti-Semitic tendency to interpret first-century Judaism in the worst possible light and the early Christian movement in the best. It is important to note that Jesus, rather than repudiating all religious officeholders of the day (e.g., the Pharisees and Sadducees), seems to have participated in the internal debates of the Pharisees. For example, in Matthew 12, Mark 2, and Luke 6, he follows the majority legal opinion of the Pharisees against another group on the issue of what was legal to "pluck with the hand" on the Sabbath. See Martin McNamara, *Targum and Testament* (Grand Rapids, MI: Eerdmans, 1972); John T. Pawlikowski, *Sinai and Calvary* (Mission Hills, CA: Benzinger, 1976); and Harvey Falk, *Jesus the Pharisee* (New York: Paulist Press, 1985).
4. For a recovery of the significance of Jewish sources for Jesus' teaching, see W. D. Davies, *The Sermon on the Mount* (New York: Cambridge Univ. Press, 1969).
5. I am indebted to Beverly Harrison, "Human Sexuality and Mutuality," in *Christian Feminism: Visions of a New Humanity*, ed. Judith L. Weidman (San Francisco: Harper & Row, 1984), for suggesting a new paradigm and sketching its broad outline. I have benefited greatly from her provocative work. There have always been and continue to be Christians who have resisted to one degree or another the structures of domination and have offered alternative interpretations and embodiments of Christian doctrines, rituals, and communal forms. Historically, I am thinking of groups such as the second-century Gnostic Christians, medieval mystics, Reformation radicals (e.g., Anabaptists, Baptists, Congregationalists, Spiritualists, Quakers, Rationalists, and Revolutionaries), and nineteenth-century Romantics and Idealists. On the contemporary scene, I am referring to Christian groups and writers who are concerned with resisting such oppressive structures as sexism (feminists and womanists), heterosexism (lesbian and gay liberation theologians), racism (black and Afrocentric liberation theologians), classism (Latin American liberation theologians), and the destruction of our earth (ecofeminists).
6. See Heyward, *Touching Our Strength*, for her understanding of God as "power in right relation."
7. Harrison, "Human Sexuality and Mutuality," 147.
8. Many other early Christian writers shared this sense. In fact, before Constantine, people such as the early-second-century bishop Ignatius of Antioch saw the Roman government in league with "prince of this world." See Cyril Richardson, ed., *Early Christian Fathers* (New York: Macmillan, 1975), 94 and 104.

9. Rudolf Bultmann, *Jesus Christ and Mythology* (New York: Scribner, 1958).

10. See, e.g., the MudFlower Collective, *God's Fierce Whimsy: Christian Feminism and Theological Education* (New York: Pilgrim Press, 1985), 40; Rosemary Radford Ruether, *Sexism and God-Talk: Toward a Feminist Theology* (Boston: Beacon Press, 1983), 234; John Howard Yoder, *The Politics of Jesus* (Grand Rapids, MI: Eerdmans, 1972); and James H. Cone, *God of the Oppressed* (New York: Seabury Press, 1975), 232.

11. Marjorie Suchocki, "A Feminist Re-interpretation of the Doctrine of Original Sin" (Robinson Lectures at Wake Forest University, 1990). See also *The Fall to Violence: Original Sin in Relational Theology* (New York: Continuum, 1994).

12. Walter Wink, *Naming the Powers: The Language of Power in the New Testament* (Minneapolis: Fortress Press, 1984); Wink, *Unmasking the Powers: The Invisible Forces That Determine Human Existence* (Minneapolis: Fortress Press, 1986); and Wink, *Engaging the Powers: Discernment and Resistance in a World of Domination* (Minneapolis: Augsburg Fortress Press, 1992).

13. Wink, *Engaging the Powers,* 6. Wink argues that the best way we moderns can make sense of the "spiritual/heavenly" and "earthly" realms referred to by early Christians is with what he calls an "integral world view." Rather than seeing these spheres of human experience as spatially separate (ancient worldview), hermetically sealed off from each other (theological worldview), or valuing only heaven (spiritualism) or only earth (materialism), it makes more sense to see these two terms as referring to two aspects of things—an outer and inner. The "earthly" aspect is the outer, external manifestation of a "heavenly" aspect, that is, a withinness or interiority of all things, which is inextricably related to the outer.

14. Wink, *Engaging the Powers,* 3.

15. Wink, *Engaging the Powers,* 62.

16. See George A. Lindbeck, *The Nature of Doctrine: Religion and Theology in a Postliberal Age* (Philadelphia: Westminster Press, 1984), for an explanation of what this means for theology.

17. Some sixteenth-century radical reformers had a similar conception. See my *Pilgram Marpeck: His Life and Social Theology* (Durham, NC: Duke Univ. Press, 1992), 148–50.

18. Wink, *Engaging the Powers,* 77.

19. Citing the work of Alice Miller, Judith Kay, in an unpublished manuscript, "Aquinas on Virtues and Their Defects," 41, makes this point with respect to our need of examining "the processes by which defective habits are created and maintained" in even very young children.

20. It is important to take note of an increasing tendency in early Christianity and in the New Testament documents to intensify the role of the Jewish "chief priests and elders" in Jesus' crucifixion and to decrease the role of, or even to exculpate, Pilate and Rome. Compare the passion narratives of Mark and Luke with the later accounts of Matthew and, particularly, John. In fact, crucifixion was a Roman punishment that had been directed at those, including Jews, who were perceived to pose a threat to the Roman domination of Palestine. This blaming of "the Jews" for the death of Jesus reflects a growing tendency among Christians of succeeding generations to project onto Jews as a whole the acts and attitudes for which only some first-century Jews might have been responsible. Historically, this distortion has served as a basis for a great deal of anti-Semitic violence by Christians. See E. J. Fisher, *Faith Without Prejudice: Rebuilding Christian Attitudes Toward Judaism* (New York: Paulist Press, 1977).

21. Taking a cue from Wink, I have here suggested a reading of the passage that substitutes "dominating system" for "world."

22. See note 10 for theologians who have a similar view.

23. This, I think, is Saint Augustine's insight in the Donatist controversy. For him, the sacraments work *ex opere operato*—that is, because they are rightly done. God, not the transformed character of the priest, guarantees their effectiveness. There is truth to that, but their effectiveness is not completely unrelated to the quality (just relations) of the community and God's immanent, transforming work there.

24. James Nelson, *The Intimate Connection: Male Sexuality, Masculine Spirituality* (Philadelphia: Westminster Press, 1988), 82.

25. Athanasius of Alexandria, "On the Incarnation," in *Christology of the Later Fathers,* ed. Edward R. Hardy (Philadelphia: Westminster Press, 1954), 55–110.

26. See Richardson, *Early Christian Fathers,* 93.

27. Saint Augustine, *City of God,* trans. Gerald G. Walsh et al. (Garden City, NY: Image Books, 1958), 456.

28. For an example of this kind of theological perspective, see my *Pilgram Marpeck,* 124.

29. See Neal Blough, *Christologie Anabaptiste: Pilgram Marpeck et l'humanité de Christ* (Geneva: Labor et Fides, 1984).

30. Augustine, *Confessions,* 21.

31. For help on this, see Ruether, *Sexism and God-Talk;* Sallie McFague, *Models of God: Theology for an Ecological, Nuclear Age* (Philadelphia: Fortress Press, 1987); and McFague, *The Body of God: An Ecological Theology* (Minneapolis: Fortress Press, 1993).

32. The development of the doctrines of the Trinity (three persons and one substance) at the Councils of Nicaea and Constantinople (A.D. 325 and 381) and of the twofold nature of Christ (two natures and one person) at the Council of Chalcedon (A.D. 451) were, I believe, attempts at holding those two aspects of God together.

33. Dietrich Bonhoeffer, *Letters and Papers from Prison,* ed. Eberhard Bethge (New York: Macmillan, 1973), 362.

34. Bonhoeffer, *Letters and Papers,* 361–62.

35. I think that the acrimonious responses to the November 1993 ecumenical conference held in Minneapolis, "RE-imagining: The Ecumenical Decade/Churches in Solidarity with Women," bear witness to this pain.

36. H. Richard Niebuhr, *Radical Monotheism and Western Culture* (New York: Harper & Row, 1943), 114ff.

37. Bonhoeffer, *Letter and Papers,* 282.

38. Carter Heyward, *The Redemption of God: A Theology of Mutual Relation* (Washington, DC: University Press of America, 1982), argues that a liberation, or redemption, of God is needed.

39. I agree here with Sallie McFague. See her "God as Mother," in *Weaving the Visions,* 139–50, for a fuller argument.

40. For help here, see Elizabeth Johnson, *She Who Is: The Mystery of God in Feminist Disclosure* (New York: Crossroad, 1994); Gail Ramshaw, *God Beyond Gender: Feminist Christian God-Language* (Minneapolis: Augsburg Fortress Press, 1994); Brian Wrenn, *What Language Shall I Borrow? God-Talk in Worship: A Male Response to Feminist Theology* (New York: Crossroad, 1989); and Eilberg-Schwartz, *God's Phallus.*

41. I am indebted to Heyward's work, *Touching Our Strength,* for this notion of God—what she calls "our power in relation."

42. See Arthur McGill, *Suffering: A Test of Theological Method* (Philadelphia: Westminster Press, 1982). McGill argues that it is "pride—and not love—that fears dependence and that worships transcendence." In Jesus, God exercises power in the mode of service, not in

domination. Further, "when Jesus stands opposed to all acts of violence and to all violent powers, and when he acts to free men from those forces which oppress and torment them, he does so as the revealer of God's own essential life" (78–79).

43. Cited in James Nelson, *Embodiment: An Approach to Sexuality and Christian Theology* (Minneapolis: Augsburg, 1978), 14.

44. Nelson, *Embodiment,* 17–18.

45. Nelson, *Intimate Connection,* 26.

46. Nelson, *Embodiment,* 18.

47. Freire, *Pedagogy of the Oppressed,* 22.

48. Nelson, *Embodiment,* 110ff.

49. Nygren, *Agape and Eros,* trans. Philip S. Watson (Philadelphia: Westminster, 1953) 61ff.

50. Nelson, *Embodiment,* 283 n. 18. Nelson notes that Rollo May, *Love and Will* (New York: Norton, 1969), identifies power and passion more with *eros* than with epithymia. Nelson, however, believes that "these qualities [passion and power] are more directly associated with the dynamics of sexual drive, and that direction and the quest for communion are marks of eros." My thought is that communion comes with a willingness to allow oneself to be known by the other.

51. Though Nelson, *Embodiment,* 283 n. 18, finds C. S. Lewis's insights in *The Four Loves* (London: Bles, 1960) helpful, he believes that Lewis, at times, "underplays the unity of love" and betrays, at points, a dualism about the body-self.

52. Nelson, *Embodiment,* 113.

53. Niebuhr, *Radical Monotheism,* 125.

54. Catherine of Siena, "A Treatise of Divine Providence," trans. Algar Thorold, in *Late Medieval Mysticism,* ed. Ray C. Petry (Philadelphia: Westminster Press, 1957), 282.

55. 1 John 4:18.

CHAPTER FIVE *Losing Ourselves to Find Ourselves: Faith*

1. I am grateful to Richard Fireman for this insight; he builds on the very helpful work on stress reduction by Jon Kabat-Zinn, *Full Catastrophe Living: Using the Wisdom of Your Body and Mind to Face Stress, Pain, and Illness* (New York: Delta Books, 1990).

2. Bonhoeffer, *Letters and Papers,* 369–70.

3. Rita Nakashima Brock, *Journeys by Heart: A Christology of Erotic Power* (New York: Crossroad, 1988), 11ff., uses the term *heart* to parallel what Alice Miller calls the "true" self and observes that the false self is the activity of a broken heart. For Brock, heart is "a metaphor for the human self and our capacity for intimacy" and involves "the union of body, spirit, reason, and passion" (xiv). The following description of "brokenheartedness" is my own; it has some affinity with hers, and I refer the reader to her provocative work.

4. Michael Meade, *Men and the Water of Life: Initiation and the Tempering of Men* (San Francisco: HarperSanFrancisco, 1993), 13.

5. Some theorists working out of the object-relations model call this reservoir "backed-up affect." John Rowe, in his "Healing Male Shame: The Pastoral Psychotherapist as Catalyst in Male Liberation" (M.A. thesis, Wake Forest University, 1993), has helped me see something about the dynamics of shame in men's lives. His work builds on that of Gershen Kaufman, *The Psychology of Shame: Theory and Treatment of Shame-Based Syndromes* (New York: Springer, 1989), and S. S. Tomkins, *Affect, Imagery, Consciousness: The Negative Affects, Anger and Fear,* vol. 3 (New York: Springer, 1991).

6. Malidoma Patrice Some, *Ritual: Power, Healing, and Community* (Portland, OR: Swan/Raven, 1993), 37.

7. Bernard Lonergan, *Method in Theology* (New York: Herder and Herder, 1972), 237ff.

8. Küng, "Paradigm Change in Theology," 25.
9. A reformulation of an insight offered by Professor George H. Williams of Harvard University.
10. These ways of looking at things correspond to Edward Farley's four hermeneutical modes in *Fragility of Knowledge*. See chapter 3.
11. Meister Eckhart, "Sermon on the Eternal Birth," trans. R. B. Blakney, in *Late Medieval Mysticism*, 177–85.
12. Elizabeth Kübler-Ross, *On Death and Dying* (New York: Macmillan, 1969).
13. Bly, Hillman, and Meade, *Rag and Bone Shop of the Heart*, 195–99.
14. Harrison, "Power of Anger," 214–25.
15. See Augustine, *Confessions*, bk. 8.
16. Catherine of Siena, "Treatise of Divine Providence," 274.
17. Saint John of the Cross, *The Dark Night of the Soul* (New York: Doubleday, 1990).
18. Augustine, *Confessions*, 171.
19. Kübler-Ross, *On Death and Dying*, 113.
20. Meister Eckhart, "Another Sermon on the Eternal Birth," trans. R. B. Blakney, in *Late Medieval Mysticism*, 186.
21. Eckhart, "Sermon on the Eternal Birth," 177.
22. Eckhart, "Sermon on the Eternal Birth," 182.
23. It is important that whatever we do, we take care of our share of responsibility to and for our children.
24. Eckhart, "Sermon on the Eternal Birth," 184.
25. Eckhart, "Sermon on the Eternal Birth," 179.
26. See David Steindl-Rast, *A Listening Heart: The Art of Contemplative Living* (New York: Crossroad, 1994), 29ff.; and Thomas Merton, *New Seeds of Contemplation* (Norfolk, CT: New Directions Books, 1961), chap. 8.
27. Merton, *New Seeds of Contemplation*, 57.
28. Merton, *New Seeds of Contemplation*, 57–58.
29. Jack Kornfield, *A Path with Heart: A Guide Through the Perils and Promises of Spiritual Life* (New York: Bantam Books, 1993), 59.
30. Augustine, *Confessions*, 151.
31. Basil Pennington, *Centering Prayer: Renewing an Ancient Christian Prayer Form* (New York: Image Books, 1980), 33, points out that the Jesus Prayer, as presented by Saint Gregory of Sinai in the fourteenth century, reproduces "even in details the *dhikr* method of the [Muslim] Sufis of the thirteenth century. . . . This dhikr method in its turn reproduces down to details the *nembutsu* method of meditation used by Buddhists in the twelfth century." He notes that there is not necessarily historical dependence; the similarities might be explained by the possibility that spiritual masters coming from related cultures evolved similar methods.
32. Pennington, *Centering Prayer*, 30–31.

PART THREE

OUR LONGING FOR CONNECTION AND A MINISTRY OF RECONCILIATION

CHAPTER SIX *Love Casts Out Fear*

1. Saint Paul (1 Corinthians 13:13) groups these virtues together as the basis of the Christian life. Saint Thomas Aquinas referred to them as the theological virtues.

2. Eckhart, "Sermon on the Eternal Birth," 178.

3. Meade, *Men and the Water of Life,* 19 and 13.

4. Meade, *Men and the Water of Life,* 10.

5. Joseph Campbell, *The Power of Myth* (New York: Doubleday, 1988).

6. For a contemporary formulation of this, see *The Book of Common Prayer* of the Episcopal church (Church Hymnal Corporation and Seabury Press), 302.

7. See Sharon D. Welch, *Communities of Resistance and Solidarity: A Feminist Theology of Liberation* (Maryknoll, NY: Orbis Books, 1985), 33–36, for her understanding of communities of resistance.

8. As a result of the Second Vatican Council, there has been a shift of emphasis in the Roman Catholic church. Before the council, confession, or the sacrament of penance, tended to be viewed primarily as a personal matter between the believer and God. Following a juridical model, the priest announced forgiveness and imposed penances that, often, were prayers to be recited privately. During and after the council, there has come to be an emphasis on sin as a brokenness in the believer's relationship to the community and to God. The term *rite of reconciliation* more adequately expresses the public and relational function of the sacrament. I am grateful to Fr. Kurt Kreml, O.F.M., and Ms. Shawn Adams for their reflections on this development.

9. Origen of Alexandria and Justin the Martyr understood baptism to be an illumination of the initiate.

10. See Margaret R. Miles, *Fullness of Life: Historical Foundations for a New Asceticism* (Philadelphia: Westminster Press, 1981), 136. For other contributions to the discussion, see Nelson, *Intimate Connection*; James E. Dittes, *The Male Predicament* (San Francisco: Harper & Row, 1985); Philip Culbertson, *The New Adam* (Minneapolis: Fortress Press, 1991); John Carmody, *Toward a Male Spirituality* (Mystic, CT: Twenty-third Publications, n.d.); Tom Owen-Towle, *New Men/Deeper Hungers* (Carmel, CA: Sunflower Ink, 1988); and William Doty, *Myths of Masculinity* (New York: Crossroad, 1993).

CHAPTER SEVEN   *On Being Body-selves: Body Wisdom and Body Care*

1. As quoted in *Men's Studies Review* 7 (1990): 8.

2. Dittes, *When Work Goes Sour,* 56ff.

3. Keen, *Fire in the Belly,* 62–63.

4. Audre Lourde, "Uses of the Erotic: The Erotic as Power," in *Sister Outsider: Essays and Speeches by Audre Lourde* (Trumansburg, NY: Crossing Press, 1984), 54, says that pornography "emphasizes sensation without feeling."

5. The summary I give here of Interplay is based on an unpublished paper, "Telling the Truth: Sex, Spirit, and Experience," written by Phil Porter for a workshop on "Male Sexuality and Masculine Spirituality" at Stony Point, New York, June 25–29, 1993. For information about publications, workshops, and performances by Winton-Henry and Porter write: Wing It! 669-A 24th Street, Oakland, CA 94612.

6. Harrison, "Power of Anger," 214–25, esp. 220.

7. Goldberg, *The Inner Male,* 120ff.

8. Cited in Nelson, *Intimate Connection,* 83.

9. Nelson, *Intimate Connection,* 83.

10. Kenneth Ring, *The Omega Project* (New York: Morrow, 1992).

11. Richardson, *Early Christian Fathers,* 105.

12. The concept of the triune brain is discussed thoroughly in Paul D. MacLean's book, *Triune Concept of the Brain and Behavior* (Toronto: Univ. of Toronto Press, 1973). This is

also discussed in Carl Sagan, *The Dragons of Eden* (New York: Random House, 1977). John Collins pointed this out to me.

13. For an excellent introduction to some of this work, see Michael Goldberg, *Theology and Narrative: A Critical Introduction* (Philadelphia: Trinity Press International, 1991).

14. I adopted this practice from Michael Meade.

15. The precise inheritance practices during this period are difficult to know with certainty. Most likely, the eldest son received twice as much as a younger son, rather than the whole inheritance. See Paul Achtemeier, ed., *Harper's Bible Dictionary* (San Francisco: Harper & Row, 1985), 421–22.

16. This is not to say that the scholarly information, usually deriving from left-brain thinking, is not important. That can be provided by persons in the group who have mastered that particular angle on the story. Here I think Edward Farley's four hermeneutical modes are quite helpful in developing a method of Bible study that is fruitful for men. See Farley, *Fragility of Knowledge*. See also Walter Wink, *Transforming Bible Study* (Nashville: Abingdon Press, 1980).

17. Stanley Hauerwas, *Suffering Presence: Theological Reflections on Medicine, the Mentally Handicapped, and the Church* (Notre Dame, IN: Univ. of Notre Dame Press, 1986), 47, believes that medicine is "the name for a tradition of wisdom concerning good care of the body. As such it is not a 'means' to health, but rather is part of the activity of health—an activity that involves as much the participation of the patient as the physician."

18. The two key numbers with respect to cholesterol are the HDLs (high-density lipoproteins) and the LDLs (low-density lipoproteins). The HDLs are the so-called good kind of cholesterol that help clear out the LDLs—the bad kind—that can accumulate and eventually clog arteries. Generally, the levels do not matter as much as the ratio of HDLs to LDLs, which should be about two to one.

19. Stuart M. Berger, *How to Be Your Own Nutritionist* (New York: Morrow, 1987), 42.

20. Unfortunately, many physicians also do not have much in the way of nutrition education. Of the forty-five medical schools surveyed by the National Research Council, only one-quarter required even one course in nutrition, and only 3 to 4 percent of the questions asked by the National Board of Medical Examiners deal with it.

21. I am grateful to Delta R. Lightner, M.S., for her insights and suggestions concerning nutritional information.

22. Jane Brody, *Jane Brody's Nutrition Book* (New York: Bantam Books, 1987).

23. Jack H Wilmore, *Sensible Fitness* (Champaign, IL: Leisure Press, 1986); Donald B. Ardell, *High Level Wellness: An Alternative to Doctors, Drugs, and Disease* (Berkeley, CA: Ten Speed Press, 1986). See also the University of California, Berkeley, *Wellness Letter* (subscription department: P.O. Box 420162, Palm Coast, FL 32142).

24. James Green, *The Male Herbal: Health Care for Men and Boys* (Freedom, CA: Crossing Press, 1991).

25. Lionel Tiger, *The Pursuit of Pleasure* (Boston: Little, Brown, 1992), 81, also 20–22.

26. James A. Weisheipl, *Friar Thomas D'Aquino: His Life, Thought, and Work* (London: Burns Oates and Washbourne, 1932), 30.

27. Alice Walker, "God Is Inside You and Inside Everybody Else," in *Weaving the Visions,* 104.

28. Olga Broumas, in a lecture for the Introduction to Women's Studies course at Wake Forest University, Spring 1990.

29. For a historical analysis, see Margaret R. Miles, *Image as Insight: Visual Understanding in Western Christianity and Secular Culture* (Boston: Beacon Press, 1985).

30. Tiger, *Pursuit of Pleasure,* chap. 2.

31. McFague, *Body of God*, 143.

32. Myer made this observation at a 1986 conference sponsored by the Smithsonian Institution and the National Academy of Sciences; it was reported by Brian Swimme, "How to Heal a Lobotomy," in *Reweaving the World: The Emergence of Ecofeminism*, ed. Irene Diamond and Gloria Feman Orenstein (San Francisco: Sierra Club Books, 1990), 15.

33. In this current ecological context, Catherine Keller, "Women Against Wasting the World. . . ," in *Reweaving the World*, 249–63, has drawn a connection between ecology (the study of the relationships among things) and eschatology (the study of end things). She asks whether our neglect and violation of the relationships between things—animal, vegetable, and mineral—have led us to the brink of the literal end of things. She further inquires as to whether certain forms of individualized, otherworldly eschatology have, in fact, contributed to our neglect and violation and, therefore, to the end, or whether eschatology can be a resource against it. She suggests that we need a "deliteralized, deapocalypticized eschatology" that harks back to an older biblical tradition of "eschatology in the context of the prophetic cry for justice." In other words, when Jesus tells us to "pay heed, watch—for you know not the time" (Matthew 24:42), we might interpret that to mean that we should "attend consciously, alert to the possibilities for relation and transformation flooding in upon us now." In Keller's words, "We need no new heaven and Earth. We have this Earth, this sky, this water to renew."

34. I am grateful to Dr. Jack Thomas of Winston Salem, North Carolina, for suggesting this image.

35. McFague, *Body of God*, 49.

36. McFague, *Body of God*, 122.

CHAPTER EIGHT   *On Loving Our Brothers*

1. Quoted by Robert Bly, in "A Gathering of Men: A Conversation with Bill Moyers and Robert Bly" (Public Affairs Television, Inc., 1990).

2. John Landgraf, *Singling: A New Way to Live the Single Life* (Louisville, KY: Westminster/John Knox Press, 1990), 81–82.

3. Aelred of Rievaulx, "Spiritual Friendship," in Bernard of Clairvaux, *The Love of God and Spiritual Friendship*, ed. James M. Houston (Portland, OR: Multnomah Press, 1983), 233–51.

4. Landgraf, *Singling*, 15–21.

5. Conference on "Male Sexuality and Masculine Spirituality," Stony Point, New York, June 26, 1993.

6. See John 21:20ff.

7. Landgraf, *Singling*, 119.

8. Bruce Hilton, *Can Homophobia Be Cured? Wrestling with Questions That Challenge the Church* (Nashville: Abingdon Press, 1992), 17, uses this dictionary definition of homophobia.

9. At least one hundred people motivated by homophobia commit murder in the United States each year. Perhaps one thousand others physically attack persons they perceive to be gay or lesbian. Hilton, *Homophobia*, 17.

10. See Ann Pellegrini, "S(h)ifting the Terms of Hetero/Sexism: Gender, Power, Homophobias," in *Homophobia: How We All Pay the Price*, ed. Warren J. Blumenfeld (Boston: Beacon Press, 1992), 44.

11. As quoted in Landgraf, *Singling*, 110.

12. This discussion follows Aelred's stages in "Spiritual Friendships," expanded by my own thinking.

13. Karen Labacqz, "Appropriate Vulnerability," in *Sexuality and the Sacred: Sources for Theological Reflection,* ed. James B. Nelson and Sandra P. Longfellow (Louisville, KY: Westminster/John Knox Press, 1994), 256–61, has developed this notion in the context of a sexual ethic for single persons. I think her reflections can be very helpful for men as we think about many different kinds of relationships.

14. Aelred, "Spiritual Friendships," 250.

15. Margaret Farley, *Personal Commitments: Beginning, Keeping, Changing* (San Francisco: Harper & Row, 1986), 45ff.

16. Farley, *Personal Commitments,* chaps. 7 and 8, provides a fairly comprehensive and very helpful discussion of this possibility and an ethical analysis of the nature of obligation in committed relationships.

17. Aelred, "Spiritual Friendship," 247.

18. Aelred of Rievaulx, *Aelredi Rievallensis opera omnia,* ed. A. Hoste and H. Talbot (Turnhout, Belgium: Corpus Christianorum, 1971), 3.109–10; as translated by John Boswell, *Christianity, Social Tolerance, and Homosexuality: Gay People in Western Europe from the Beginning of the Christian Era to the Fourteenth Century* (Chicago: Univ. of Chicago Press, 1980), 225–26.

19. Aelred, "Spiritual Friendship," 244.

20. There are several anthologies that might be particularly helpful here: Michael S. Kimmel and Michael A. Messner, eds., *Men's Lives* (New York: Macmillan, 1989); Keith Thompson, ed., *To Be a Man: In Search of the Deep Masculine* (Los Angeles: Tarcher, 1991); and Franklin Abbott, ed., *New Men, New Minds: Breaking Male Tradition* (Freedom, CA: Crossing Press, 1987).

21. Osherson, *Finding Our Fathers,* 15, says that more involvement with our sons helps heal "the father wound" for us.

22. Ashahi News Service; reported in the *Winston-Salem Journal,* January 19, 1991. The center is funded by contributions from the men it serves.

23. A helpful resource for starting and maintaining men's groups is Bill Kauth, *Circle of Men: The Original Manual for Men's Support Groups* (New York: St. Martin's Press, 1992). For a guide that includes spiritual and religious perspectives, see Cecil Murphy, *Mantalk: Resources for Exploring Male Issues* (Louisville, KY: Presbyterian Publishing House, 1991).

24. Meade, *Men and the Water of Life,* 11–13.

25. Sam Keen and Anne Valley-Fox, *Your Mythic Journey: Finding Meaning in Your Life Through Writing and Storytelling* (Los Angeles: Tarcher, 1989), xv–xvi.

26. Keen and Valley-Fox, *Your Mythic Journey,* xix.

27. Robert Brizee, *The Gift of Listening* (St. Louis: Chalice Press, 1993), 24–26.

28. Brizee, *The Gift of Listening,* x.

29. For example, see the work of Michael Clark, *Beyond Our Ghettos: Gay Theology in Ecological Perspective* (Cleveland: Pilgrim Press, 1993); Gary Comstock, *Gay Theology Without Apology* (Cleveland: Pilgrim Press, 1993); Chris Glaser, *Uncommon Calling: A Gay Man's Struggle to Serve the Church* (San Francisco: Harper & Row, 1988); and John McNeill, *Taking a Chance on God* (Boston: Beacon Press, 1988).

30. I am grateful to Charlie Kreiner for this insight.

CHAPTER NINE *On Loving Our Sisters*

1. This passage is taken from a poem entitled "Empowered" written by Lisa Allred, Rape Crisis Counselor and Volunteer Coordinator, Family Services, Winston-Salem, North Carolina, for the Rape Awareness Speakout, Wake Forest University, February 1993.

2. Farley, *Personal Commitments,* 62.

3. Farley, *Personal Commitments,* 62.

4. David Smith, "Split Inside and Out: Pastoral Psychotherapy with Men and Affairs, Utilizing Object Relations Theory and Gender Theory" (M.A. thesis in Pastoral Counseling, Wake Forest University, 1994), has helped me understand some of these dynamics from an object-relations perspective.

5. The National Organization of Men Against Sexism, 54 Mint Street, Suite 300, San Francisco, CA 94103, has task groups on reproductive rights and male–female relationships. Participation in any of these groups, or local chapters of the National Organization for Women, will help in identifying some of these practices and what can be done about them.

6. Ellen Goodman, "Fear of Sexual Assault Creates a New Barrier to Equality for Women," Summer 1993.

7. For further ideas and networks for involvement, see Poling, *The Abuse of Power: A Theological Problem* (Nashville: Abingdon Press, 1991), or contact the Ending Men's Violence, Sexual Harassment, and Pornography task groups of the National Organization for Men Against Sexism. See also Joanne Carlson Brown and Carole R. Bohn, eds., *Christianity, Patriarchy and Abuse: A Feminist Critique* (New York: Pilgrim Press, 1989), for analyses of the relationship between violence against women and children and certain formulations of Christian doctrine.

8. See Michael S. Kimmel and Thomas E. Mosmiller, *Against the Tide: Pro-Feminist Men in the United States, 1776–1990* (Boston: Beacon Press, 1992), for examples of men, many Christian, who have worked with women for an end to political and ecclesiastical discrimination.

9. I think Dinnerstein's analysis also helps explain women's resistance to women ministers.

10. Nelson, *Intimate Connection,* 26.

11. See Nelson, *Embodiment,* chap. 5, for help in framing sexual ethics. See also Nelson and Sandra P. Longfellow, eds., *Sexuality and the Sacred* (Louisville: Westminster-John Knox Press, 1994) and Christine E. Godorf, *Body, Sex, and Pleasure* (Cleveland, OH: The Pilgrim Press, 1994).

12. There is much that can and should be said about the historical practice of celibacy. Without going into a discussion of the positive and negative aspects of the practice and its effects, I simply note that temporary or permanent celibacy holds some important possibilities for men. By choosing not to engage in a primary sexual relationship with a woman, we have the opportunity to focus our energy and attention on other kinds of relationships, thus moving out of the isolation in which many of us find ourselves. By taking a moratorium on the dynamics of what I have called our "monorelational psychic structure," we have the possibility of developing deeply intimate relationships with many other people. See Steindl-Rast, *A Listening Heart,* 24ff., for a discussion of the role of celibacy in building community.

13. McFague, *Models of God,* 106.

14. See McFague, *Models of God,* 206 n. 22, where she cites Phyllis Trible, *God and the Rhetoric of Sexuality* (Philadelphia: Fortress Press, 1978), for the Hebraic use of the "breasts" and "womb" of God as metaphors of divine compassion and care, and Caroline Bynum, *Jesus as Mother: Studies in the Spirituality of the High Middle Ages* (Berkeley and Los Angeles: Univ. of California Press, 1982), for the use of such imagery among twelfth-century Cistercian mystics. She also rightly points out that female images of God should include, but not be limited to, mother images (99–100).

15. Victoria Secunda, *Women and Their Fathers: The Sexual and Romantic Impact of the First Man in Your Life* (New York: Delta Books, 1992).

16. Secunda, *Women and Their Fathers,* 430.

17. Another very helpful resource in this area is Kyle D. Pruett's *The Nurturing Father: Journey Toward the Complete Man* (New York: Warner Books, 1987).
18. Heyward, *Touching Our Strength*. Heyward and James Nelson (*Embodiment; Intimate Connection;* and *Body Theology* [Louisville, KY: Westminster/John Knox Press, 1992]) are among contemporary theologians who are rediscovering the powerful connections between sexuality and spirituality. Their work points in interesting directions as we reevaluate the pervasive sex- and body-negativity of much of the Western Christian tradition. Saint Augustine, after a long and tortured struggle with his own sexual expression, concluded that sexual relations between men and women are fraught with alienating dynamics. He was, I think, right. The question Heyward's and Nelson's perspectives raise is whether those alienating dynamics are produced by the mysterious, biological transmission of lust (alienated sexual passion) or by sexist structures of inequality that were endorsed or left unquestioned by figures like Augustine. In other words, is it possible that while the church rightly condemns lust, or objectified sexuality, it nevertheless contributes to it when it supports sexist attitudes and behaviors?
19. For a helpful approach to structuring honest exchange between women and men, see Aaron Kipnis and Elizabeth Herron, *Gender War/Gender Peace: The Quest for Love and Justice Between Women and Men* (New York: Morrow, 1994).
20. Publishers-Hall Syndicate, Chicago. This article appeared in the *Winston-Salem Journal* in 1990.
21. Muriel James and Louis M. Savary, *The Heart of Friendship* (New York: Harper & Row, 1979), as summarized in Landgraf, *Singling,* 112–13.

Epilogue

1. An example of one way to understand this theologically is the view of John Calvin, who believed that the eternal Word of God, which became human in Christ, was active in the world before the incarnation and continues to be active in the world beyond the incarnation and its extension in the Church. While the ascended Christ rules the Church through the Spirit and the Word, the eternal Son of God rules the world even outside the Church. This is what Heiko Oberman has called the "extra calvinisticum." See Oberman, "The 'Extra' Dimension in the Theology of Calvin," *Journal of Ecclesiastical History* (1970): 43–64.
2. Keen, *Fire in the Belly,* 176.
3. See Paul Tillich, *Christianity and the Encounter of the World Religions* (New York: Columbia Univ. Press, 1963).
4. Hacker, *Two Nations,* chap. 1.
5. For very helpful analyses and suggestions, see Robert W. Terry, *For Whites Only* (Grand Rapids, MI: Eerdmans, 1975).
6. For a historical perspective, see Marc Saperstein, *Moments of Crisis in Jewish-Christian Relations* (Philadelphia: Trinity Press International, 1989).
7. For helpful materials about Jewish–Christian mutual understanding, contact the National Conference of Christians and Jews, 71 Fifth Avenue, New York, NY 10003.
8. See King, Maynard, and Woodyard, *Risking Liberation,* 72ff.

Index

acceptance, 136
Adam and Eve story, 80–81, 86
Adams, Kenneth, 62
addictions, 168–69
Aelred of Rievaulx, 178, 179, 181–83, 212
agape, 120, 121, 147
aggression, 25–26, 80
Ali, Muhammad, 29, 30
Allred, Lisa, 202
American Baptist Convention, 93
anger, 11, 133–34, 159–60
Anselm of Canterbury, Saint, 90, 130
anti-Semitism, 14, 47, 48, 49, 230; in Christianity, 241 n. 3, 242 n. 20
Aquinas, Thomas. *See* Thomas Aquinas, Saint
archetypes, 75, 238 nn. 3, 10. *See also* capacities
Arendt, Hannah, 25
Athanasius of Alexandria, 112–13
athletes, 29–30. *See also* cultural images
Augustine, Saint, 15, 119, 130, 136, 194, 216; bargaining by, 134; on boyhood, 18, 30–31, 37, 69, 80; on God, 13, 100, 101, 115, 141; on need for connection, 44; on responsibility, 96, 225
authority: in mutual paradigm, 118–19; in objectified paradigm, 89

"banking" concept, 34, 165–66
baptism, 150–51
bargaining, 134–35
Barth, Karl, 173
Becker, Ernest, 161

biographies, personal, 194–95. *See also* storytelling
Bly, Robert, 5, 9, 12, 79, 133; on emotions, 127, 163; as translator, 122, 143, 176
bodies: addictions by, 168–69; alienation from, 155–57; health care of, 169–71; limitations of, 161–63; listening to, 158–61
Bonhoeffer, Dietrich, 116–17, 123, 126, 138, 163, 188
Boyd, Stephen B., 4–8, 24, 137; childhood of, 27–28, 34, 38, 205–6; mentors of, 187–88, 215–16; perspective of, 9–10, 34–35; seven theses of, 3–4
Bradshaw, Jack, 33
Brantley, Bill, 162–63
Brizee, Robert, 196
Brock, Rita Nakashima, 127
Bultmann, Rudolf, 106

Campbell, Joseph, 6, 77, 146, 149
capacities: compassionate connection as, 73, 74, 75–76, 130–31; distortions of, 74–75; intelligence as, 72, 73, 76–78; justice as, 72, 73, 78–79, 238 n. 4; men's inherent, 72–74; strength as, 72, 73, 79–80
caring: for bodies, 168–76; in friendships, 184
Catherine of Siena, Saint, 15, 119, 122, 135–36
celibacy, 214, 250 n. 12
centering prayer, 141, 142, 245 n. 31. *See also* meditation

Certik, Richard, 189
chiropractors, 171
Chodorow, Nancy, 60, 61, 62
cholesterol, 170, 247 n. 18
Christ. *See* Jesus
Christian theology, 15; in mutual paradigm, 103–19; in objectified paradigm, 87–91
church, 231–33; and men's spiritual longing, 14–15; seven theses on men and, 3–4; women as leaders in, 91–94, 211–12
classism, 14, 37, 47–48, 49, 229–30
Clement of Alexandria, Saint, 130
coed groups, 220–21
Collins, John, 187–88
commitments: to caring for body, 168, 169, 171, 174; to friendship with women, 204; to listening to body, 158, 161, 163; to spiritual friendships, 183, 184
competition: and competitor, 39–40; in education, 32–33; in relationships with men, 201
"compulsive relational fantasies," 58, 237 n. 16
conditioning, 26; in education, 30–35; about gender roles, 26–27. *See also* socialization
Cone, James, 79
Confessions (Augustine), 69, 80, 134, 141, 194
connection, compassionate, as capacity of men, 73, 74, 75–76, 130–31
Conroy, Pat, 1
conversion, 126, 129–31, 142
covert incest, 62
cultural images: masculine, 24–25, 36; values of, 29–30
cultural invasion, 33–34, 84

daughters, 218–19
death, 161–63. *See also* grief
Decroux, Etienne, 177
denial, 2; of church leadership role for women, 91–93; as stage of grief, 132–33
dependence, on women, 65, 67, 168, 179, 205–8

depression, 135–36
Descartes, René, 106
"desperate lover," 11, 44–45, 66–68, 70; diagram of, 48, 147. *See also* identities
Dinnerstein, Dorothy, 60–61, 63, 84, 211
discrimination, against women in workplace, 211–12. *See also* racism; sexism
Dittes, James, 156
domination, 87–88; Christians against, 241 n. 5; internalized, 83–84, 86, 93; male, 61–62
dominative masculinity, 3, 224–25, 235 n. 17; versus kenotic masculinity, 95–97; and women as church leaders, 91–93
drumming, 165, 166, 194

Eckhart, Meister, 15, 131, 135, 150, 196; on spiritual experience, 136–37, 147
ecology, 174–76, 248 n. 33
education: antidialogical, 32, 33; "banking" concept in, 34, 165–66; conditioning in, 30–35
Ehrenreich, Barbara, 11, 35
Ehrenreich, John, 35
emotions: and gender-role polarization, 26–30, 52; numbing of, 29, 127–28; responsibility for, 206–8; wounds of, 127–28. *See also* feelings
eros, 120, 121, 219
Eucharist, 113

faith, 100, 126, 142, 146
family, 60–63. *See also* fathers; mothers
Farley, Edward, 77, 79
Farrell, Warren, 18, 56, 195
fathers: and mentor relationships, 188–89; respect of, 187; as role models, 23–24
fear, 177, 179, 225. *See also* femiphobia; homophobia
feelings: door to, 12, 129, 132; and justice, 78–79; rituals for connecting to, 164–68; sexual, 66–68, 160; trusting, 131–32. *See also* emotions
femininity, 51, 52, 53
femiphobia, 29, 45, 48, 49

financial provision, unequal sharing of,
    54–55. *See also* public sphere
Fire in the Belly (Keen), 8
Forbes, James, 229
Freire, Paulo, 32, 100, 114, 120, 165–66;
    on "cultural invasion," 33–34, 84; on
    liberation from oppression, 83, 85, 86
friendships, 177–78; with gay men, 198–
    201; in men's groups, 189–90; in
    mentor relationships, 186–89, 215–
    20; personal, 185–86; spiritual, 179,
    180–84, 198–201, 212–15, 227, 228;
    with women, 202–4, 212–15; worldly,
    178

gay men, 162–63, 198–201. *See also*
    homophobia
gender: and education, 34, 35; roles
    polarized by, 26–29, 52
gender dance, 51–53; origins of, 60–63
gender reconciliation groups, 220–21
genitalization, of male sexuality, 36–37,
    67
Gillette, Douglas, 74–75, 238 n. 10
God: Augustine on, 13, 141; female
    images of, 218; kingdom of, 102,
    110–11; love of, 118, 119, 122, 147–
    48, 225–27; as masculine, 88, 115–16;
    188, 240 n. 28; in meditation, 141; in
    mutual paradigm, 115–19; Niebuhr
    on, 100–101
Goethe, Johann Wolfgang von, 122, 154
Goldberg, Herb, 160
Goodman, Ellen, 210
grace, 91, 109, 227
Green, James, 171
grief, 12; as door to feelings, 129, 132;
    stages of, 132–35
guilt, 11–12; and kenotic masculinity,
    93–97

Harris, Sydney, 221–22
Harrison, Beverly, 78–79, 103, 134,
    159–60, 219
health, and alienation from bodies,
    155–56
health care, 169–70
heart, 127, 244 n. 3. *See also* emotions;
    feelings

henotheism, 101
herbalism, 171
heterosexism, 14, 37, 228
heterosexuality, compulsory, 36, 37
Heyward, Carter, 101, 219, 220
hierarchy, in objectified paradigm, 89–
    91. *See also* patriarchy
High Level Wellness (Ardell), 171
Hillman, James, 150
Hirooka, Yoko, 189
Holm, Bill, 223
homophobia, 14, 36, 37, 48, 49;
    expanded definition of, 45–46, 179–
    80; overcoming, 162–63, 198–201. *See
    also* gay men; lesbians
hope, 146–47
household chores, 54, 205–6. *See also*
    private sphere
How to Be Your Own Nutritionist (Berger),
    170–71
hugging, 197

identities: contradictory, 11–13;
    separative, 236 n. 1; strains with
    dual, 69–71; stress from defending,
    124, 138. *See also* "desperate lover";
    "lonely warrior"
Ignatius of Antioch, 113, 162
initiation, 148–53
institutions, civilizing, 4, 87
intellect: and gender-role polarization,
    52, 58; socialization about, 30–35
intelligence, as capacity of men, 72, 73,
    76–78
internalized domination, 83–84, 86, 93
internalized oppression, 83, 84, 86
interplay, 158–59
intimacy, 66–68. *See also* connection,
    compassionate
Iron John (Bly), 8
isolation, 11, 12–13, 44, 48–49

Jacob and Esau story, 166–67
James, Muriel, 222
Jane Brody's Nutrition Book (Brody), 170
Jesus, 123, 127; and mutual paradigm,
    109–14; and objectified paradigm,
    90–91, 101–2, 104
John of the Cross, Saint, 4

Jung, Carl, 119
justice: as capacity of men, 72, 73, 78–79, 238 n. 4; of God, 102; in objectified paradigm, 89, 90

Kaufman, Michael, 33
Kay, Judith, 26, 72, 83
Keen, Sam, 50, 156; on friendship, 180, 227; on storytelling, 194–95; on "warrior psyche," 33, 194
Keller, Catherine, 58
kenotic masculinity, 93–97
King, Paul, 34
Kingdom of God, 102, 110–11
Kohn, Alfie, 39, 40
Kornfield, Jack, 140
Kreiner, Charlie, 26, 36
Kubie, Lawrence, 202, 203
Kübler-Ross, Elisabeth, 132–36
Küng, Hans, 130

Landgraf, John, 177–78, 179, 185–86, 222
Lawrence, D. H., 97
lesbians, friendships with, 219–20
Levinson, Daniel, 177
libido, 120, 121, 219
listening, 195–96
"lonely warrior," 12, 69–70, 123–24; diagram of, 42, 124, 142; as masculine role, 41–43; Ralph as, 19–23. *See also* identities
Lonergan, Bernard, 129
longing, men's, 13–15
love: of God, 118, 119, 122, 147–48, 225–27; in mutual paradigm, 120–22; in objectified paradigm, 91, 240 n. 30; romantic, 64–65; of self, 124–25
Luther, Martin, 4, 114, 173, 231; on Fall story, 80–81, 86–87; three estates of, 4, 87

Machado, Antonio, 176
marriage, 63–66, 221–23
masculine role: dysfunction in, 38–41; as "lonely warrior," 41–43; as punishment for sin, 80–81, 86. *See also* patriarchy

masculine socialization and conditioning. *See* conditioning; socialization
masculinity, 2, 88; dominative, 3, 91–93, 95–97, 224–25, 235 n. 17; kenotic, 93–97; mature and immature, 72, 74–75
massage, 197–98
Maynard, Kent, 34
Mays, Willie, 29, 30
McFague, Sallie, 174, 175, 218
McNeill, John, 179
Meade, Michael, 127, 149, 150, 194
meditation, 139–41, 142
men: oppression of, 3, 85–87; restlessness of, 11–13; seven theses on church and, 3; spiritual longing of, 13–15; violence as natural to, 25–26, 235 n. 10
men's groups, 189–90; activities for, 194–98; guidelines for, 190–94
men's movement, 8–9
mentors, 186–89, 215–20
Merton, Thomas, 138–39
metanoia, 116, 126, 129
midlife crisis, 7–8, 15
Miedzian, Myriam, 25–26, 80
Miles, Margaret, 216
militarism, 14
misogyny, 29, 49, 61
monorelationship psychic structure, 50
Moore, Robert, 74–75, 177, 186, 238 n. 10
mothers: and friendships with women, 215–18; and gender dance, 60–63
Moyers, Bill, 8
mutuality: in private sphere, 205–8; in public sphere, 208–12
mutual paradigm, 130; Christian theology in, 103–19; God in, 115–19; grace in, 109; Jesus in, 109–14; love in, 120–22; sin in, 103–8
Myer, Norman, 174

National Conference of Catholic Bishops, 93–94
Nelson, James, 119–21, 155, 162, 213
Niebuhr, H. Richard, 88, 100–101, 117, 121, 131

NOMAS (National Organization for
    Men Against Sexism), 9
nutrition, 170–71
Nygren, Anders, 120

objectification, 65; of female sexuality,
    57; of male sexuality, 36–37; of
    selves, 123–24; 138–39
objectified paradigm, 130; Christian
    theology in, 87–91; and Jesus, 90–91,
    101–2, 104
O'Neill, James, 39
oppression, 82; dynamics of, 83–84;
    internalized, 83, 84, 86; of men, 3,
    85–87. *See also* victimization
overfunctioning, in public sphere,
    208–12

pain, 7, 158, 168–69. *See also* grief
partners, relationships with, 63–66,
    221–23
patriarchy, 224–25. *See also* masculine role
Paul, Saint, 72, 107–8, 146, 155; on
    alienation within, 69, 71; on
    reconciliation, 100, 114, 126
Pedagogy of the Oppressed (Freire), 83, 100
Pennington, Basil, 141
philia, 120, 121, 183, 208, 219
physical life: and gender-role polariza-
    tion, 26–30, 52, 53–55; ideal
    masculine, 26
physicians, 169–70
Pleck, Joseph, 39
Pollak, Felix, 68
polytheism, 101
Porter, Phil, 158–59, 160
powerlessness, 12–13
Prince of Tides, The (Conroy), 1
private sphere, 52, 63–64;
    underfunctioning in, 205–8. *See also*
    "desperate lover"; household chores
Promise Keepers, 8
public sphere, 52, 63–64;
    overfunctioning in, 208–12. *See also*
    financial provision; "lonely warrior"

racism, 14, 229–30; against African-
    Americans, 46–47, 48, 49; in church,
    79; in sexuality, 37–38

Ralph, 25, 125, 178; grief of, 127–29;
    as "lonely warrior," 42–43; role of,
    54–55, 71; story of, 18, 19–23, 44,
    69; success of, 23, 38–39, 76,
    78, 80
Rank, Otto, 161
rebirth, spiritual, 136–38, 150
relationships, 35–36, 41, 201; blockage
    of, 48–49; and gender-role polariza-
    tion, 52, 58–60; mentor, 186–89,
    215–20; with partners, 63–66, 221–
    23; and vocation, 227–28; with
    WOMAN, 48, 49–50. *See also*
    friendships
restlessness, men's, 11–13
retreats, 164–68
Rilke, Rainer Maria, 143
rituals, 164–68
role models, 23–25
Roman Catholic church, 92
Rumi, 43

sacred spaces. *See* sanctuaries
sanctuaries, 163–65, 166, 180–81
Savary, Louis, 222
Scarf, Maggie, 59, 204
Schweitzer, George, 129–30
Secunda, Victoria, 218–19
segregation, of boys and girls, 28
Seidler, Victor, 78
self, 42, 103. *See also* identities
self-justification, 124–26
self-love, 124–25
senses, replenishing, 171–74
Sensible Fitness (Wilmore), 171
sex, 119–20
sexism, 14, 45, 48, 228; and distorted
    images of God, 115–16; and kenotic
    masculinity, 93–96; renouncing
    privileges of, 209–12
sexuality, 120; compulsiveness in, 36,
    157; feelings with, 66–68, 160; in
    friendships with women, 213–14;
    and gender-role polarization, 36–38,
    52, 55–57; and intimacy, 67; and
    spirituality, 119–20, 251 n. 18
sight, 173–74
Simpson, O. J., 67
singlehood, 178–79, 222

sins, 14, 71; dominative masculinity as, 3; in mutual paradigm, 103–8; in objectified paradigm, 90; patriarchy as manifestation of, 80–81, 86, 224–25
smell, 173
socialization, 2, 26; connections blocked by, 48–49; on gender roles, 27–29; of "lonely warrior," 18. *See also* conditioning
Some, Malidoma, 129
sound, 173
Southern Baptist Convention, 91–92
spiritual friendships, 179, 180–83; commitments in, 183, 184; with gay men, 198–201; grace in, 227; sanctuaries for, 180–81; stages of, 181–83; as vocation, 228; with women, 212–25. *See also* friendships
spirituality, 120; and sexuality, 119–20, 251 n. 18
sports, 29. *See also* cultural images
Sternbach, Jack, 24
storytelling, 165–68, 194. *See also* biographies, personal
strength, as capacity of men, 72, 73, 79–80
stress, from defending identity, 124, 138
success, 38–39, 156; and compulsive work, 40–41; defining, 23
Suchocki, Marjorie, 106, 108
SURGs (screwed-up religious guys), 95
Swaggart, Jimmy, 67

taste, 172–73
Thomas Aquinas, Saint, 72, 173, 239 n. 18
Tiger, Lionel, 172, 174
Tillich, Paul, 207, 229
touch, 66, 171, 172, 196–98
truth, 119

underfunctioning, in private sphere, 205–8
Unitas, Johnny, 29

Valley-Fox, Anne, 194, 195
values: of athletic cultural images, 29–30; in education, 34
Valverde, Mariana, 57, 219
victimization, and protests, 12. *See also* oppression
violence: and alienation from bodies, 157; in conditioning, 3, 25–26, 30–35; in friendships, 183–84; in socialization for sex roles, 26–29; against women, 210–11
virtues, theological, 146
vocation, 13, 227–28. *See also* work

warrior psyche, 33, 194
Whitman, Walt, 201
Williams, George H., 40, 187
Wingo, Tom, 1, 14
Wink, Walter, 106, 107, 242 n. 13
Winton-Henry, Cynthia, 158–59, 160
WOMAN, relationship with, 48, 49–50, 67
women: as church leaders, 91–94, 211–12; fear of violence among, 210–11; friendships with, 202–4, 212–15; as partners, 63–66, 221–23
women's studies, 34
Woodyard, David, 34
work: and bodies, 156–57, 169; changing, 230–31; compulsion in, 40–41, 156–57; as private space, 206; violence in intellectual, 33. *See also* financial provision; vocation